ENTREPRENEUR SECRETS TO A GROW GET GIVE LIFE

BY MIKE SKRYPNEK

Book Cover, Inner Design and Layout by Jenna Anderson

Formatting for publication by Run + Jump Books

runandjumpbooks.com

Editing by Sarah Rose Sinclair

Published by Fit Family Enterprises Inc. Publishing:
info@mikeskrypnek.com

Disclaimer:

This book contains the opinions and ideas of the author and is offered for information purposes only.

The author and publisher specifically disclaim responsibility for any liability loss or risk personal or otherwise, which is incurred as a consequence, directly or indirectly, of the use and application of any of the contents of this book.

To my wonderful wife Sherri and our incredible children, Madison and Coen, I sincerely thank you.

Sherri, you always make the journey more smooth, enjoyable and comforting as I choose the excitement of a bumpy road. Patient, kind and loving your unconditional love for me always lifts me. You are my partner, my lover, my friend- forever and always. I swore I'd never write another book, and it was you who pushed me through my second and now after five, look what you've done. Our life together is an adventure; I am honored to enjoy it with you. Thank you.

As parents we strive to be good role models, mentors and guides for you, but Madison and Coen, the truth is you inspire me every day. You inspire me to strive for more, to build good habits and to smile and have fun along the way. I have always stressed that you must live your passion. You are both doing that. I am proud to share the lessons you've taught me with anyone who will listen. It is beautiful. I can only hope it is as pure for me as it is you. Thank you for who you are and who you will become.

To all you impact-minded entrepreneurs, dreamers and innovators. I wish you strength, courage and unbridled enthusiasm as you move forward and make waves in business and life. How will you make your big impact?

GROW GET GIVE

Praise for Mike Skrypnek and his GROW GET GIVE Philosophy:

"The most successful entrepreneurs have a millionaire mindset and a road map to achievement. Mike clearly and thoughtfully helps his readers find their connection to their purpose and passion. The secrets to grow, get and give are written simply and powerfully. I recommend this as required reading for any entrepreneur."
- T. Harv Eker, #1 NY Times best-selling Author of Secrets of the Millionaire Minds™ #secretsofthemillionaireminds

"Mike Skrypnek's tremendous book, Entrepreneurs Secrets to a Grow, Get, Give Life, is a total WINNER! For any individual wanting to make a difference in industry and life will benefit from the many secrets and tips that will help you do the things that lead to greater happiness and success. Every person that reads this book will benefit from it. It is a fun read and a great gift to those you care about."
- Steven R. Shallenberger, author of the #1 National Bestseller, Becoming Your Best, the 12 Principles of Highly Successful Leaders and founder of Becoming Your Best Global Leadership.

"Mike's book "Entrepreneur Secrets to a Grow Get Give Life" is one of the better books I have had the chance to get my hands on as it combines a tremendous motivational message with a clear plan of attack to take your "entrepreneurial game" to another level. Mike does this for you in such a way that you can immediately incorporate the lessons into your life and your job."
- Kevin Eastman, International Corporate & Sports Team Speaker; Author; former NBA championship coach and executive.

"Not only is Mike endlessly insightful and constantly my 'mirror into the future', but he also serves as an anchor on many occasions as my little business is tossed around in the sea of uncertainty that is entrepreneurship."
- Geoff Starling CSCS FMS - Owner / Director, Every Body STRONGER.

"Mike is a true leader both in spirit and action, who provides a high level of integrity and professionalism. He is a brilliant strategist that embraces practical and proven solutions to solving complex issues. He cares about you and your business and is success oriented in his approach. I would encourage you to read all of his books as they will make a significant difference in your life."
- Dan Holinda - Regional Executive Director-Prairies, Canadian Cancer Society.

"*Mike's ability to communicate common sense, helpful and real-life examples in his book makes this a must-read for every entrepreneur, no matter if they are starting, in or ending their business. Learn what any successful business person will confirm; it's not all about the money.***"**

- Gabrielle Loren, CPA, CGA, Founding Partner Loren Nancke, Chartered Professional Accountant and Former President West Vancouver Chamber of Commerce

A Special Gift For You

To help you live you own GROW GET GIVE life, I've put together additional free bonus resources for you at:

www.GROWGETGIVE.com/secrets

To unlock the secrets, enter code: **G3SECRETSFREE**

Enter the code and get access to:

- Free video interviews with Mike sharing secrets to implement your GROW marketing strategy, executing your GET freedom for your strategy, and the step by step directions on taking your own GIVE back action.
- Free video interview with one of North America's elite business and philanthropic leaders.
- Mike's proprietary G3 Assessment of your GROW GET GIVE business.

Go to **www.GrowGetGive.com** and enter your code in my Live Chat box: **G3SECRETSFREE**

GROW GET GIVE

Share This Book!

Share the Secrets to live a GROW, GET and GIVE Life!

Retail: $24.95

Special Quantity Discounts:

5 – 20 books

$19.99 each

21 – 99 books

$17.97 each

100 – 499 books

$14.95 each

To place an order, contact:

(604) 898-6340

GROW GET GIVE

Hire Mike

A professional speaker you can rely on

for your next event!

If you're serious about getting the most out of the people you serve, employ or entertain, then Mike is the ideal person for a keynote or training experience.

To book Mike to speak:

Mike Skrypnek
Grow Get Give Coaching

Squamish, BC
604-898-6340

info@mikeskrypnek.com

www.GrowGetGive.com

www.Sea2SkySummit.com

GROW GET GIVE

TABLE OF CONTENTS

GROW GET GIVE

BOOK TWO

GET MORE FREEDOM

BOOK THREE

GIVE BACK

An Important Note from the Author – Read This Before Anything Else

I've always been Coach Mike...

...but only understood why when I recalled the week I feared for my life.

The Shift from Hoarding to Giving

During the biggest global stock market crisis since the Great Depression, my life went through a major transition. Amidst the pressures of the 2008 market losses and stresses on my investment management business, I was battling with partners who had declining businesses and poor work habits who were selfishly enjoying the benefits of my intense work to keep our income coming in and assets growing.

I wanted a business divorce from them, but as in most break ups, there is one party who wants out, while the other holds on. When a path to that exit was clear, I transitioned my business to another firm two months ahead of the bottom of the worst market decline in eighty years. Fear was at its pinnacle.

Despite the intense pressure of moving my clients during that time, the transition was a new beginning for me. My business had been growing in spite of the market collapse, although it was not progressing in the meaningful way I had hoped. With the disruption and climate of fear, a large portion of my clients simply were not willing to add moving to a new company with me to their concerns.

We spent years building a business on the basis of sound investment strategy and convincing clients how smart we were. We were proud of our commitment to the science of investing and built a substantial business. But the focus we had on the merits of our "product" left us vulnerable to the overwhelming fear in the downturn.

A connection to the minutiae of the investments had inextricably linked our value, in clients' eyes, to portfolio returns only. There was much more to the guidance we gave clients. We provided them what they needed, but neglected to learn enough about what they wanted. When things went poorly, our relationships became strained. This was particularly challenging for me. No matter how much I cared, or the work I had done to help my clients in the past, it felt as though I was somehow to blame for the impact of the global market meltdown. It was a painful reminder that I would be measured for what I could not control. I always hoped it would be my value in the relationship.

There had to be something bigger and better for me to find more impact for myself and my life. 2008 had reinforced the fact that I wanted to share my philanthropic desires for our community by giving back during my day job, not just my evenings and weekends. I had wisdom to share.

I could help charitable organizations govern and manage their endowments so they could better connect with donors to make a bigger difference. I wrote down my new commitment on the whiteboard in my office: "Give $1 million per year to charity". I could give time, money and influence.

I was about to build a new core for my business - serving charities and their donors – by focusing on estate and legacy planning. I first turned to The Strategic Coach™ program for guidance. Inspired with clear direction, I quickly created a proprietary system, wrote research papers and within a year published my first book called *Philanthropy; An Inspired Process*.

This served as the connection between my passion to give and purpose to make a big impact by taking action through my investment management business. It was part of an effort to engage a community of philanthropists, impact-minded entrepreneurs and giving families to give them the impact that they sought. I was determined to give a million dollars away to charity every year helping others. It felt good to build a brand new unique business focusing on one specific and important niche.

I knew nothing about how to give a million dollars away to charity and even less about building a business in the investment industry that would help to do it. In order to serve the non-profit industry, I needed to learn. I sought and hired the best suited coaches, who had done it before, to train me. Those mentors provided me kinship and wisdom.

My advisor peers were more in the business of hoarding capital than giving it away. They called serving charity the "no-profit" industry. I was determined to prove them wrong. They dismissed my aspirations, didn't understand what I was doing, and in some cases, they even chuckled at my goal. Caring and giving was not really the standard of the industry. It often seemed more like rape and pillage, or rather, "make-and- take" (clearly, I had become jaded). Many of my coworkers' most important clients were themselves.

I don't suffer fools and care even less for the selfish and self-centered. Early on, I did not have industry partners or allies in my heart-centered drive to build a business on an impact-focused vision. The market collapse, the move and the unscrupulous behavior of former colleagues left my business beaten.

You see, in 2010 when my first book was published, my business book of clients had been decimated and was a fifth of the size it had been before my move. My trailing revenue had dropped to only 10% of two years prior! I had a ton of work to do and an eye to make a bigger impact in my life and the lives of others. I was ready.

Fast-forward six years to 2016. I was grateful to be a catalyst integral in nearly $12.5 million in charitable giving, and became a dominant player in philanthropic estate planning in Alberta. I published three books on business and philanthropy, grew my revenues ten times bigger and diversified my investment advisory away from the single revenue stream linked to market performance into multiple unique ones that rewarded my expertise and added value to my client families.

I could never have gotten anywhere without hiring coaches to help me figure that out.

Working with strong mentors was probably one of the most important parts of my growth as a human being. Once built, it would have been simple to stay in my business. However, there was still something holding me back from realizing my true calling. I considered what I was most passionate about and how I might be able to gain further leverage to make an even bigger impact. My attention shifted from overseeing investments and serving families who had already made money and were planning to pass it on. I would focus on helping those who were building wealth and planning their rich futures. These were the entrepreneurs and business owners - the change makers.

For the previous six years I was helping people who were transitioning and preserving their wealth, passing it on to future generations. They were planning for their estate, and together we were making good strategic decisions. This work was technically rewarding, but I was seeking more freedom as an entrepreneur, more connection as a human and greater reach for impact.

The structure of the financial industry felt confining and the daily routine was soul-sucking. Working with entrepreneurs and business owners always intrigued me. Conversations with them were optimistic and hopeful. I boost their trajectories by them advising them on finance, capital markets and strategic business planning, and running business successfully. I was able to share valuable wisdom from my accomplished baby boomer philanthropist clients who had the hindsight of what they would have done better twenty years earlier.

Rebuilding a business with a new passion from an $80,000 per year to an $800,000 per year business required a lot of work. I did it with a two-person support team, with consultants and by outsourcing with the help of incredible mentors. I invested nearly $180,000 over a ten year period to learn from some of the best coaches in North America. It was clear through that process I could leverage my abilities and direct experience to help more people. What made my business grow, how I was able to take more time off than ever before and the impact I was able to make could be taught to other entrepreneurs just like me when I started my journey.

I learned that with more freedom in my work, I could think and be creative. I needed to do things in life that made me happy by aligning with my passion. I envisioned helping one hundred impact-minded entrepreneurs earn more money and guiding them to re-direct one million dollars in taxes from profits to charitable causes. We could make a $100 million difference. That seemed like an achievable goal and I set out to do just that.

Getting To My 'Why'

For years, the goal to give more to charitable causes is what I considered my 'why' as I transitioned from legacy advisor to business coach. It was my mission. Shifting my focus to work with entrepreneurs was to help them see the opportunities beyond themselves for big impact. It seemed to be an admirable goal, but conversations with one of my coaching clients, my wife and a new friend turned my attention back to why I chose coaching over remaining in the investment industry.

After a couple years of focusing my energy on building my coaching business, things were going well, but there was something missing. I felt I should be working with about five times the number of people by that point. On the surface, I had done all the right things: developed a sound process, a marketing system and a model that attracted prospects to events. It worked well and I had a clear method of engaging them as clients. The approach was validated and repeatable. It was scalable and I was on my way. However, it was an event-driven process and while my contact list was growing, I ran into challenges trying to get bigger audiences to attend. Large audiences would be proportionately able to drive even more business, but attracting them was a challenge. 'Frustrating' was a gentle way of stating my situation.

I was experiencing exactly the thing I know many entrepreneurs do. I understood it was my marketing message, but I didn't quite know what part to improve. Then a series of conversations allowed me to understand what might be happening. You see, my $100 million goal was an honest and admirable passion, yet it didn't explain much about why I could help. It wasn't clear why I should be considered over other coaches. The big number didn't inspire or compel busy growth-focused business owners to want to start working with me. Then three conversations in thirty days happened.

Conversation one: I helped Launa write her book, *Getting Up,* that helped others get up and get back to working after major life illness or trauma and recovery. We worked well together, enjoyed wine and good food with our spouses and became great friends. She once told me, "You are intimidating, and people think you are a bit intense to approach." She then assured me, "Until they get to know you." Wow! I had never thought of myself that way. I suddenly became very aware of the perception people had of me and started smiling more. Seriously, smiling more!

Conversation two: I invested $97 for a one-hour conversation with Vaughn, who is a stellar guy, and new friend. He worked as a corporate team trainer and professional emcee. I wanted to get to know him better and maybe do some work with him on a project. I invested the money in the session he offered and I asked him to walk me through his coaching process. His first stop in the discovery was my 'why'. We didn't get further than that.

He was someone who didn't know me well, but was quite intuitive. He dug in and asked me if the goal to redirect more and more money to charitable causes was so important, "Why don't you just stay in the financial services business? It seems to be an effective platform for it. Why not just serve entrepreneurs instead of baby boomers in that role?" He wasn't altogether wrong, yet I did not want to manage investments any longer and I certainly did not want to be judged on the value of basis points versus wisdom and impact. Inspiring the minds and hearts of motivated people was my jam. The investment side got in the way of big ideas and even bigger impact. He asked again, "Why do you coach?" Then it became clear to me. I had been contemplating this question already, but I hadn't quite put my finger on it until then.

I did a lot of different things in the investment management world for twenty-two years. While excelling in the profession, I didn't enjoy it. I researched and studied to understand the science of investing, even learned from Nobel Laureates. I made prudent decisions for people in the management of risk and investment, but never liked that part of the business.

It always seemed that measuring performance down to single basis points did not reflect the value that I brought to the table. Vaughn pressed me harder, and he said, "Why do you care? You could go back to your old business. You have knowledge of finance. In fact, you know of all kinds of money-related things that you could create a business on. Why coach people?" And then it clicked for me. I thank Vaughn Pyne for unwittingly allowing me to share a story that I have kept close to my heart for a long time. I am going to share it with you.

Conversation three: My amazing wife, Sherri, and I were driving home from a speaker's club event I was hosting one night in Vancouver. She was always at my side at events as my business partner as well. We were marveling at how enjoyable the evening was and the stories that were shared. At the same time, I was disappointed with the low attendance compared to the high RSVP list. People confirmed they were attending, and then didn't show up.

This happened a couple times and my frustrations were coming out. I vented to Sherri. "Why the fuck won't people show up? If they only knew how great the experience was, how much I can help them and how much I care, people would flock to these events." My clients and club members knew this. I wanted to help many more.

Sherri said, "You are a great speaker. Your stories are entertaining, and people love them, but you don't really get to the heart of things. You don't tell your real story."

She was right. Two decades in the financial service industry preserving a professional image and avoiding true vulnerability had prevented me from an honest explanation of my 'why'. From that moment, I would lay my intentions bare.

Why I coach

Sometimes I get a little emotional about this whole conversation. In fact, I often lose my composure when speaking this truth out loud. I want to ask you,

"Have you ever worried, or have you been fearful in your life that you would be killed? Not that you might die from some known or discovered illness, not as a result of an accident, but that you feared your life was endangered because you might be killed by someone you know, in a predetermined kind of way?"

Not many people have, and for the few of you who experienced this, my heart is open to you. I am sorry you had to live through that.

At 23, I was in a pretty good place in my life. A couple years out of university, armed with a Kinesiology degree, with a rapidly growing personal fitness training agency business, good friends. I was having a ton of fun and didn't have many concerns in the world. I had moved back home to live at my parents' place, was working long hours and playing deep into the nighttime as well.

My work life balance didn't consist of much sleep and was excessive. It didn't take long before my body reminded me of my mortality and I suffered a serious bout of mononucleosis. It was a stark reminder that

I was living life a bit carelessly and it highlighted how little I knew about running a business. When I was sick, I couldn't even get off the couch. In fact, I felt like a captive watching the entire OJ Simpson trial. The drama was riveting and I was shocked at the outcome. It was during that time I began my path as a lifelong learner. Prior to that, I hadn't read much and didn't have any basic business knowledge.

I discovered three amazing books, *Think and Grow* Rich by Napoleon Hill, *Seven Healthy Habits* by Stephen Covey and *Guerilla Marketing* by Jay Conrad Levinson. Today, during my talks and workshops, I speak a lot about this period in my life. It is both a cautionary tale and one of enlightenment. I had always spoken of being ill and refocusing my life and my attention on business and marketing. But I'd never, ever talked about what was also going on at the exact same time until recently.

There I was, living back at home in the basement of my parents' tiny home. A fit, young man who was strong and healthy (aside from catching mono), who was pretty sure of himself. But for five evenings, in the middle of the darkest days of winter, before going to sleep, I would lock the door to my basement room. I locked it because I was worried that my father would come down the stairs and kill me in my sleep.

Today (and back then, as well) my father is a thoughtful, caring and kind man. He was suffering a major depression at the time. I thought he might be contemplating suicide, and extrapolated in my imagination that he would take other actions.

I thought if he were to actually go through with it, he might think the pain may be too great for his family to continue on, so I made an assumption that he would think it was better to kill me and my mother and then take his own life. I figured in some delusional, illogical way that could make sense to him. These were dark times and I envisioned the worst outcome. I believed this nightmare could happen and was genuinely worried. If need be, I could easily stand up to the man physically, but in my sleep, I wasn't much of a challenge.

You see, my dad has schizophrenia. He has endured his mental illness since its unrelenting appearance in his late teens. When I was in my first year of university taking psychology, we had to do research papers and my choice of topic was electro-convulsive (shock) therapy or ECT. Our parents told me and my sister about dad's mental health challenges when we were in our mid-teens. While I personally think they waited many years too long to tell us – we obviously knew something was not exactly right with our father – they were more likely concerned that we would speak about it with our friends and the resulting stigma that came with it in the community.

Keeping mental illness a secret was normal back then. It was a shame, really. Once the elephant sitting in our midst was revealed, we were able to discuss it, demystify it and ask questions.

As intense as you might guess this was, it was also hilarious sometimes. Some of the incredible stories of my dad's life with the disease were also comical. Like when he was living in transition from the institution where he was locked up for a year getting shock treatments: my mom told me the story of how his roommate, who was also recently released, was a "Peeping Tom". So you had the schizophrenic and the "Peeping Tom" living together. One was thinking he was seeing things and one voyeuristically watching things.

As part of the research for that psychology paper, I asked my dad about his experiences. One of his favorite actors to this day is Jack Nicholson. He described his early experience when he was diagnosed with depression and schizophrenia, spiraling into insanity, as exactly like the movie "One Flew Over the Cuckoo's Nest", only with a hundred times more shock treatments. He told me that had it not been for the ECT, he would not be sitting there telling me the story.

As crude as that was, he said it was the only thing that brought him back to reality and saved him from an institutionalized life. His manageable form of schizophrenia allowed him to function at a pretty high level and we occasionally saw glimpses of his "Beautiful Mind" – without the paranoid delusions. We luckily had Jack Nicholson from the "One Flew Over..." institution and not Jack from "The Shining". For this I am eternally grateful. With medication, my dad was (and remains) a functional, successful human, retired small business owner and a loving parent.

My father is a good man, a caring grandparent, a wonderful father and a genuinely decent, kind-hearted person. He is, by all accounts, a mental health success story. But in that little window of time in 1994, what was going on for him (and my mother) was, at a point, probably heavier than anything anyone might be able to bear at that time. During that time, I feared for my life, my mom's life and my father's. The medication he took for years, that kept him functioning, was giving him Parkinson's-like symptoms. He needed to change it so began trials with a number of different medications to find different solution so he wasn't headed down this Parkinson's road. But getting the chemical balance right, as you might well understand, is extraordinarily challenging.

At the exact same time, his psyche was vulnerable; my parents were losing their business. They ran a portable sign and installation company and the bylaws had changed dramatically. Essentially, in their tenth year of operations, they were working twice as hard for half the money. When it's -

20 degrees Celsius and you're still slugging away, your business is going under, your house is at risk, you're making half the money for twice the work, and you're in your early fifties, you wonder why you are doing what you're doing.

For my dad, the gravity of all of it was simply too much. He disappeared into his bed for weeks on end. My mom was left to run the rapidly failing business, maintain the household, hold off the creditors and overcome her challenge every single day. The body was on life support and she was making a valiant effort keeping the heart ticking. I was consumed with my own fledgling business. I was working hard and partying hard and likely self-medicating along the way. But I thought I was clear on one thing at that moment: my life was endangered.

Why is this moment in time important?

When I was between the ages of 20 to 28, my father was pretty much incapable of providing me mentorship, personal guidance and even a stern word from a caring parent. He was dealing with his own business challenges and mental illness. Because I was a pretty confident man with my own ideas, it is possible that I might have told him to back off if he tried to give me advice.

Even the attempt or whisper from him asking questions like, "Are you sure that's the right thing to do? Have you considered this?" would have been helpful. If only he was not sick and able to see that several of the individuals that I ended up working with as I shifted into the investment management business didn't have my best interests at heart. Maybe he would have said something.

He could have even said, "Mike, you might think they want you to succeed and have success, but they really only want that so that they benefit. They don't care about you." He would know - he was a smart man who experienced a lot and he might have shared that with me. My dad couldn't take me under his wing by identifying some things that I did extremely well and help me do more of that.

My sister and I have a good upbringing. We always heard, "Just be great at everything. We'll support you in everything you want to do, from music to sports to academics to lifestyle to relationships."

As a result, I had success with a lot of things, but I didn't have any understanding of that **one thing that made me unique**. My dad couldn't do it, and my mom was so busy holding everything together that she couldn't do it either. I had no strong external mentors in my life during that window of ten years. It might have removed some of the challenges in my life. While I know they wanted to be, my mom and dad couldn't be there, and no one else was there for me at that important time. It could have been the moment when it might have made the biggest difference.

It wasn't until I was in my forties that I finally began working with people who were helpful coaches and there for my best interests. They were hired to ask questions, listen and help by sharing their wisdom.

I realized that was why I coach. I ask important and sometimes pointed questions, listen, share my wisdom and provide guidance with a deep and practical understanding of the tools needed. The one thing that separates me from my coaching peers today.

I am committed to be the objective mentor who has the right combination of knowledge and experience, which listens and truly, truly cares about your success. I will be there at that moment when you need me the most.

Had I received that input at the right time, my adult life might have shifted twenty five years earlier to do the best thing for me and avoid a ton of the wrong roads, wrong choices and wrong mentors. I could have profoundly affected the lives of so many more people so much sooner. But I have that chance now and am making good on it. The life experience was great, but I see no valour in the school of hard knocks. There is more value in the school of good decisions, positive experiences and strong guidance. Experience is one thing, but avoidable tuition is another.

I have some knowledge, understanding, and you might even call it wisdom. The first twelve years of my investment business could have been skipped if I could have learned what I did in the last ten, but without those first years, I might not have been ready for the growth of the past decade. My early years provided a lot of great stories, but boy, a lot of those earlier years are a cautionary tale and demonstrate what not to do. They are certainly no "how to" manual.

What I'd like to do is offer my help so that you speed ahead with progress and do things right first. Believe me you'll still make your fair share of your own missteps, but they won't cost you as dearly as some of mine cost me.

My journey has given me knowledge; the tools and experience that may help you move things forward constructively so you can enjoy growth in a way that you never thought possible. You can get the freedom you were hoping to have in life and with your family. You'll discover you can think creatively and innovatively, and enjoy the freedom of time so that you can give back to have the greatest impact that is suitable for you and consistent with the values you bring to the table. That's it. That's my true reason for coaching. Now when I'm asked, I can share my truth. What is yours? This story has yet to be fully written, as I am a work in progress. I hope that sharing this provided clarity for when you hire me or you work with me, as you know what you're getting. I genuinely care.

You're getting someone who wants you to succeed and works every single moment that we spend together (and in the time when I am away from you) to understand better what it is that makes you tick, what it is that makes you unique. When we figure out what it is that makes you special and valuable to this world, we can connect it with proven strategies for success, ideas for freedom, and techniques and tactics for impact. Let me be that guide. Allow me to be your mentor. You'll be happy you did.

I created Grow Get Give Coaching to share my philosophy of business and life. I want to help teach entrepreneurs how to GROW their unique businesses larger and quickly connect their message with their ideal customer, how to help them GET more freedom to enjoy their lives and their families, and how they can GIVE back to their community and the causes they care for most.

A friend of mine, Biaggio, met with me just after my first workshop in 2014 and the launch of my third book and told me, "You know, I really like your Grow Get Give philosophy." I hadn't thought of it that away before. But from that moment, I have chosen to live my life in a way that allows me to check those boxes all the time.

My decisions around business, life and money are made considering whether I will continue to live a Grow Get Give life and how my actions will lead me further along such a path.

What exactly is a Grow Get Give life?

Living a Grow Get Give life is an aspirational philosophy that I believe should be pursued by everyone. Where you, as an entrepreneur, enjoy the growth of your business, your wealth and your impact. It is when you can share your true passion and purpose for what you do and what you offer to the world clearly. It is when you are working with or selling to the right customers all the time and building your wealth based on a positive combination of serving and selling. The result is that you experience true personal and professional growth.

Entrepreneurs are enticed by one goal – to get more freedom. Doing what you're passionate about, when you want to and with who energizes you is key to that. Controlling your time and energy and removing a ceiling on what you earn are also primary drivers for us. When you get more freedom, you can be more creative and innovative. Such freedom gives you more time to enjoy life while working less and earning more. True entrepreneurial freedom is realized when you are an owner and not when you have a job. People and processes are key to this. I invest my time and work only with those who feel it is their responsibility or calling to give back. I call them impact-minded entrepreneurs. The result of any successful business is **profit**. Beyond financial freedom, profit, in my world, is the means to make your impact – philanthropic or otherwise. When you get entrepreneurial freedom, you can live your dream for impact.

Giving, however, isn't only based in the philanthropic. It is also about improving your quality of life. Give back to yourself in ways that ensure your health and happiness. Give to strengthen your family and community relationships. Give back to the causes that matter most to you to make your big impact. Incorporating a Grow Get Give philosophy of life into your business planning is simple and your business plan should be too.

There are two rules of business that will help you build any business plan:

Rule #1: Attract clients + Rule #2: Delight clients

All things in business boil down to that. Build the strategies and tactics to accomplish those goals and you will find success. Design processes and implement systems to make attraction and delight repeatable and predictable. Often when I am working with owners, they become overwhelmed and focused on details that don't point in those directions. Expanding those two key rules will allow you to answer any questions about how you should build your business, products and services, how to sell, how to structure things and how to serve. After the two rules of business are clear and a business is in motion, entrepreneurs face very basic challenges that can be described in two more words: growth and freedom.

Build your mountain

Reaching any summit requires a mountain to climb. Your business must have the bedrock that everything else lies on. That bedrock then gives way to layers that raise the height of the peak. The highest mountains necessarily have the biggest bases.

For example, climbing Mount Everest doesn't even start until you reach base camp which is 5,364 meters above sea level and it takes three to four weeks to get there. Only then can you begin the forty-day endeavor to summit the peak, which is another 3,500 meters to reach the top of the highest mountain in the world at 8,848 meters! No mountain can stand tall without an incredible base. The pyramidal base of Mount Everest is roughly 15.7 km in circumference. The distance of 25,200 meters around means it is three times the size of its height.

Strong businesses have strong foundations. The goal of business is to make profit and the result of profit is impact. That is your summit. If you want to reach the highest peak, then you have to have the largest base. Your mountain starts with the foundation. That is about you, your customers and the people who support the business, including employees, shareholders and all other stakeholders. How you start and build your business is about establishing that base. Connecting your vision with what you do for others or how your products help people is the first step. Next is positioning your message to reach more and more people while developing a better or more attractive offering. This will result in many struggles, opportunities and challenges as you build your knowledge and experience. Defining your business and attracting your ideal customers starts here. As you move past your base, climbing higher, there are more needs: strengthening your position in the market, spreading the ideas, and marketing to a larger and larger audience. Selling is needed to earn money to grow the business. Delighting customers allows you to keep them, make them happy and retain them for future sales.

In order to coordinate your climb, you need preparation and a plan. Doing things as efficiently as possible will be the key to reaching the highest peak. You can't get closer to your summit if you are weighed down, exhausted and out of supplies. Building processes allows you to do all the above predictably; adding systems and people allows you to do this on a larger scale. When you get freedom from these concerns you can move swiftly to your goal.

When you stand atop the summit of your mountain you are alone, but you didn't get there by yourself. Your summit is where the profit is. There are no competitors, no noise and nothing but blue sky. You have reached your goal, made your profit and can contemplate your impact. At this point your actions feel effortless, and you experience the ultimate freedom by working less and making more.

A vast and sturdy foundation is what I've built in three decades. Knowledge gained from training, experience, coaches and mentors allows me to contribute to business owners and entrepreneurs in a myriad of ways. This is a deep resource that can be mined by my clients. The culmination of this allowed me to become an expert in business marketing, time management, finance and impact. This book is actually three books. Within them, I share what I've learned in my life and what I learned from other amazing people along the way. I shine light on a few things you should avoid, while giving you the secrets that worked to build a successful business for me and for others.

Along with these books, speaking, mastermind groups and my Grow Get Give Coaching business, I am thankfully and humbly positioned to enable others to make their own incredible impact. I urge you to read on, to learn, and to join me in pursuit of your own Grow Get Give life. You can find out so much more when you join us live for our annual two day Sea 2 Sky Summits and other training. Start by registering for your first transformational experience with me at:

www.Sea2SkySummit.com

www.mikeskrypnek.com

www.GrowGetGive.com

About Mike

Wouldn't it be great if there was someone in your life who could help identify what it is that you do best and how you might turn that passion and your natural gifts into success? We all hope we'll be seen for the amazing people we are and that others will hear or see our vision for our best life.

At the same time, we wish that special individual might be able to help us achieve it. Finding the combination of someone who listens, can see our true abilities and unique self, then understands how to make it our reality is rare.

Mike is that unique, intuitive person who listens and sees your true self. He learned a long time ago that his greatest strength is seeing the potential in others, understanding the gifts that are unique to you and developing ways to help you passionately build your business and life around them.

In thirty years of working, consulting and coaching others, and experiencing his own entrepreneurial failures and successes, Mike has developed the knowledge, expertise and skills needed to help you achieve your business goals. Imagine that: A custom toolkit full of strategies <u>and</u> tactics. He is committed to be the person in your life who "gets you" and gives you a chance to be the best you can be.

Mike is an accomplished business owner, entrepreneur, five time author, international speaker and coach. He's both a risk taker and a trusted steward. He is recognized as a leading authority and business coach for entrepreneurial and personal **GROWTH**, showing people how to **GET** freedom for their lives and families and helping families **GIVE** back to their community and causes that matter most to them.

He is powerful speaker and has delivered hundreds of motivating presentations. Mike has shared his **GROW, GET, GIVE philosophy** with <u>thousands</u> of entrepreneurs, business owners, advisors, charities and the millionaire businessperson next door.

Mike's quick learning style and innovative marketing ideas helped him envision and **GROW** a dominant niche legacy planning business focused on helping others **GIVE** to the non-profit industry. He sold that business a number of years ago in his quest to share his business and philanthropic knowledge with entrepreneurs like you, who's unique vision, needs a champion.

For his own **BIG IMPACT** in business, he was the guide for entrepreneurs and affluent families to redirect $12.5 million in **Big Impact Giving** to charitable causes between 2012 and 2018. His work with passionate entrepreneurs like you will help grow this to over $100 million in the next decade.

Mike understands how to differentiate and succeed. Through public speaking and training, he has shared his insights and knowledge of sales and marketing with hundreds of passionate, impact-minded entrepreneurs to gain top of mind positioning with their prospective customers and **GROW** their own unique business. Mike can teach anyone how to manage their time and their talent better to **GET** more freedom to enjoy their lives and their family. Life without passion, purpose and action is a life wasted.

GROW GET GIVE

BOOK ONE

GROW YOUR BUSINESS

GROW GET GIVE

Introduction

Fundamental to any business is the base upon which it is built. Like a mountain, there is no summit without a strong and sturdy base. The reason an owner entrepreneur does anything is at the heart of this. It aligns with their passion and purpose. WHY you do what you do, WHAT it is you do and WHO (in some cases WHAT) you do it for comprise the foundational elements of your business. Your vision for success, your impact and benefits to your customers and society need to be clear and, if possible, inspiring to others.

The goal of commerce in business is to exchange something of value in return for monetary compensation. A product or service can be a necessity (like water) or perceived to have value (like cucumber infused water) to the consumer. In any case, your goal is to convince and persuade your future customers that your product or service is what they want to exchange their currency for. Generally, there is a buyer for any service or product. The key is will there be a disproportionate number of buyers for yours? Can you make the product and sell it at a price that attracts buyers and allows you to make a profit?

Profit is the goal and when considering growing your business the goal is to attract more customers, sell more products and earn more money. You then can decide if you want to continue to grow the business to serve more people and make more money. For the impact minded entrepreneurs I help grow their business, they draw a straight line between profit and impact. The better they do the more impact they can have. It seems pretty simple, doesn't it?

Well, growth can be challenging. Early growth is always possible because it is easy to establish exponentially more revenue than the almost zero you have when you start a business. Gains in growth and sales often happen rapidly in start-ups and then taper off at some point. When tapering happens, challenges become clear. The top things entrepreneurs cite when considering their growth – or lack of it – is they either can't sell as much as they want, or they don't receive the price for their services that will give them the profit they need. This boils down to marketing.

Growing your wealth and impact requires selling something. We all sell, convince, or persuade others to buy our products or services. Success is measured in profit, but energy and time are also important barometers of growth. Understanding how your passion and purpose express your vision to the marketplace and knowing how to position your business in front of your prospective customers is tough. This first section, GROW Your Business, is written to help you think differently about how you can position your business to generate more sales and market to attract the right kind of customer for your business.

I was recently presenting to an audience at one of my two-day business building Sea 2 Sky Summits for entrepreneurs. Time and again, a self-described branding expert in the crowd kept beaming about the internet and social media as the only modern way to market and sell. In fact, it is true there are an overwhelming number of people who use the internet to sell, get their news, find information and communicate. In fact, they often think the internet will sell their goods for them. They believe a simple "social media strategy" or Google ad or Facebook ad campaign is what everyone needs. We differed in our opinion of the power and role of the internet in sales. I posited that the internet and social media, as powerful as they are, are simply tools for marketing. They are modern day TV, and TV was the modern version of radio and radio was the modern day version of the soap box and newspapers and magazines and print ads used along the way. The medium you choose to use for selling over time will change and something new will come along. Why you do what you do, what you say and how you say it matters more. I am tool agnostic. While biases will arise in terms of where your customers' eyes and hearts and wallets are, I won't suggest any one thing is better than the other. If your marketing is ad hoc and your messages are random and do not connect with your customer, then it doesn't matter how many followers you have, or how many likes your last post received. Nor does it matter how many drive-by impressions your bus stop ad or billboard got – if those driving by won't ever want what you're selling.

Email marketing and social media is like cold-calling without the immediate rejection…err, feedback. They are definitely more scalable, but they are still a "spray and pray" approach without true engagement – personal connection.

The answer is clear yet multi-faceted: Know why you make, produce or offer what you do, know who you are selling to, know what they want, serve them and communicate a message that connects. Do this any place your prospects and customers spend their time, get their information or network.

To help you think about how you can GROW your business, I have shared 30 secrets that I have learned and put to effective use to make more money and direct bigger impact that will help you. Use what you need or can implement, park the ideas that aren't right for you now and discard those that don't fit for you.

GROW GET GIVE

1. Your Why: Why You?

Our philosophical belief systems form the foundation for what is important to us. Understanding what this means to us is important in shaping our connections with staff, stakeholders, and customers. Our "*why*" is a connection between our principles — our personal and philosophical values — and our vision for the future. Jim Rohn once said, that "Philosophy drives attitude ... attitude drives action ... action drives results ... results drives lifestyle". While the process of getting to the heart of who you are and expressing it in a public manner can be a bit challenging and even uncomfortable, you'll be surprised at how liberating it is to be you professionally and personally.

Show people, unapologetically, who you are and why you are passionate about what you do.

My most complete business building experience was driven by a clear and unwavering "*why*". When I was serving families as a Portfolio Manager and Wealth Advisor, it took a long time to build up the courage to share my desire to help others give and work philanthropically, while in the investment business. For most of my career, my peer group were largely from the "greed is good" way of thinking and having a heart was a bit too touchy-feely. So, I suppressed my desires to do more, until the markets crashed. When that happened the hollowness of chasing returns and crunching data became clear for me. There *had* to be something bigger and more important for people; I knew it and wanted to help. My dedication to making a bigger impact was an intentional step that my colleagues stayed away from. My "*why*" was simply to help others realize their big impact. How I would do that manifested in a decision to help people give money away, and it was the opposite of my industry peers. I would flip our industry norms by changing the approach from hoarding to giving.

All personal service industries are sales businesses. To fulfill your purpose in business, you must sell, convince or persuade. Simon Sinek, in his book, *Start with Why: How Great Leaders Inspire Everyone to Take Action*, he said, "People don't buy WHAT you do, they buy WHY you do it." The essence of why a leader does what they do is the magical difference between success and average. To make a big impact, I couldn't settle with average.

It took me six years and I basically started from scratch. I began with a simple goal, my "*why*", and I wrote it in the last chapter of my first book: "*to help others make their big impact by helping to re-direct one million dollars per year to charity for the rest of my life*". I built a wealth planning business around connecting charities with the donors who love them. I was happy that beyond my own personal gain, my business was built on my "*why*". That allowed me the opportunity to affect the lives of thousands and thousands of people over multiple generations. A mission heart attracted families with shared values to join me in multiplying their impact. When you are clear on your "*why*", energy finds you every day.

Today, it is the same. Why I coach comes from a very personal place. My life experiences good and bad drive me every day. When others don't recognize your true potential and won't help you achieve success, I will be the one, who cares and possesses the tools and knowledge to lift you up.

2. Be Passionate

Loving what you do makes the doing enjoyable.
People are attracted to those who have passion about their work.

Your WHY is defined by your Passion.

You immediately know when you are in the presence of someone who is passionate. We are drawn to them. They are so damn crystal clear about why they do what they do. Without question, you will always recommend them to others. Passion is referable! There were people in my life that I would hire and hang out with because they were so passionate about what they did.

My dentist, now retired, was a man who was obsessed with doing the best possible work. He loved the craft of dentistry. I always felt I was in the best hands when sitting in his chair. Prior to Danny, I hated dentists and was horrified by the thought of having work done. I was sad to see him retire. His replacement was skilled, friendly and competent, but her passion simply did not match her predecessor. I became indifferent and returned only out of habit, for lack of knowing a better option.

There's an accountant I knew who I would highly recommend. He was passionate about the Income Tax Act. He loved every single line of the Act. To him, spreadsheets were foreplay and the lines in tax returns were like porn. He vociferously defended Canadian business owners and would quote every single word in the Act. I never personally needed or used his specific service, but his passion for the work would lead me to recommend him to anyone who needed him.

Lastly, we had a man who worked in my past investment firm as our company receptionist. That's right - a middle-aged man ran our reception desk in a typically male dominated industry and heavily conservative Canadian Caucasian clientele. He was from the Caribbean, which meant he stood out in a big way in a brokerage firm in Calgary. He loved that everyone meeting him for the first time was a bit surprised. Dexter was the most passionate person you would ever find when it came to his desire to make the customer experience memorable and special for every single client who walked into the lobby. He woke up every day with a positive energy and enthusiasm about his role in making the day special for everyone he met. His passion was contagious.

The words artistry and craftsmanship are synonymous with passion. The pursuit of personal achievement through what you do and drive to excellence cannot be realized without passion. Uncover yours and express yourself. Show passion to your customers, your family, and to yourself and your ideas. Live with passion and embrace the energy it provides. Passion is addictive. But, keep a clear mind as you indulge this in your business. Don't fall in love with your passion if no one else will buy it. Passion alone can make you poor.

Leading with passion can produce great outcomes. Paul Alofs, the President of Canada's HMV enterprise in the early nineties, had had vision and successfully carried HMV Music through the changing times in the retail music industry. The company increased its revenue from $30 million to $200 million. In his book, "*Passion Capital*", Alofs quantified passion as energy plus intensity plus sustainability. He went on to describe seven basic principles to which passion must be applied to generate a spark and wrote that passion capital is the foundation upon which all other forms of capital are built. I largely agree with Paul and ultimately believe that without passion there is mediocrity. This should instill caution for the enthusiastic entrepreneurs in the crowd. Alofs didn't have success simply by being passionate about what he did. He took very measured steps to apply his passion to successful business-building principles. Beware: passionate people go broke all the time. It isn't enough to be passionate; you must execute smart, effective, money-making ideas well. People must clearly understand what your passion is through how you share it, communicate and the actions you take. This must be unmistakable.

Passion + Purpose + Action = Success

My passion for coaching was so strong it forced me to change the direction of my life, just as I was reaching a peak in the growth of my investment business. Day after day, I could not focus on managing money when I only wanted to guide people and share the wisdom I had gained over decades of experience. When I was just starting to make the transition to coaching and was writing my third book I shared the ideas I was passionate about with my business coach, James.

I had been mulling the idea of shifting to build niches for entrepreneurs and helping them give back. I wanted what I had a passion for to be right there for everyone to see so I created what I thought was a catchy acronym for my passion program. I called my idea *DYN&MIC* training — "*Dominate Your Niche & Make It Count*". I sat with James in his home. He first had a look on his face like, "What?!?" He then asked me to explain this in 30 seconds… well, I began some long-winded explanation about how niche building is powerful and entrepreneurs need to learn this and when they become rich they can give the money back. And I would be the person who would train them. All this might be true, but boy, did my explanation land with a thud. I was passionate about my intentions, but it was clear no one would get it. We needed to simplify and clarify. People would never invest their hard-earned money in what I couldn't explain — just because I lived it with passion and believed it would be good for them.

The objectivity my coach brought to this allowed us to come up with my original Big GROWTH Big IMPACT. It said it all. I helped people get big growth and make a big impact. That's what I was passionate about. Helping entrepreneurs GROW their business, GET more freedom, and GIVE back to their community. My passion was undeniable, but until then, I had no idea how to present it.

> *Passion is crucial, but passion that connects is powerful.*
> *"If you don't have your dream, then others won't be able to have theirs."*
> - *Rudy Rutiger, focus of the biographical movie, "Rudy".*

It all comes down to passion. It is what drives you to move forward, to dive into a subject or market, and inspires lifelong learning. If you're not able to connect your passion with a vision of the future in a way that is better or ideal for you, then you are not able to pursue it. If you learn how to share it clearly with others, they will be able to benefit and enjoy their dreams as well. Your passion will support them, lifting them up, enabling them. Without the passion of you pursuing your dreams, you can never help others to pursue theirs.

3. 'Hey smarty pants. No one cares!'

Passion plus purposeful action equals success. Your passion is your why, your purpose is your what. Think of this as your professional skill set; it is what you offer of benefit to your potential customers in your chosen field of business or in the marketplace. Do you serve and guide? Or do you lead through your products? Do you support and assist in the products or services you provide, or do you create them? Having a clear understanding of what it is you've been trained to do is important. There are certain skills you have that others may not, and your future customers will want.

People are compelled to follow passionate leaders. They will want to work with a company or person they trust, that they perceive to have their best interest at heart, and who are competent. When you are hired as the authority or expert, you are expected to have the skills needed to carry out the task. With my dentist, or accountant, or even the receptionist, I was comforted that their passion drove their expertise, but I did not share the passion they had for their craft. As such, I did not care to hear all the intricacies of their work that made them great at it. In fact, if they decided to go into elaborate detail about what they did, it would bore me, and I would lose interest. When they could simplify what they did, I remained interested. You must always understand that:

*Your customers want you to know what you're doing, but they often do not care to hear the intricate details about it. They are most interested in **their experience** as a customer.*

Keep this in mind the next time you feel compelled to explain how great you are, what you know or what you have accomplished in your academic life. Be mindful of what your customers want.

What I "*do*" has two parts. The first and most important is my unique ability — personal connections, probing conversations to uncover true goals and values, identifying unique ability and developing practical solutions to achieve those goals. The second is my professional skill set. I have extensive technical expertise in corporate structure, marketing, investment, finance, cash flow, retirement funding, estate planning, charitable giving and planning, tax strategy, and estate planning. My skills support the implementation of appropriate tactics identified in our discovery and strategic planning process. The last thing most people want me to detail in our discussions is how smart I (think) am at this, how the science of the tactics work, or why the theory or models I use to make decisions is better than other options in the marketplace. They want to hear about themselves, their own problems, and gain confidence that what I can do for them will get them closer to their goals.

When your passion is backed up with purpose, you can lead others to higher goals. In fact, when you are clear, you can inspire others to their own purposeful action. There was a story once that described Kennedy and his entourage touring NASA after hours. They were there to review the progress of Kennedy's moonshot plan. As they walked through the darkened halls, they encountered a janitor pushing his broom and pulling his cart. They stopped to speak with the man and questioned him as they had been doing with others. They asked him what he was doing at NASA. He didn't recite the details of how he cleaned the floors, or emptied the wastebaskets, he responded, "I am helping put a man on the moon". He was 100% clear that his purposeful actions were part of the bigger purpose of what NASA was doing. He was inspired by the simple goal to put a man on the moon and he summarily understood that the explanation of what he did would be more usefully described as helping to put a man on the moon.

GROW GET GIVE

4. Build A "Mountain of Credibility™"

Stand atop your mountain — become credible in the eyes of your customers. Authority positioning is a blend of experience, expertise, and perception. Your experience allows you to position yourself in markets where your expertise can be leveraged by customers who perceive you to be the most credible authority on the subject. Building your Mountain of Credibility™ can be done in many ways and you must start now if you wish to secure your position as the subject matter expert in your field or market.

To build and climb your own Mountain of Credibility™ is the key to gaining top of mind positioning with your prospects and clients. It really is like "scaling the peak of a mountain". In the 60+ years since Sir Edmond Hilary and his Sherpa, Tenzing Norgay, were the first to reach the summit of Mount Everest, over 4,000 people have successfully done so, over 300 people have lost their lives attempting, and literally billions of people have never even tried. When someone says they've climbed Everest, we are still in awe of the achievement. In fact, that adventurer even becomes credible for things outside of their area of expertise. For example, if they were mingling at a conference of jellybean flavor testers and were asked their opinion of the chemical blend that makes bubble gum flavor possible, anyone within 20 feet would stop to listen to their insights on the matter. It is amazing.

Reaching the top of the mountain in a marketing sense is extremely challenging. From speaking, to writing articles, to appearing on radio or television, to being interviewed or endorsed by an expert or celebrity, there are many ways to begin the climb to credibility. However, despite thousands of books being published every year, writing a book still creates instant credibility and places the author at the very peak of the mountain immediately.

The accomplishment of having written and published a book presents you as a perceived authority on a topic.

It is something so many people want to do and hope to, but writing, finishing, and publishing a book eludes most of those folks. Everyone has a book "in them" but proportionately, few get one "out of them". In this accomplishment, people are impressed. Oprah took this acknowledgement to a whole new level and redefined how a celebrity endorsement of a book written by you will place you on the highest peak as the recognized authority. I won't lie, while it sounds very simple, it can be extremely difficult to write a book. I found that simply putting words on paper was not too challenging … and even organizing thoughts and ideas wasn't that difficult either. How many times have you heard someone say they have been working on a book, but you never see it completed? The only thing harder than starting to write a book is finishing one. It doesn't have to be an epic, or the century's greatest novel. To be effective for building credibility, it must be a complete, sensible and topical book. When asked about some of his "smaller" books, my business coach, James always responded to the typical critic by saying,

"The tiny little book I wrote is a heck of a lot better than the book my competitors didn't write".

There are thousands of authors published each year. In order to write their book, they had to do the research. Thus, they have become an authority on that subject. When it is a published work, people recognize and respect this for its completion. Finally, a book is content. Content is in huge demand. Quality, helpful content is invaluable. An author makes themselves a valuable resource for others who seek to <u>learn</u> more on a subject, or <u>market</u> one.

When the stock market crash of 2008 hit I was working to establish myself as a credible authority in the planned giving and estate planning space. Cold-calling and introducing my thoughts on why a charity or endowment needed to work on their governance with such a smart guy as myself got me nowhere. Then I decided to write a white paper on the biggest challenges of the time faced by my target clients (charities and their endowments struggling to attract funding during a recession).

Before I wrote my first book, *"Philanthropy; an Inspired Process"* in 2010, I was still struggling to gain a foothold in the non-profit marketplace. I was perceived as the fox in the henhouse. They distrusted my entire profession, my peers and me. In order to serve them, I needed to reach the influencers – the board of directors – to share my knowledge and ideas for a better process. Traditional marketing did not open the door wide enough with this market. The negative perception was too great. I needed to capture their attention as a useful resource.

Then, I wrote my book on the philanthropic journey taken by famous iconic philanthropists and donors moving from involved giving to committed philanthropy. It became the most meaningful "business card" I had ever possessed. Almost instantly, I gained credibility. I was invited to speak at numerous industry events and conferences. I was interviewed on the radio, in magazines. Executive directors of charities would meet me in my office! I also received numerous opportunities to present to the board of directors of organizations I wanted to work with. Getting their ten minutes was elusive before. Writing a book seemed magical. And it was. It was because it was hard. There is respect for the effort and an understanding that you've done the difficult work to become the authority. Always remember: the book you write is exponentially more powerful than the one your competitors won't write.

4b. Carry A Magical Business Card

The author stands at the top of the Mountain of Credibility™. Your book places you in the upper echelon of accomplishment. Authors are revered for the accomplishment. I have the pleasure to meet Jack Canfield and speak with him personally. He is the author of *Chicken Soup for the Soul* and the co-founder of one of the biggest book franchises on the planet. He knows about the power of books and being the author. To be the author is to be the perceived subject matter expert.

"When smart people want to find answers they go to books, and when they want to hire the expert, they hire the author".

This is paramount wisdom gleaned from Jack.

His company has half a billion books in print worldwide!

Upon completion and publication of my first book, the results were magical. Presto! In markets or in board rooms I had been shut out of before, I was welcomed. Those few minutes of attention needed to become introduced as a valuable resource to my prospective clients was offered to me and inevitably it was extended to 30, 60 or 90 minutes.

Being an author was no less than a miracle. It became the unquestionable reason why I was "in the room" and it changed my business, my revenue and my life profoundly. With complete conviction I can say that my book created tenfold growth in an expedited time for me. Without it, all marketing and my effort to sell would have been a never-ending grind and the timeline to success would have seemed to be forever.

J. Conrad Levinson wrote one of the first influential books on marketing that I read. "Guerilla Marketing" was a staple on the shelves of entrepreneurs everywhere in the 90's. When asked about the power of books and "how much he made from selling his books", Levinson responded that he made $10 million! He said he had only sold about $35,000 worth of books, but that he made and estimated $9.965 million from the sales of courses, speaking engagements, services, products, etc. that came as a result of his book. That was the magic of writing a book for him. It can be your reality too.

Once you've written one, you will want to write another and another. If you are an entrepreneur moving into new markets and creating unique offerings, it will be something that you do every time you make a shift. My second and third books were part of my evolution from charity advisor to charity and donor consultant to entrepreneur and business coach. My fourth was a collaborative effort to deepen my expert positioning and my last three-book set – this one – was used to re-introduce myself as a valuable coach while expanding into new markets. All my books placed me at the top position as an authority in my chosen market and continue to act as the best business card I have ever owned. Handing a new prospect or contact or future partner your book – instead of that 2" x 4" hunk of cardboard – is the most effective and magical first impression you can consistently make.

Be an author.

5. Focus on your unique ability

What is it that makes you unique? Arguably it is locked up in your DNA, your fingerprints, your eyes. Physiologically speaking, there are many ways we are naturally different from one another…yet in basic carbon composition, very similar. Psychologically, the combination of our genetic make-up influenced by the environment and personal experiences throughout our lives offers us more diversity. How we view the world and interact with it become traits that enhance our personality. When people can focus their energy on these things, they stand out. In business, those that differentiate themselves from others, shine. Often, identifying what it is that makes us unique eludes our attention. When we are not aware or do not focus on what we do better or differently than others in business we are left wondering how our competitors seem to frequently attract the right people and opportunities to their lives while we don't.

Kathy Kolbe, renowned for her work in what is called "conative" skills identification and measurement, launched a rating system called the Kolbe A Index™. It provides a rating of the Four Action Modes® she identified that represent human instincts used in creative problem-solving. The premise is simple.

If you hope to get the most out of people, place them in situations and careers where their strongest attributes are used.

Their natural behavioral tendencies will likely provide them more engagement, more possibilities for success, and greater passion for their activities. The Strategic Coach™ program's first step for all new members is to have them take their Kolbe A Index™ test. This gives their "students" an excellent idea of what they should be focusing on to begin their coaching experience. There are four key areas identified.

They are:

1) "Fact Finder" – detail and complexity, providing the perspective of experience.
2) "Follow thru"– deals with structure and order, and provides focus and continuity.
3) "Quick Start" – deals with originality, risk-taking and uncertainty.
4) "Implementer" - deals with physical space and ability to operate manually, and provides durability and a sense of the tangible.

In fact, coaching members even walk around with name tags that have their Kolbe scores noted right on them. This behavioral testing focuses a person on what The Strategic Coach™ labelled the concept of "Unique Ability".

There are many methods of testing your personality and behaviours, ranging from the Myers Briggs test, to Tom Rath's "Strengths Finder", and more. I have found the Kolbe A Index™ to be the most revealing when it comes to entrepreneurs and business. I require all my clients to take the test, and you won't get past the first interview working with me unless you have taken the test either. Finding out your "score" doesn't tell us everything we need to know. However, we must combine that behavioral knowledge with our skills, experience, and practical applications of what it is we do and the industry we work within. Identifying what you do, how you do it, and what you are naturally inclined to do matters. A person who is attracted to systems and processes and feels better crunching numbers on a spreadsheet is not the person you look to drive innovation in the organization. Their contribution might be integral to innovation, but their role would help the visionaries in providing the background and data needed to make sound judgements. Knowing your strengths and learning to embrace them and exploit them will help you rise to more success. Do not resist this.

Kids, students, and even adults who become narrowly focused and "obsessed" with specialization are often ostracized. They are considered out of touch with everyone else, or ignorant of what others are doing or feeling. In society, an emphasis is also placed on addressing weaknesses. Somehow there is a belief that applying energy to improve the things we're worst at is better invested there than applying the same – or less – energy to that which we do well. The words well-rounded have become a compliment, though one could argue that it basically means average, or status quo. To be well-rounded in a social or emotional context is a huge advantage in life, generally. But when it comes to the skill or thing you do best, specialization is incredibly valuable.

In my life I have been a poster child for the jack of all trades, master of none. I was good at sports, music, academics and good at inter-personal relationships. I never intentionally focused on and developed specific areas I had real talent for — mostly because I couldn't figure out what my real talent was. No one helped me figure this out either. I would say I was a high achiever … not an overachiever.

Later in life I learned my Kolbe A Index™ score. It was 2-3-10-2 and it placed me in very select company. Had I understood this as a young adult, I could have realized powerful results early on. Knowing it was natural for me to pursue multiple opportunities, adapt to changes and synthesize many ideas or concepts to come up with action, might have led to incredible success early on in life. I gravitated to settings that fit my profile, but without intention, I made cognitive decisions that weren't consistent with my conative strengths. Business coaching allows me that dynamic environment and my purpose is to help others discover their unique qualities and embrace them.

You will find throughout this book and in my storytelling, there are many times that I reference our children. They provide so many life lessons, but also their lives have focused around the unconventional. Their passions and pursuits as well as unique skills have leaded them to explore career paths that are highly specialized. In my last book, I discussed school and grades. As much as we desire our children to be "well-rounded" citizens, we expect their top grades and focus at school will be on the skills that best positions them to explore their unique abilities, allowing them to excel in those areas. Interestingly, their grades in all subjects rose when they spent more time focusing on improving their best attributes.

When people focus their energy on their strengths, they develop habits and skills to excel at them. Those habits get applied to every other area of their lives and they then see improvements in other areas. Our daughter Madison exited elementary school with a diagnosed learning disability significantly affecting her math and reading comprehension. She worked with tutors, applied herself conscientiously and developed incredible behaviors and skills to enable her to learn. Six years later, she ended high school with marks in the 90%'s and early acceptance into film school as a result. She focused on her unique ability to "do art" and specifically, special effects makeup artistry. She has become self-taught and developed to a level of professional quality before formal schooling, because she understood how to excel by focusing on her unique "thing".

The habits she has put in place will carry her through her lifetime as her professional skills develop. Focusing on her unique ability got her noticed and selected for more opportunities for excellence in the areas that come naturally to her and which she is passionate about.

GROW GET GIVE

6. Squeeze Your Niche

Once you have identified your unique ability and how it supports the way you do business and how you construct your vision for the future, embrace it and look for as many ways as possible to enhance that specialty. The closer you move to your unique offering or ability, the more attractive you become. It sounds a bit counterintuitive; in **order to grow and happily succeed you must narrow your focus**. You'd think if you were more common, with a larger reach, you'd have more sales...true, if you consider manufacturing in China. But with it comes a perception of low value, the lowest common denominator, the biggest headaches and most often, the lowest margins. Even then, if that is your unique ability – being the top mass producer on a global scale or being "everything to everyone" – you are a specialist in a way. In most cases, however...

...a race to the bottom is a race not worth winning.

What I mean by bottom is the lowest price point, the broadest customer base and the biggest selection – a commodity. You can choose to go there in business, but it will result in challenges with profit margins, lack of differentiation, vulnerability to competition and stress with scale, processes, and energy. Specialty and niche businesses scream value. There is a higher premium to be gained. Think of your own business. If you had fewer clients who were paying a little bit more and complaining less it would be a good thing, right? What if every time you added a new ideal client, they increased your profit and reduced service demands while stimulating your mind and as a result allowed you to make a bigger impact? You would enjoy your business more while having more time and energy to create, innovate and grow. Also, the further you squeeze into your unique offering the deeper your customer relationships can be.

Think of how this has been done on a large scale with premium brands. Look at BMW, Mercedes, Apple, Patagonia and Four Seasons go to great lengths to differentiate themselves from their competitors. Real or perceived specialization works. These brands act like and make the claim that they are unique and therefore special. Their marketing goes out of its way to show that. They build a cache around their image. They invest more money into appearance, function and marketing. People pay more and value their products above others.

Want to know why more businesses aren't doing this? Not every brand or business needs to be the premium brand…nor wants to be. One reason is fear. The fear is that you will lose or alienate current customers and there won't be enough new ones to make up for that perceived loss. Squeezing your niche more and more requires a dogged belief that what you are offering will be valued and desired by your future customers.

Often value is perceived rather than real. The quality versus reliability of a car is no different to those who simply seek transportation and view vehicles for their utility. In fact, to many people, a high-end auto might be viewed as wasteful and unnecessary– even unappreciated. However, there are those who admire, appreciate and seek quality. They look at driving as an "experience" and enjoy the message a luxury car sends to others. Whatever the reason, someone will pay tens of thousands more for the difference. Once you have squeezed hard enough and built a business that supplies true value to a niche customer, your competitors are few and far between.

In their famous paper turned book, "Blue Ocean Strategy". Professor W. Cahn Kim and Renee Mauborgne made a great breakthrough in using this metaphor to describe this opportunity. Consider if you are swimming in blood filled "red oceans" where the sharks are all feeding in fertile waters where they must compete viciously with each other to survive. In business your competitors want to "consume" you. In fact, your customers can't even see you through the proverbial blood in the water. As a result, you spend all your time treading water, hoping to survive the onslaught of competitors, the indifference of customers and the cost of sharing the waters. Then your business dies quickly, but you experience a slow "death" of realization. You should be swimming freely. The reason people use multiple products, multiple contractors, multiple advisors and believe their eggs would be better off in many baskets, is because they can't tell the difference. The blue ocean is where you swim alone, in fresh and uncharted waters to stand out. You are unique and available to those who appreciate your vision and buy what you offer.

GROW GET GIVE

6b. Do the dirty work

Do the things that others won't do. Put the effort and time and energy into learning and doing projects, tasks and skills that very few people will do. By doing this, the expertise you develop builds a competitive moat around your business. Standing out in your niche, but then acquiring skills or talents that others do not have, will ensure you get the highest compensation for the service or product you provide. People invest more in specialists. Be perceived as the subject matter expert and you will attract deeper engagement and larger sums for doing what you love.

Our young adult daughter, Madison, is a beautiful young lady. Strong, determined and caring, she's curious about nature, art and the world around her. School never came easy, so she developed great habits and ways to focus her attention. When she found certain things interesting, she would learn them in all their intricate detail. She always had an interest in science. When she was twelve and in grade seven, she came home from junior high school, full of wisdom and excitement to share what she learned that day.

She said, "Dad, do you know anything about niches (pron. "neesh-es")?" And I said, "Niches (pron. "nitch-es")?" She looked at me with kind of a sideways look and kind of gave me the *"aw dad, come on, really?"* in her newly developing teenage girl voice. She rolled her eyes. I said, "Okay, niches ("nitch-es"), niches ("neesh-es"), whatever." At the same time, she goes, "Okay, well whatever." Nearly exasperated, "Anyways, Dad, here's the thing. Do you know anything about the dung beetle?" I said, "Yeah, I kind of know about the dung beetle, I haven't seen one in person before, but what do you mean? Tell me more."

She went on to say, "We learned in class that the dung beetle has guaranteed its survivability among its predators, its prey and its competitors." I responded, "Madison, please tell me more because it sounds kind of interesting." She said, "Well, what happens is the dung beetle rolls up the poop of other animals into balls and stores it in holes in the ground. It then has a saved and secured food source. Yes, they use poop as food. So, they always have this food source available to them to get by on and quite frankly, no other animals or creatures want to be in the poop business. Because of that, they guarantee their survivability. So that's their niche." I said, "That's perfect Maddie. You really understand the idea of niches." She REALLY got it!

When I think of niches, I think of business niches. What I would suggest to any entrepreneur, is when you have identified that quality, that unique thing or that unique product that you create or sell, you must squeeze harder, squeeze that niche. People value things that they perceive as rare, unique or special. By doing those things that others won't do in securing and exploiting your very own niche, you build a dominant position in your market. Ultimately, we want to be in the poop business. It's better to be doing the dirty work, with no competitors, no peers, standing alone, than it is to compete with people doing nothing extraordinary, nothing unique and nothing new in a race to the undifferentiated bottom. Excelling at things others don't want to do, or won't do, is a quality in life personally and professionally, that will see you through

Choose the poop business for yourself.

7. See it differently and build it yourself

It has been described by Trout and Ries in their book, "The 22 Immutable Laws of Marketing". That is Law #2: The Law of Category, when everyone is battling it out for a market, take a different spin on it and create your own category – which you then dominate. It requires that you maneuver to create your own market. This can be a large shift or subtle one. Moving to one category removed from the mainstream competitors can be all that is needed to differentiate your offer to succeed and open a niche opportunity. If you can't own the category, create your own. Think back to doing the dirty work. This is a very similar concept, although where the dirty work can be done in the competitive market where similarities abound – but your differentiator is that you simply do more, better. Do what others **won't do**. In the new category, **effort goes into doing what others haven't done before**. When you create your own category, you have carte blanche to do it the way you want to and the way it is perfectly fit for you. In this case, you will have to work harder or faster than anyone else because you're paving the way in an area to create expert positioning, and credible authority. You might have a head start for a while, but when others finally realize your success, some will want to model it. Second movers get a break, because they simply don't have to innovate as you do. The key is there is only one recognized leader.

The law of category requires you validate your presence in that category by providing tangible proof that you deserve to occupy the space, that it is your **indisputable category**. By creating your own unique category, you have a chance to simultaneously create all the barriers to entry to your niche. No one paid attention when you started out. It was imperative you donned blinders and earplugs while your peers were wondering why you would enter or create this market.

By the end, they'd be saying to themselves, "Holy cow! How did they accomplish so much? How did they attract so many ideal customers, and why can't I do what she's doing?" By then it is too late for them, you own your own category, built your Mountain of Credibility™ and now you stand atop in plain sight attracting your ideal customers at will. By the time anyone realizes what you've done; the barrier to entry will be too great. At this point competitors will be too lazy, too uninspired, and perceive that they're not able to compete with you in that space. Law of category is crucial.

8. Master the perfect pitch

"In Japan, the hand can be used like a knife, but this method doesn't work with a tomato. " Suddenly the hand tries to cleave a plump tomato.

Splat!

– Barry Becher and Ed Valenti, founder of Ginsu Knives.

"Order now!" "Operators are standing by," "But wait, there's more!"

*(*All trademarked by Becher and Valenti*)*

Kevin Harrington is known as the founder/inventor of the infomercial and "As Seen On TV". To figure out how to better use television to sell more products, Harrington considered – very late one night – investigating advertising on TV in the late-night, time slots that seemed to be test patterns or repeat programming. He found out he could buy those time slots for his use and negotiated extremely low costs to do so. He would use the ultra-cheap time to create mini programs with which to showcase products he wanted to sell. It was then that he started the **infomercial**. One of his first and most widely known products was the Ginsu knife. He saw Barry Becher working his magic at tradeshows and how he pulled huge crowds as he sliced through steel and tomatoes with the Ginsu knife – "the only knife you will ever need". He instantly knew that this demonstrative selling approach would be a great thing to put on TV. He crafted an extra-long commercial of the entire live presentation. It was a smash! Kevin Harrington began his huge impact on TV and selling at that moment. He would turn the products AND their "pitchmen" into celebrities. He also discovered Tony Little, a brash, ponytail-wearing fitness trainer and turned him into a marketing celebrity. Kevin launched his three decades long career and a $2 billion fitness product marketing empire. Funny thing…after I graduated kinesiology, I got my dream job working in professional sports right out of school. Unfortunately, that career was interrupted, and the league's season ended early due to the majority owner being indicted for embezzlement. The entire league folded, and I was left looking for work. It was the best five-month gig I ever had, for sure! Without a job, I ended up working in the produce department at a grocery store to pay my bills. At that time, I was offered a job as a personal trainer and turned it down. My naïve logic at the time was that I was educationally overqualified to count reps for the rich and overweight. It was also because I didn't want to be perceived as a "ponytail-wearing Tony Little" pushing the "ab-roller". My academic snobbery and a desire to seek perceived credibility over aggressive marketing was clearly a questionable decision…Tony has a multi-billion empire now…and me, well, not quite.

Without Kevin Harrington and his decision to create what we all know as the infomercial, we probably wouldn't have bought the Ginsu Knife, the Sham Wow! and Slap Chop, or anything that Tony Little was hocking as a fitness product. For the '90s and '00s, the infomercial became the new advertisement. It was one of the most incredible shifts in the use of media and television for sales that had ever been done. Almost everyone can tell a story of what they bought late at night because of a compelling and entertaining infomercial. Hey, in the 90's, I even bought the entire 80's music CD collection late one night after a great evening out. I was mailed one over-priced CD per month for years before I stopped my subscription. Kevin Harrington turned the infomercial into his own multi-billion-dollar business success and went on to launch "As Seen On TV" and many more successful ventures, not to mention his appearances as a "shark" on ABC's entrepreneurial pitch show, "Shark Tank".

He said that one of the most important things about selling on this platform is that the infomercial puts you on the spot and forces everybody to master the perfect pitch. In other words, you must completely understand your audience. Know what they **want**, not what they need. Know what they what they desire, what they have-to-have. Package your product or service, what you offer, in a way that is desirable to them, so that they're willing to part with their capital <u>immediately</u>. In other words, make an undeniable and meaningful trade for the value they perceive and convince them to buy that instant. Kevin Harrington says,

"Tease, please, seize."

Tease. Tease with what they want. Tease with the desire, what people are looking to achieve in their life, the benefit to them. *Tease* by gaining attention with a problem. Identify the prospective buyer's pain, demonstrate that you understand it, and show how your product or service will relieve it. Show that there's promise for them to achieve success or relief…and you are the one to help them.

Please. Deliver a solution or a product or an idea that connects their goal with reality, the potential, of achieving that success. Connect the dots for them. You must, ALWAYS *"please"*. Use unique benefits and testimonials to convince people that what you offer is something that may help them achieve this relief of pain or relief of the challenges in front of them in a way that would be reasonable for them.

Seize. Seize the opportunity to ensure that they act to do what's good for them and what they need in a way that gets the sale closed. Create access, create flexibility, and create the open opportunity for a buyer to make that purchase. *Seize*. Make an irresistible offer. In other words, make an offer that they can't refuse, that they must act on, that they absolutely would be missing out if they didn't, and in other words, close the sale.

When you're considering mastering the perfect pitch, consider those three words.

9. Build A Reputation, Build A Brand

"A Coke and a smile", "Just Do It", "I'm Lovin' It", "It gives you wings", "A Diamond is Forever"

Let's talk about *branding*. Almost everybody I talk to in business say that they want to *launch their brand* or that they must *work on their branding*. They will say "this is part of my branding effort". As much as we would all want to be a household name, this is something that can be extremely costly. It is possible when you get to a point where your business, product or service has become so incredibly compelling and sought after that you start to achieve this status. However, attempting to draw comparisons to your small business and Coke, or Apple, or Macdonald's or Red Bull, must stop. Modeling what your largest favorite brands do is a good thing. Building your own business by applying the best of what they do is great and recommended but spending money as part of a branding campaign could very likely make you broke.

Effective branding can be a billion-dollar activity - or at least a multi-million-dollar activity – when done properly. Branding is what Nike and Red Bull do. It's about investing long term in a ubiquitous presence to embed their image in our psyche. It takes a continual, year over year, daily – even hour by hour – application of marketing across all possible mediums, globally. You can pursue that if you like, but they throw millions and billions of dollars at branding, which makes their logo, their trademarks, their trade names and their businesses omnipresent. We might wish that our business names, our logos and our jingles would become part of popular culture, but it is like becoming a viral hit online…it just doesn't happen often or for many. That doesn't mean you're settling for less by not focusing on branding per se. What it means is that you will direct your focus and your resources to making sales, building a lasting reputation and becoming referable as the sought-after product and/or expert. One could say this is the essence of brand building.

Your brand is your **reputation**. We all must make every effort to build it. Your energy is best applied to building your company, your following, your service, your marketing language and your networks.

No brand is "branded" until it is established.

Any business owner and entrepreneur without a team of marketing and branding experts, or a large budget devoted for this, should consider the power of positioning. The heart of it is the use of marketing to build your brand. It is your representation of who you are, what you sell and what you offer to others (your customers). It all begins by constructing a reputation. Build a reputation for what it is you do, who you are and how you serve your customer. Develop a following of people who are at the very least, slightly interested in what you do. At best, those who are attracted to your brand become completely engaged in what you do.

Instead of worrying about traditional branding, build a reputation for yourself in your community. It will attract prospects to you. Then build your family of customers. They're important to you in your livelihood beyond anything that you would imagine. Again, your reputation is what you're known for and why people will pay more. They'll pay you for **who they think you are** rather than just what you are.

Your reputation doesn't only have to be earned; it can be assumed. Start by calling yourself the best – and believe it. You can lead by reputation, good or bad, before anyone meets you.

Cassius Clay aka Muhammad Ali was one of the most expert branding people ever. He didn't need a billion-dollar campaign. All he did is say, "I'm the greatest," repeatedly, and people eventually agreed. Not everyone bought in, but a LOT of people did. He kept saying he was the greatest, and then he backed it up by knocking people out and winning exciting fights. The audience was predisposed to believing he was the greatest, so any impressive feat simply secured that belief and the legacy was born. He may not have been the best boxer in history, but when you think of him, you think of his incredible brand: Muhammad Ali, "the greatest". Muhammad Ali, the champ.

GROW GET GIVE

10. Define Your Ideal Customer & Write It Down!

How can you serve anyone, sell anything or make any money if you don't know who your customer is? This is your perfect fit, or right fit customer. They are IDEAL for you. They are your match for millions of dollars. You will make more money, have less stress, and enjoy your work more when you work with the right customer. You don't have to meet them all, nor do you have to meet them all, but you certainly must know their "type".

To be sure you are clear about whom you will serve; you must create a detailed written description of whom you are selling your products, goods, or services to. Many businesses now go as far as creating their very own ideal customer avatar. Giving your ideal customer a virtual appearance with attributes that are both descriptive and visual will help to create a clear image of them. Adding detailed data and specific demographic information will practically make them real. Getting to know them personally, intimately, is the key to attracting them.

When writing your description, include their demographics, their gender (if applicable), likes/dislikes, fears, concerns, greatest challenges, buying habits, values, and aspirations. You can create just one or have multiple versions of your ideal customer. One great place to start would be to…

Identify those who are already your ideal customers and simply replicate them in your written description.

Then publish it!

Going further, identify how many of your potential ideal customers are out there, what they are trying to achieve, and how you can help them. Interview your current customers and write, in their words, what they value about your services or products. Share this information with all prospects in your marketing.

11. Position Yourself With Credible Partners

Who influences and serves your ideal customers? Can you make yourself valuable to that partner and help them serve their customers? Those are important questions that will guide you to your credibility partner.

Too often the approach taken is to first ask these centres of influence for something. They are not about to give you a referral or give you access to their customers. In many misguided descriptions it almost feels like the recommendation is to infiltrate your partner's business to convince them to serve you. There are many versions of this that end up being "pay-to-play" or even where you offer free services in exchange for access.

This blatant quid pro quo is fraught with risk and in some cases, unethical. Except for few situations, your desired partners will see right through this approach and block your attempts at all turns. If they are trusted gatekeepers to your ideal customer, then they will view you as the fox-in-the-henhouse. They are wise to these old school "tricks".

In order to *earn* this important positioning, you must learn how you can *serve* the organizations, or people, which will provide you with a credible endorsement. Your input must *help* this partner achieve their goals. Help them serve their customers or stakeholders, and they will allow you to work as a partner with them in their efforts to improve their own customer relationships while tacitly endorsing your authority in a marketplace. Become a useful or helpful resource recommended by someone they trust and respect.

As simple as this seems it is difficult to do well. There is little room for error here. Remember,

"It takes a lifetime to build a good reputation, but you can lose it in a minute" – Will Rogers.

How do people make decisions to buy or to use a service? They do research. Where do they look? Today, they look to the internet, primarily. But for a lot of decisions, many of us still require the input of other people to become comfortable with who we work with or what we buy.

The comments and reviews sections matter a lot. Your customers will be influenced by the overwhelming facts, by the "cool factor" attached to something or by the ratings it or they are given. They might look to the "likes" or number of "views" or "retweets" or try to identify if your offering is liked by others they respect or want to be respected by.

If they don't know you, how will they trust you? In a commoditized industry, there might be hundreds of services or products like yours. The endorsement of you as an authority or respected supplier by a source your customer trusts is powerful. In a roomful of strangers, that becomes your differentiator.

Just think, if you were to walk up to someone who you thought might be a good customer at a social event and introduced yourself, the person might be hesitant to even speak to you or acknowledge you in a professional context. Even if you were to get past hello, convincing them you were someone they might want to work with can be a difficult task. They might even smile and agree with everything you say and demonstrate a need for your services, yet still not become a customer.

Now if you got a re-start and obtained an introduction from one of their personal friends or a respected colleague as a credible resource, they might immediately be inclined to hear you out. If they agree with your perspective or like your products, they would consider you. But they will most likely move toward becoming a customer when they recognize you as an authority that can help solve a problem or challenge for them.

If you can show you are there to serve them and your partner, your chances go higher.

The power of partnering with credible and trusted authorities will place you top of mind with potential customers.

In my legacy planning business, I followed an elegant proprietary process called the Donor Motivation Program™, created by one of my business coaches, Scott Keffer. The essence of the program was becoming a serving partner with charities by helping them provide helpful tax and estate planning information to their donors to protect their wealth and fulfill their desire to leave more to charitable causes.

To earn those relationships, though, I also studied the non-profit industry, wrote white papers, special reports, two books about giving, and volunteered with industry leading organizations. I spoke regularly at conferences and events. The program was great and it gave an outline of how to engage with and serve charities and their donors as the expert, but unless I had done all the other work to earn the right to partner with them as a legitimate resource, I never would have been able to succeed.

By serving both the charity and the donor, I became a valuable resource. When you are positioned in this way, there is no need for direct endorsement or referral. It was a win-win-win and the ultimate outcome was that everyone is enabled to make their very own big impact.

Stop asking for referrals from your current customers. Stop asking these things of your circle or influence. Do not try to infiltrate or convince your partners. Be of value and serve. It will result in the natural and positive connections you desire. When you ask for referrals or endorsements, your customers or sphere of influence don't know how to sell you anyway. Even if they like you and respect you, they might not want to sell you to others. Identify, engage, and serve your future credibility partners. You will build better relationships with future customers while removing the added dynamic of asked-for referrals from your customer relationships.

12. Celebrity Attachment

The age of social media has made everyone a pseudo celebrity. The infatuation with celebrity might be at an all-time high. It never ceases to lose its allure. There's something about those who achieve fame in the media, entertainment, business and sports world that continues to intrigue us. We all have our own attractions. Whoever you are, there are rock stars you want to be like, or to be near. You might have wanted to hang with Aerosmith's Steven Tyler – or genius Stephen Hawking. By keeping company with them or being seen with them, it would somehow bolster your own credibility. If they endorsed you or offered testimony to what you did or sold, others would place you at a higher standing than your competitors without such attachment.

The strong motivation of FOMO (fear of missing out) lends itself to an even greater attraction for celebrity connection. People aren't posting themselves online doing the mundane. They post happy or interesting pics, or their version of them doing cool stuff. We are all attracted to this. Celebrity has permeated our psyche and when present, such connections improve our view of the person who is connected. In a November 2011 study in the Australasian Marketing Journal, Jasmina Ilicic and Cynthia M. Webster concluded that, "Celebrity attachment is associated with positive attitudes towards advertisements and brands, while both attachment and the number of endorsements influence purchase intent."

Most people, it seems, want to be famous. Those fifteen minutes of fame is happening to reality TV personalities all over, but it wouldn't even be a thing if people didn't value the celebrity that it brings. The truth is everybody has some form of connection to celebrity in their own mind that makes it attractive, interesting, and desirable. Wherever you can create celebrity attraction, do it.

Celebrity attachment is something that works when you are trying to engage others. Before society became more enlightened and in touch with the negative impact of capturing and containing large marine creatures, SeaWorld understood the importance of celebrity when they featured Shamu the killer whale. Multiple daily shows attracted millions of people to come to the park and walk through all the vending and other attractions to get to the big stage – the aquarium. Come early – seating is limited. The best view is available for those who get there early. People would come from all around just to see the main attraction, but they would stay all day and go see the turtles, the stingrays and other fish. They would buy lunch and merchandise and tickets for other attractions just to be there in time for the big show – to watch Shamu. The other attractions were just as good, in fact often they were better and more informative and even more interactive, but the reason people came was to see the killer whale. Who is your Shamu? Who are the celebrities you will bring to the stage?

Attaching yourself to people who have instant public recognition and will attract folks to the event of a business you own. You might already be able to get an audience of your ideal prospects/customers when you host an event, but celebrity attachment will draw an even bigger crowd. A bigger crowd gives you more chance to serve others, deliver what you do and more opportunities to sell.

Ideally, the celebrities you connect with will be engaged with or endorse you. They might, in fact, approve of what you're doing and be willing to tell others. Any time you have a chance to become connected with a celebrity, serve them and utilize the relationship of a celebrity in a way that positions you with your potential customer, your audience, your buyer, your prospect, and even your current customers. You should make that effort.

I can put "butts in chairs". It isn't always predictable, but it can double or triple for every degree of celebrity that I host. If I bring a top-level celebrity in, an event I would normally get 40 or 50 people to, I could expect multiples of that. Bringing in multiple high-profile guests will further increase your attendance.

Don't expect your celebrities to market or advertise for you. It is amazing if they do, but it is highly unlikely they are going to share your event with their audience. You might be able to build some marketing into the appearance contract, but they are in the driver's seat and most will have zero interest in promoting your event.

What types of celebrities are good draws? Well, widely known public figures or performers, local media types and athletes are a good start. Think of an Olympian or pro-sport athletes from your hometown. Even well-known artists, musicians, news people or local TV celebrities are an attraction. Well-known local business owners can also be those folks. Finally, well liked authorities or industry specific authors can help you attract a crowd as well.

The next level, of course, is a nationally known TV personality, radio personality, someone that people look up to, aspire to be like, and are inspired by. Then of course, the top level would be the knockout superstars. They key is that celebrity "size" doesn't always matter much. You don't need Oprah – and you likely can't afford Oprah. You don't need to spend $400,000 or $500,000 on an appearance from one of the top celebrities in the world. It takes a little bit more celebrity than you, and someone who's recognizable by a very large audience or everyone for who they are or something they did. If you are connected somehow that is best.

When you bring them into your life, they are not just there for the "photo op". They are there because you have served them in some way. They are there to work with you to connect with other people you have attracted, to meet them, greet them, and see them – to be seen with them and have their pictures taken. Of course, you must be discerning to be sure that your chosen celebrity or celebrities can actually "do the gig". There is some homework to be done. A celebrity with no personality who's not a good speaker, or a celebrity who has no qualities other than recognition, may not be as powerful for you. They might not deliver much to your business, for your product, or for your service, or with your audience. A better choice is someone who is interesting and engaging, and willing to do more with you and your audience will be a better choice.

Before you brush this off as fluff, consider whether you think you are immune to the awe or spectacle of celebrity. Bars, restaurants and businesses will pay hundreds of thousands of dollars for appearance fees for famous people, even pseudo-celebrities like the Kardashians, to simply show up for an hour or an evening at their venue. This draws hundreds of people to the event, builds goodwill with thousands more in marketing and results in more sales and the ability to use this celebrity attachment repeatedly in the future. Being close to the celebrity gives all your guests a story that they will share at some point in the future. A smart investment in celebrity attachment will give you exponential return.

13. Testimonials

Not so far off the celebrity attachment theme, the testimonial is one of the oldest and most tried and true methods to build credibility. It is valuable "social proof". This is the foundational component of what I call your "Mountain of Credibility™" and it is of it. People who say good things about their experience with you through testimonials are keys to marketing. A simple statement that they benefited buying your product or working with you will move others to want the same, to enjoy the same experience, and to have and use the same products. Wherever you can obtain a customer testimonial: get them. You can get two types of testimonials or endorsements.

One form is the "same-as-me" testimonial, where people share the same wants as well as appearance, values, challenges or personalities as your ideal customer. Prospects want to know they are not alone in deciding to work with you or buy your products. They need others who are *just like them* to test the waters and validate their future decision to buy. Seeing others like them have success, gives your ideal customer courage to make the purchase. It also gives them an "out" if they experience buyer's remorse. Others did this, so "I'm not so stupid to do it either"; "It just didn't work for me".

The more testimonials from people like your ideal customer give people that social proof. Again, social proof through testimonial is the foundation of your Mountain of Credibility™. As Josh Kaufman, author of "The Personal MBA: Master the Art of Business" wrote,

"Testimonials are an effective form of social proof often used in business to close more sales."

Getting that social proof is just like dating. Take it from me, I am living proof. You see, I'm married to an incredibly wonderful woman. Sherri is such a nice person, a kind soul, a decent human being, and wonderful to get along with. Whenever people meet me and we speak, I am engaged in the conversation and pay attention to who I am conversing with. I am also warm and I like people. I've even been told I have a good sense of humor. At the same time, I'm a businessperson with a business-mind. I have lots going on and prefer to get to the point. I don't suffer fools and do not naturally have a lot of time or patience for excess in day to day encounters. When people meet me, they're often engaged and interested, they might even consider working with me. But when they meet Sherri, they're convinced they made the right decision. She provides social proof that a wonderful human being is married to this man, has had children with this man, and I am worthy of their personal investment. This connects them to me in a way that would never be possible, or at least take more time. It would never be as immediate as it happens with her.

When you have people or customers in your life that provide that for your prospects, it's invaluable. Social proof is the critical piece, and testimonials must be used when you get them. Plaster them everywhere. If someone has something nice to say about you, share it with everyone, everywhere, all the time.

Testimonials traditionally come in written form, but quality video testimonials are even more powerful. Be aware, though, that the video testimonial isn't for everyone…and quite frankly, you don't want everyone to ramble on, stumble, appear stiff or have a need to over-edit. You must understand the people you hope to gain a testimonial from and choose the right medium.

How do you obtain testimonials? When you ask for testimonials or comments on your book or a project or an event or a presentation, especially if it's going to come from a celebrity or some other notable person, one of the big recommendations or one of the keys is to make sure that **you do the work for them**. Create the basis of the testimonial for them. Give them a foundation, something to work with, because they're busy people. They don't want to invest their time in your project and, while you wish it were so, they don't go through their days thinking about how great you are or creating new ways to sell you. They may be willing to support you, but they're not going to think through some elegant or eloquent message about their experience with what you did for them. You must provide them structure.

Make it super easy for them, by even writing the testimonial for them and have them review it and approve it, but ideally you want the endorsement to be as authentic and genuine as possible. But you also want it done, so providing guidelines is important. One key strategy that I would recommend, however, is to guide them to consider something that is more "generic" rather than precise. This is a testimonial that could be used in many ways in your current and future marketing efforts. Instead of a testimonial specifically for your <u>book</u> about fishing, it would be better to have a more general statement. For example, "*Mike's ideas and principles about fishing are amazing. I would recommend Mike to help you master the craft of tying flies,*" would be better than "*Mike's book, called The Joy of Fishing, shares the wisdom of tying flies in 2020*". You see, "*Mike's ideas and principles about fishing*" would be a much better body of the testimonial because you can repurpose it for so many more products, marketing, or events in the future, than if it were more specific.

Once you've put yourself into a box, you have wasted your celebrity attachment and diminished the use of your testimonial for future marketing. You've narrowed yourself into only a specific use of the testimonial. Always consider using any testimonial, any photograph, video, any celebrity attachment. Use anything you can possibly get that endorses you with social proof. You want to have the ability to reuse and repurpose what is said about you. You want to be able to plug and play wherever. In articles, web pages, social media, marketing, books, events, whatever. You want to be able to use that testimonial without breaking the quote, without misquoting. Versatile testimonials are powerful marketing tools.

14. Go "Customer" On Your Market

Get market intelligence. Do not think that because you know your business well that you become so ignorant as to ignore what your competitors are doing or where you operate. The saying, "don't worry about what your competitors are doing" is a load of BS. Focus on your thing and don't pay attention to all the noise, but you better know what your competitors are doing because they are either whispering or shouting in your future customers ears. Don't willfully lack the knowledge your prospects already have. Pay attention to what the average and the best in your category and outside your industry are doing. Learn the landscape you and your competitors share. In learning this, it will also help you understand the psyche of your customer. With this knowledge, you can better differentiate yourself and your business as their desired solution.

Your current and future customers know what your competitors are doing and expect you to be at least the same as everyone else, but hope you'll be different — better.

Taking on a "customer's eye" allows you to see what is considered "normal" (a.k.a. expected) in your industry. When you do this, you see the full landscape of options. Think of every great business that enters a highly competitive market segment. The owners/founders might say they started the company because they "were tired of how every single…in the industry would do things this way. They wanted to change things…and so they launched…" Uber literally upended the entire paid transportation and taxi industry with their vision, the simplicity of their app and ease of payment as well as the incredible accessibility of ridesharing over the traditional taxi service model.

When you understand the landscape, it is easy to take action to rise above your competitors. Think of coffee and coffee shops. Over thirty years ago, coffee in North America was something that you paid a quarter for from a donut shop, truck stop or cafeteria en-route to wherever you were headed. The norm was cheap, no fuss, and utilitarian. The coffee shop wasn't a destination, it was a convenience.

Enter Starbucks. When the company launched and began a break-neck speed expansion in the late 1980s and 1990s, they took the simple coffee shop and turned it into the "third place". Their stores became community focal points — social hubs. They sold coffee and specialty drinks that cost anywhere from $1 to $6 per cup! They smashed the norms and set the new standard. Some say they were "disruptive", but they really just differentiated their offering, listening to the customer, with an emphasis on "place" and enjoyment of coffee as a beverage to be savored. They knew their market, understood their competitors, and set out to build their own standard for how their ideal customer would enjoy a simple cup of coffee.

"To stay vigorous, a company needs to provide a stimulating and challenging environment for all these types: the dreamer, the entrepreneur, the professional manager, and the leader. If it doesn't, it risks becoming yet another mediocre corporation."
— Howard Schultz, *Pour Your Heart Into It: How Starbucks Built a Company One Cup at a Time*

15. Always Be Learning

Sometimes you meet certain people who are fountains of wisdom, gained through decades of teaching. One person I continue to hear great insights on coaching and life happens to be Kevin Eastman, International Corporate & Sports Team Speaker, author and former NBA championship coach and professional sports executive. I have quoted Kevin many times before. As a past player and college basketball coach, and through his role as an assistant coach with the NBA for over 12 years, he was an observer of great players, great coaches and great leaders. It is no surprise that Kevin has an arsenal of amazing insights. One of the many that stuck with me is how he gathers, collects and records all that he has learned in what he calls his WILT books. That is "What I Learned Today". Each day, Kevin writes down the one thing that he learned that day. He said the journaling process is not just a way of preserving his experiences, but the concept of writing what he learned, forces him to seek learning. It becomes a daily pursuit of knowledge. This is not identifying trivial factoids or useless information; although from time to time that can be helpful too, it is actual learning about useful things. For Kevin, it goes beyond the basics. If there is something he does not know, he doesn't only seek the answer and memorize it, he looks to how or why things are the way they are and learns for him.

Be a "learn-it-all"

Kevin aspires to be what he calls a "learn-it-all" as opposed to a "know-it-all". "Know-it-alls" never really have that success or that enjoyment or satisfaction in life that we strive for. They are content with knowing what they know and blocking any disruptions to their belief patterns. "Learn-it-alls" become successful people with an insatiable desire to learn, in their lives and in their businesses through constant improvement. As a result of their ever-expanding knowledge, they experience success, they have enjoyment, they have fulfillment.

After hearing Kevin speak, I wanted to begin my own WILT book and, sure enough, I started with great success…this lasted a solid month, before I started to literally wilt in my writing. A little travel, business distractions, deadlines, holidays and suddenly there were gaps. Large enough to change my habit before it was fully formed and then ultimately prove to be a challenge to even start up again. Constant marketing keeps me looking for new ideas and novel ways to connect, so I am always learning and sharing it. If you can build this into you daily routine, it is a great habit, while formalizing it through the regular writing is powerful.

Whether it is a "what I learned today" book, a diary, simply journaling, or daily blogging, the message is the same. What didn't you know in the morning that you learned in the day? I'd suggest while you're at it that you add your own gratitude entry to that daily routine, but the essence of the WILT book is about pushing yourself to learn about something new that you didn't know already.

Your WILT will help push you because you want to make that entry into the book that helped encourage you to try new things, to expand horizons and the learn things that you never knew before. So start your own "what I learned" book.

16. Learn The Language Of Your Customer

WIFM. This is a frequency everyone is dialed to. Serving your customer is a priority if you wish to create lasting relationships, stronger professional ties and more predictable, long term income for your business. Identifying your ideal customer is the best starting place, then understanding their needs to serve them better, and finally, having a concrete grasp of the landscape and marketplace your customers see and that you occupy. The last secret to success is to learn the language of your customer - that's the What's-In-It-For-Me station. Let's say it is the "Duolingo" of customer relationships.

We all are on our own WIFM frequencies. And they're all different. We're in business to sell products and services, expand our reach, and expand our impact, but our personal priority is not on the mind of our prospects or customers. As a result, when communicating, we cannot speak in our own language, reflecting our needs. We must tune in to what matters to them. Even then we aren't going to learn their language solely by what they are saying, because often they don't share all their thoughts. We must develop a process to extract the truth about what our customers really feel and learn the language they think. Learning how they perceive your products or services and how that benefits them is to understand the language that conveys whether you are a value to them, or not.

So, tune in to station WIFM on your marketing radio. It will require research to learn how the buyer thinks. You must consider yourself a consumer of your service or product so that you can think like them, be like them, and understand their language. Dial slowly and pick up their frequency.

Do the research. Since it isn't quite as simple as downloading a language app and rehearsing, although that is part of the process, you must gain the market intelligence of your customer. Some of it will be done by analyzing data such as census information, demographic trends and buying patterns.

You can also do it directly through soliciting testimonials, surveys and interviews. One of my favorite ways to begin a project positioning yourself as an authority in a marketplace is by interviewing your prospect. Ask them directly why they make purchasing decisions, what their needs are and what else is on their minds while they consider your product or service. Depending on your ideal customer, this might be easily done, or challenging. If you happen to be focusing on high net worth, or ultrahigh net worth individuals, then gaining access to that group for these direct personal interviews might be tough. They likely have gatekeepers. The same can be for these whose target client is an appointment-based profession…from dentist to electrician; they do not have much time during the day to answer your questions. One way to increase your odds of gaining that interview with hard-to-reach customers is request an interview to gain their knowledge for a research paper or special report you are writing to help people just like them. There are few people who will decline when asked for their expert opinion. It is human nature to talk about topics what we know. Our favorite topic is generally ourselves and our experiences.

When I decided to focus my efforts in the wealth management industry to serving charities and their donors, I did exactly that. I created a list of experts and influencers in the city, explained that I was doing research for a white paper discussing the communication challenges and opportunities between charities and their donors and requested brief 10-

minute interviews. I had five key questions to ask them and would they be interested in meeting me to do this? If they declined a meeting, they would often take a phone call. Remarkably, most took the meeting. That ten-minute meeting would always be extended to 30 or even a remarkable 90 minutes. Simply by asking them their opinions and experiences and then shutting up and listening, they would divulge important market information readily while thoroughly enjoying our time together. This provided me with a wealth of information and an understanding what my ideal customers thought, their experiences and things that were most important to them. I was able to learn their language in their words.

One of the most powerful outcomes of the interviews and the special report or whitepaper was that through the process I was able to demonstrate a level of respect, proving that I truly was genuinely interested in their challenges and insights. They became sources of referrals to the next interview, they were the first people I reached out to when the paper was complete, and they became advocates or influencers within the community I wanted to serve.

When I listened, I learned to speak in their words. I was able to speak from a shared experience and used "we", "us" and "our" when explaining the information I unearthed. Their language became our common language.

I became one of them by understanding the radio frequency of what was in it for them. By doing so, I was able to tune them into my marketing, communicate clearly and demonstrate the value of the opportunities that I presented for them with my services and products. Because of this, I was able to effectively position myself as a helpful, credible authority who could serve them.

GROW GET GIVE

17. Always Be Marketing

Formerly featured on ABC's "Secret Millionaire" TV show, James Malinchak, is always asked how he can get so many people to attend his business seminars or workshops and boot camps. His college and business speaking events are extremely well attended. During them, he sells programs and courses at an amazing pace. He is one of the most skilled "sell-from-the-stage" professionals I have ever met. His conversion ratio is incredible. While this means he can predictably earn income from his live events, it is all about scale. He can forecast how much he might earn in a day, or weekend, based on the amount of qualified people there are in the room. No different than a restaurant owner who knows precisely how much they will likely earn if they fill their eighty seats with customers on any given night. James knows that the only way to assure he has that opportunity to sell is to fill the room. With five hundred people at an event, James can earn over a million dollars in just a couple days.

Naturally, people want to know the absolute single best way to get five hundred prospects to an event. Malinchak says, "I don't know one best way to get five hundred sales, but I sure know fifty ways that each get ten people — and I do all of them!" There are no miracle cures you can find, or silver bullets to get big results. Success requires effort and planning. It is just that the people who get the biggest results work right by working smarter and sometimes harder than others to produce those results. They also quickly learn what works and what doesn't. Then, they focus their effort and energy on what does. You won't know fifty different ways when you first start out, but you will learn a new way (or more) every time you set out to sell something.

By using multiple methods, techniques, and approaches to marketing, you will find that you are also always marketing. Think of James again. He'll only spend thirty minutes making a direct offer and sell a million dollars of products in a four-day event. The rest of the time during the months prior, every moment of the event and in all his communications, he is marketing and setting up the opportunity to sell. No communication, action, conversation or material happen by accident or randomly; they were planned and designed to move uninterested people to become interested, then to engage them as prospects and, ultimately, as customers. Some methods are blunt instruments and others are surgically specific. You must use all of them in a defined process to build predictability, repeatability, and reliability to your sales efforts. Once used, you gain intelligence about their effectiveness and adjust, then repeat.

Wayne Gretzky was the NHL's best scorer of all time with 894 goals, but it wasn't because he was the most accurate. The are many other players who could claim that title, Wayne wasn't even in the top twenty of all time for accuracy, but he was in the top thirty. He was accurate but took the seventh most shots on goal ever. The stats also don't show all those shots that just missed and weren't counted as "on goal", which I would guess might be even double the 5,088 shots he took. If he thought he might have a chance to score, he would always take the shot.

As a Calgary Flames fan growing up, I saw more of Gretzky and the Edmonton Oilers than I wanted to. I'll admit it was tough to watch the "Great-One" and the Oilers keep Calgary from going deep in the playoffs, all but one year late in the 80's. He took shots from the front of the goal, from close range, from the side and even – notoriously – from the behind the net! There were areas that were high percentage, but others weren't.

Because he took them, his stats soared. Think about that, 4,194 failed attempts, for 894 goals and that is the BEST ever!

Besides the score and the time remaining in the game, the most important statistic that is posted on all time clocks is the shots on goal. More shots = more chances to score. This is the same with marketing. The more impressions, touches, asks, and conversations — the more sales.

You can hold out for the quality chances all you want, but as such you must settle for longer sales cycles and likely fewer conversions. This is an energy and enjoyment thing, but let's all agree that an empty net goal at the end of a close game is just as important as a full-strength goal in the first five minutes of the game. Take the shots.

My motto on marketing and in life has always been, "You don't ask, you don't get". As "Coach Mike" I teach others how to score more. Sometimes, the goals or successes don't come quickly, or they even are low quality. There are even periods of drought. The lack of sales is often a result of lack of asks as opposed to making the wrong ask or technique. Let's consider Gretzky again. He couldn't take the shots, or make the goals unless he was in the right position on the ice - not to mention being on the ice to begin with. His skills as a player, his constant rehearsal and practice performance gave him the ability to play on the top line as one of the best players on the team, always. As a result, he was in the right place at the right time a lot. He worked incredibly hard for most of his life to place himself in the best position for success.

Once you have prepared and developed your skills you must get yourself in the right position. In its essence, that is marketing. Marketing puts you on the ice and in the game. For Gretzky, his marketing was showcasing his incredible skills and work ethic day in and day out to justify the coach's faith in having him on the ice. He always practiced right and performed right.

Rehearse over and over until you do things instinctively. Thus, in a game, nothing happens by accident. The same applies to sales and marketing. If you never market, and never ask for the business, you will never sell anything. If you don't prepare or you use the wrong marketing techniques to sell, you will also have limited success. It is not enough to practice - you need to apply the right techniques. Then set up a measurable process and repeat. Sales should rarely happen accidently … only accidents happen by accident. When you have a message worth sharing and the ultimate effect of your efforts is to add value, make an impact, and enrich the lives of others, it is okay to market yourself and your business in any way possible to ensure you share your message with those who will benefit.

Marketing is not something you do to other people; it is something you do FOR them.

18. Learn To Speak In Public

Almost all of us must sell, advocate, lobby or convince. You will never be able to share your value, offer your benefit or make your impact if you are unable to communicate. Public speaking is one of the most important skills an entrepreneur can learn. I'd like to share a portion of a great article published in Inc. Magazine in 2017, written by Carmine Gallo, Keynote speaker and author, *'Five Stars: The Communication Secrets to Get From Good to Great" wrote in an article from Inc. online magazine* (https://www.inc.com/carmine-gallo/the-one-skill-warren-buffett-says-will-raise-your-value-by-50.html)

Carmine asked, "Imagine working on one skill (in 2017) that--once you improve it--will raise your value by 50 percent. The one skill is public speaking."

He went on to write, *"The dividends on the investment you make in sharpening your communication skills will pay off for the rest of your career. Don't take my word for it. Listen to billionaire Warren Buffett's advice to a class of business students Columbia University back in 2009:*

"Right now, I would pay $100,000 for 10 percent of the future earnings of any of you, so if you're interested, see me after class." After the laughter subsided, he turned serious.

"Now, you can improve your value by 50 percent just by learning communication skills--public speaking. If that's the case, see me after class and I'll pay you $150,000."

Buffett's point is that mastering the art of public speaking is the single greatest skill to boost your career."

Public speaking for Buffet was terrifying and he sought out public speaking courses and coaches to train him to be a better speaker. There are many resources available to you to improve your public speaking such as Dale Carnegie's public speaking courses and Toastmasters International, as well as local speakers' clubs and groups. TED Talks™ was formed out of the demand and need for great storytelling. It provided a stage for some for the most powerful talks of our modern age. The platform has launched careers (i.e. Simon Sinek), showcased expertise that the world needed to hear, and given a platform to activists like Greta Thunberg and humorists like Reggie Watts around the world.

You can even seek out improvisation groups or performance and actor training. Whenever you can practice your material in front of a live audience, you should. The feedback you get is powerful, no matter if your audience is, as I always say, *"nodding or nodding off"*. I have been speaking in public for decades. From a young age in music, not only was I comfortable on stage but shone as a performer. I wanted the solo in the big performance. It was the same for me in sports. I wanted the ball or to play when the game was on the line. The highest pressure brought out the best in me. I might not always have "practiced well" but when it counted, I always rose to the occasion.

I launched Speak 2 Sell in 2018. The clubs are designed for entrepreneurs looking to improve their ability to communicate, pitch and sell their products or services. I believe it is such an important skill, that I incorporated public speaking training to my coaching programs and events. If you are building a business and selling a product or service and developing messaging around it, you must be able to articulate it clearly. Seek out opportunities to rehearse your message so that it connects with the audience you are trying to entertain, persuade or sell to.

As you rise to success, public speaking becomes a natural extension of your expert positioning. When you have built your Mountain of Credibility™ and written your book(s) you will be asked to present your knowledge. People will defer to you and seek you out to help them and others. This is a chance for you to shine – or fade. It is important to be prepared and rehearsed when offered the stage. When you are prepared you will shine. NEVER pass on a chance when the microphone or stage is offered to you. The message is clear: if you want to become a success, become great at public speaking.

GROW GET GIVE

19. Help Your Customers

Become a serving leader in all you do. Leading is not confined to your staff and people around you; it also includes a responsibility to your customers. To be helpful to your customer it will require that you understand them. It is critical that you

learn what they need, what they like, and how you can help ease their pain or fulfill their desires to be better.

Become the trusted advisor or resource for them by guiding in their self-discovery. Teach them how you will be able to help them. Making a commitment to serving your customer will position you closer to them. When you solve their biggest challenges, offer what they want, and give them what they need, you move from a commodity to a resource. When you help your customers achieve their goals, they become connected to you in a personal way. You become more than a supplier or vendor– you become a trusted advisor. It is the same for personal services as it is for consumer products. When Apple introduced the iPod and iPhone, they made utilitarian technology (a phone and a music device) hip. People wanted to be fashionable and feel cool. But they also needed usability. While Apple brought cool, they also delivered intelligence and practicality. Their products were simple and easy to use. People perceived more and paid more because they valued the offering. By offering an experience, Apple helped a generation move deeper into connectivity. They re-inspired music, they changed social media and brought people together…in a cool way.

Serving your customer is also critical in a professional service role. For example, if you're a financial advisor, you serve by helping to ease pain and reduce fear. People WANT to be secure, feel confident about their finances and their future. People NEED a plan and tools to make that happen. When you are in the role of trusted advisor, it is because you have been able to identify the challenges faced by your clients, clearly articulate the ideal outcomes and have the necessary tools and knowledge to make that happen. When you have that ability, you have a moral responsibility to use your knowledge, skills, and expertise to define goals for them based on their vision of the future and to deliver all they need to accomplish those goals. Helping people achieve their financial success becomes your mission.

20. Be Of Value

We have all heard this – be of value. But furthermore, be of value to valuable people. That's a Jim Rohn piece of wisdom that wasn't an overused quote like "If you don't like how things are, change it! You're not a tree." as much as it was something that Kyle Wilson, his business partner and master marketing guru of 18 years, said. I heard Kyle speak in 2017. He was one of Jim's closest friends and business associates when their business was at its highest levels. He shared his observation of something Jim Rohn lived every day. He said,

> *"To make a living, learn to be valuable to the market.*
> *If you want to be wealthy, learn to be of value to valuable people."*

I'll say that again. To make a living, learn to be valuable to the market. If you want to be wealthy, learn to be valuable to valuable people. That comes down to how you serve. How do you know when you're not of value?

You are not of value when you're cramming products and services down people's throats.

You are not of value when you bait and switch your prospects.

You're not of value when you lead every conversation with "I" or "me".

You're not of value when you speak first and listen later, if at all,

You're most definitely not of value when you are constantly planning for how **you** will benefit before you learn how others might benefit from what you do, or how you can help them.

You are of value when you find out the things that matter most to people and seek ways to serve them. Learn the things that your customer views as the most important benefits for them. Know the things that they need to have success. Understand these things and deliver them to them. At the very least deliver access to it in some way through whatever it is you do. You become valuable when you're viewed as a resource, as someone who's a trusted resource that helps them, guides them, and improves their lives.

21. Provide Process-Driven Solutions

Once you understand what your clients want and what they will need, you must identify the best possible solutions for them. This requires that you develop the skill to listen and learn. You are an expert, behave like one. Experts use their knowledge and experience to connect the dots in a strategic planning process and provide intelligent solutions.

Every process starts with a clear vision for an ideal future outcome.

W. Edward Deming, an American engineer instrumental in inspiring the powerful Japanese post-war economic industrial recovery, famously stated that "If a person can't explain what they're doing as a process, they don't know what they're doing." When marketing, your process will most often start with uncovering the pain being experienced by your customer and the ideal vision they have for their own future. Desire is also a strong motivator for people, but in most cases, pain will be a greater motivator for action, so get to the pain first. Connect their present situation with their ideal future and the outputs of a strategic process will identify solutions (tactics) that are right for them. Offer them a real, customized, and attainable solution that will remove their pain. Using processes to get there provides comfort. This is realized as trust in you and your service or product.

Remember your business planning: Get Clients – Keep Clients. A strategic approach with an identifiable process attracts people to your business. The same process-driven approach affirms why they bought from you, gives them comfort that they are in good hands and increases their trust that you are there to help them.

Marketing using a process that is describable in simple terms clarifies the approach you take to make decisions. Customers find this particularly reassuring. The biggest challenges are listening and observing what the customer is really saying in order to start drawing the road map for them. It is the same for how we might think of our financial, health or life goals.

When we review our own goals, we might not be happy with the way things are now, but are afraid that we, or even someone else, might do something in ignorance that puts us at greater risk. We also know what we hope the future could look like for us — our "Norman Rockwell" painting. The biggest problem is, because we're not experts in what it is that we're tackling, we have no idea how to get to our ideal from where we are today.

The authority who listens to us and uses an explainable process that gives us a clear strategic map to reach our goals will give us comfort. Because we are assured, we will gladly pay even more for their services. In order to ensure this, they must understand what we like and don't like. They must understand our biggest fears or concerns, and we must believe they see our vision for the future almost as well as we do.

22. Be Talented — Do The Extra Work

I have already quoted Kevin Eastman once in this book. He is a wealth of knowledge from his personal exposure to greatness. Years ago, when I first met Kevin, he was speaking to my mastermind group in Los Angeles. Kevin was working with famous coach Doc Rivers at the time and had moved with Doc from the Boston Celtics to the LA Clippers. They guided the Celtics to the World Championship a few years prior. Kevin was sharing the wisdom he had gained from his observations of top performers he had worked with over the years and shared his insight on talent.

We were sitting in a room full of entrepreneurs who had talent and they competed daily in business with others who also have talent. In Kevin's mind there is a clear distinction about those who have talent and those who are talented. He used his observations about Kevin Garnett, one of the NBA's biggest and most dominant stars of the last decade. Garnett redefined the power forward. He was a big man who could dribble, pass, shoot, defend and was a monster in the paint. Lebron James is partly "Lebron" because Garnett cleared the way. Eastman used Kevin to illustrate his point. It was extraordinarily difficult to reach the NBA and those who did were all exceptional basketball players. He said while everyone had talent, Kevin Garnett was talent**ed**. He made the distinction of talent versus talented. Eastman spoke of a practice, deep in the playoffs. Garnett, who had been working extremely hard all season and needed some rest ahead of a string of important games, was running the normal drills that the second string and rookies were participating in during an optional practice. They needed to learn the plays to be prepared in case they were called upon in a clutch situation. The coaches determined Garnett needed rest more than work and encouraged him to sit out for a while. He forcefully declined and kept playing. This went on for a short while and eventually, he was mandated to stop and allow others to run the drill. As the team restarted the practice, a few moments later, everyone could hear the breathing, squeaking of shoes and ball hitting the floor in the distance while they were going through the drill. Eastman looked up and saw Garnett, alone, in the darkened practice court, running the entire drill — end-to-end, full out — against imaginary opponents.

Kevin Garnett is easily one of the greatest NBA players ever, with incredible talent, yet he was running a basic drill on his own, until he got it right. What Eastman summarized was that

*...the talent**ed** do what others with talent won't.*

They will put in the reps; they will perfect their craft and deliver their absolute best — always. The result of course, is that Garnett gained that slight extra advantage over his competition. He has incrementally more success on the court and has exponentially more success on the pay scale. At that time, the average pay of an NBA player was just over $1mm per season. Kevin Garnett was making over $9mm and while the others were collecting only their salaries, Garnet was easily bringing in over ten times more money than that in endorsements. The difference between those with talent and the talent**ed** was literally a factor of 100!

What are you doing to rise above all others? Are you doing just a bit more to keep that edge? If you are a successful entrepreneur doing well and making a decent living, you will undoubtedly be surrounded by competitors who also have talent. When you do more and step up your game in practice as well as in the game, you give yourself a chance to rise above your competitors and achieve more. Remember incremental improvements can lead to exponential rewards.

GROW GET GIVE

23. Resilience

Re·sil·ience: The capacity to recover quickly from difficulties.
Toughness, a.k.a. a "thick skin".

This is not to be confused with perseverance or determination. Resilience is that "thick skin" developed over the years, built layer by layer, experience by experience. Calluses on your hands build in time through use, as the stresses of the world impart its force upon your once soft and supple skin. The hardening and thickening of your dermis are important protection for your hands. It provides resilience to the elements you are exposed to. Calluses are not destructive - they are designed to protect your body and reduce sensations, to enhance performance. They grow to allow you to continue to work at whatever it is you are doing. The resilience is adaptive, not limiting.

Our kids are downhill mountain bikers and our oldest daughter, Madison, also trains and fights as a Muay Thai fighter. Her hands have developed calluses as she has gotten stronger, but what always amazes me when I hold her hands, is just how soft and gentle they are at the same time. She is strong and protected, but her hands and personality are soft and inviting. People might tell you resilience hardens you. They are wrong. The true meaning of resilience is accepting the world and forces that affect us with the adapted protection of experience to shield ourselves from harm – not hide from it.

Stress is an important component of personal development. For some people, they simply have not been exposed to enough of it. They wither or become injured (personally or physically) under duress. They crumble or hide when pushed. Their dreams are constantly halted or never attempted because of the perceived imminent threats they face. Without stress they don't build resilience.

Successful entrepreneurs and business owners constantly build resilience. We are sometimes told we won't succeed. People look at you as you describe your goals and ambitions and they might sneer or fold their arms in judgment. They'll poke holes in your plans; they'll say you don't know what you're doing. These will be people close to you. They'll be people who you look up to or might have viewed as your peers. In fact, the worst thing, the saddest thing, is that it's often your family, your friends, your immediate peers who are probably whispering in your ear that maybe you shouldn't do what you're doing. "Why would you do that?", "Isn't that risky?" "Do you really know what you're doing?" They'll say almost anything to draw to your attention that maybe you shouldn't be taking on a risk that you view as an opportunity.

When you have a clear vision of your own future as an entrepreneur, a lot of people won't really understand you. Most people aren't hard-wired for entrepreneurship. They don't understand what it means to look at an opportunity and see the blue sky versus all the red flags. In order to exist in a world where you are exceptional and viewed as different, you must build resilience. You are not erecting walls. You don't want to ignore the people that are around you and don't tune them out, turn them off, or close them out of your life because they're in your life for a good reason. Your friends and family are with you for the long haul and they may be able to provide you with so many other things such as emotional support, acceptance and encouragement that you otherwise wouldn't get from strangers.

You will find as you become more successful, more popular, and your products or services are seen, purchased and exposed to more people, that people you have never met will manufacture and share their own opinions about you that aren't accurate. How you deal with this - the strategies you put in place and the calluses you build - determines whether those voices become prophecy, fuel, or simply noise.

The internet and social media platforms like Facebook, Instagram, LinkedIn, Twitter and YouTube are platforms where everyone has an opinion to share. These are massive online aggregators for people to share opinions and comments. Not all of them will be kind or supportive. Opinions are like assholes, everyone's got one, and some people choose to be one – an asshole, I mean.

In order to drive forward and succeed with your vision for your best life, you must become resilient. Resilience requires intestinal fortitude beyond the basic strength that it takes to wake up every day and plow a new field or set a new course as we do as entrepreneurs and business owners. Choose to be resilient in the face of not only adversarial feedback, which gets our competitive blood flowing, but plain old negative feedback. Someone else's notion of what they think our lives or our business should be or what our opportunities are should not define us. We shouldn't allow them to dictate our successes or dictate our commitment.

During my career as a wealth manager, when I turned my focus on giving back, most of my investment industry peers and corporate partners did not support my efforts. They didn't understand what I was doing. Their preconceived ideas and experiences prevented them from seeing the upside of my path. Some passed judgment and some were skeptical. Some unscrupulous ones would wait until I inevitably miss-stepped or produced marketing they didn't understand just so they could complain to our management team about what I was doing. Negative feedback was pervasive. Ironically, I was attempting to do "good", by helping charities and their donors realize their philanthropic dreams with a mission heart.

I did not listen. I built my calluses and chose to seek out support from those who were positive, who would lift me up. I ignored the negativity. Shit, I didn't have time to listen to others' negativity when I was already constantly questioning what I was doing! Without resilience to protect me from those naysayers, I could not have persevered. It was not easy. I spent the first couple of years doing so many things wrong. Spending and investing in my business and education to become the subject matter expert. There was so much doubt. It took time to build the right processes, systems and team to support the business. Incredible determination, dedication and commitment made me known as a valuable resource. None of the charitable impact, neither the happiness in my life nor the reward in my business would have ever been possible if I didn't have resilience. Without resilience I would've given up. I never would've had that experience; we would never have been able to accomplish such great things and it probably wouldn't have set me on the course I am today.

24. Build A Tribe

Give me raving fans — maybe even raving fanatics!!! Ok, maybe not quite fanatic…but where fan meets fanatic, count me in. This is where the daily wisdom of Seth Godin, author, speaker, and marketing guru, rings so true. From his "Purple Cow" to "Tribes: We Need You to Lead Us", Godin long touted building your tribe as the best way to market and sell ideas, goods, and services. This concept is centered in highlighting your unique "thing", putting it out there, attracting like-minded people who would benefit from you, and doing it over and over. In his daily blog, Godin frequently instills that any entrepreneur or marketer should produce their best work. They should strive to create and innovate rather than commoditize. When combined with your unique ability, it is also the differentiator that attracts people to you. You become the leader of your tribe by producing great work. As in any organization, culture or business, the leader of the tribe set the tone. It takes courage and passion to do this. Others admire it and will follow the things you do and what you say.

Tribes are important. They come in all shapes and sizes and provide the members a sense of community, of belonging. In time, tribes develop their own language. They might even create their own customs and practices. Looking at my tribe, we discuss concepts in certain terms and use language that everyone in the tribe understands. We also have events and rituals that we do over the course of a year as we get together for group or individual coaching, training and mastermind sessions. There are behaviors that are understood as well, such as confidentiality, respect and support.

In time, more and more people who see things the way you do will gravitate to what you were saying or doing. Your tribe will grow if you nurture it. Your tribe is your biggest advocate and one of the best teachers you might access during your career. As you build your tribe, resist the urge to sell to them. Ideas, not products, grow connections within the tribe. Develop and nurture your relationship with your tribe and over time you can introduce opportunities or products or services that might be helpful to them or desired by them.

Your tribe is the essence of permission marketing and selling.

Historically, tribes have formed by word of mouth, personal connections or recruitment. The maturation of the internet has given almost everyone a platform to lead with their uniqueness. Remarkably, they often find that there are many people who think and feel like them. Social media has had a compounding effect on reaching like-minded people. There are tribes for everything; all you have to do is look, from the most obvious things like fantasy football groups, or opera fans, to comic book fans (Comic-Con) or Star Trek lovers, "Trekkies", to wine-lovers, or book clubs. I belong to tribes too. From the family of mountain bikers we hang with, to ones I lead such as my Speak 2 Sell club members and my coaching and mastermind clients. My members share aspirational elements such as wanting to make a bigger impact in their lives and the lives of others, choosing to learn to better position themselves and their passions in front of others so they can serve and sell to them, and adding techniques to their lives to increase their happiness by gaining more time for creativity and personal pursuits. They want to grow their businesses, get more freedom and give back while to making more money, gain more energy and making a big impact.

Building your tribe will give you a platform to share and help, and to make offers that will benefit the members. This ultimate permission-based marketing platform is powerful. When people have joined your tribe, they have moved from the uninterested masses to the fully engaged.

You must always take care to nurture your tribe; they are not to be taken for granted. Serve them and give generously. They will reward you, and you will not need to rely on elaborate marketing campaigns or sales processes to make offers that they will consume. They sign up, they show up and they buy – because they want to, period. For example, if your tribe is robust and you have an event coming up, all you need to do is share a save the date notice and most of them immediately sign up. Whereas, if you have not built your tribe, it will take extensive marketing campaigns to educate, inform and sell each and every time.

GROW GET GIVE

25. Meet People

Make space in your life for new people by opening your time, energy and mind. Meet new people in new environments whenever possible. There are opportunities all around us each day to meet new and interesting people. Most of our lives and days begin and end purposefully as we move through our necessary work, obligations, appointments and pastimes. We don't often stop to introduce ourselves to new people or accept unknown people into our busy days. It is often through travel and the time in between the busyness that we allow openings in our minds and our schedules for the wonder of new people and new experiences. If you travel for work, you will agree that the process of getting from one place to another is often not enjoyable. It is bad enough that we are moved like cattle through security clearances, departure gates and traffic. Unfortunately, travel has moved from a luxury to a necessity. Away from our families and friends, we are herded along with strangers in - often uncomfortable - confines. It isn't surprising that when traveling we don't want to engage. A flight can be a real long test if you're stuck with someone who doesn't quite fit the personality you want to spend time with. The seat lottery, or more appropriately roulette, in a flying, airtight cylinder can be cruel. This might not be the best meeting ground, but occasionally it works out.

While I frequently avoid interaction on planes – mostly because I like to read or work as I travel – it is a joy when you do connect with someone you just met. Most times, your destination provides you with opportunities to meet new people. I suggest you attempt to meet someone new whenever given the opportunity at events, conferences, seminars, workshops, boot camps, mastermind sessions, etc. These environments are natural places to engage. It is acceptable to move beyond the "Hi, my name is…" kind of stuff and really engage. Make the effort to identify that person or people who you might learn something from, or simply be entertained by and say hello. The best way to move quickly from meaningless to meaningful is to ask someone why they decided to make the trip, or what they were hoping to achieve or learn by coming to the event or destination.

This is networking. It is something a lot of us simply hates doing. I will admit I do not like it at all, yet to build new businesses or relationships it is a must. It doesn't have to be awkward or superficial. Throw out your immediate objections to this old school, business card shuffling exercise. Networking is simply the business word for initiating and building relationships, finding ways to serve others. It's just like Simon Sinek, author of "Start with Why" said,

> *"It's not about how many people that you can meet while networking, but how many people you can introduce to others."*

The only way you can effectively have someone refer you is if the person you are trying to help perceives you as a trusted resource, knows that you won't risk their reputation and likes you. To get to there quickly with new people you must engage and make connections. You must genuinely learn about the person you've just met. You can't make meaningful connections if you don't understand the people that you've met. Ask a single personal question and they will be slightly put off guard and curious but respond. Ask about them and they will talk about their favorite subject for a while – them. Shut up and listen to make clear mental notes about them.

You might even try making written notes. I've done this many times immediately after meeting someone. In my next trip to the bathroom, or the moment I leave the event, I'll quickly write a few key points about them – often on the back their business card or in my phone as a calendar reminder a day or a week later. That helps remind me to circle back to this new relationship.

When first meeting someone, my attention goes to mannerisms, appearance and the way people behave, not on their other details. I must write those things down quickly, so I don't forget them. My wife, Sherri, is incredible at gathering personal information and recalling it. I love it when we're out together meeting new people, because I can describe how and who they were while she can tell me what they were all about and their connections. If you can't recall important personal details or have no interest in the things that are important to them, then you're not of much service to them early on or down the road. You wouldn't know how to introduce them to people, and they certainly wouldn't introduce you to anybody meaningful because you just don't have the connection and understanding of who the fit may be perfect with.

When meeting someone new and you've made the decision to engage, then truly engage. Listen, learn, and ask questions. Sometimes, there won't be a connection. It is also okay to disengage quickly too. The sooner you get to that point, the better. Be aware. Too often in these situations, time is wasted talking about yourself and never really learning whether your new connection can benefit from getting to know you – or vice versa. We all want to be liked, but it is egocentric and quite frankly inconsiderate to ramble on about yourself to people who won't engage, or who you won't likely ever speak with again.

Using basic probing questions such as "What it is they hoped to find/learn at the event?" or "Why they chose to do what they do?" will allow you to get some deeper answers fast, without offending or interrogating. Once you've started the ball rolling, get out of the way. Intentional listening gets you to a conclusion about this person quickly and you can both do away with obligatory pleasantries if it is clear there is nothing there for either of you. Simply and politely excuse yourself and move on.

The best outcomes are when you learn something you never learned before or meet someone who will become an important connection in your life. You might simply get an interesting story out of the exchange. At worst, you must bid farewell and start up a conversation with someone else. Move on. Until you've spoken to those strangers you will never know. So, take the time to meet people, take the time to understand. You never know who might happen.

26. Build Barriers

Unique processes, offerings or originality will distinguish you from your competitors. Your Mountain of Credibility™ will elevate you to top of mind with your prospects and customers, while building barriers to block your competition. When they perceive the effort is too great to compete with you, they are no longer a threat. It is up to you to stoke that perception. This is not an overnight thing, it takes time. Think of it as building a brick wall. Each brick is laid beside another, then stacked row on row. By acting purposefully to achieve one more notable thing after another, you are piling up bricks. As you add another accomplishment, achievement or even relationship you keep building your barrier. The bricks represent an interview, a referral, testimonial, then another interview, then an article, an award for achievement or community service, your book, an endorsement, a new sales record, your home, new car, vacations, happiness, and impact. All these things added onto one another create a visible barrier that competitors will shy away from. The weak competitor will shy away and quietly wonder how you did it. The formidable competitor will rise to the challenge, shift and make their own category...often avoiding direct competition, but adding options to allow prospects to filter out and decide to buy from you or your competitor. Embrace those who will accept the challenge because few will, and you can learn from those who do. When your competitors rise to the occasion and differentiate themselves from you, they help do the work to filter your ideal customers for you – and to you.

Create barriers by educating your ideal clients, and their peer group, how you are different from the others. During my work as a financial advisor, almost every first meeting I had with a prospect, I heard "I already have a person … but they don't do that", or "You sound different." In less than an hour, the difference became clear to the prospect. I was the author, the radio professional, the speaker, the celebrity endorsed advisor and the strategic expert. Their person was just a tactical implementer. Or worse, their so-called "advisor" was only a product salesperson. Do you know how hard it would be for their advisor to re-position themselves as the strategic advisor to compete with me? Who would you think the client will be more inclined to seek valuable advice from after that comparison?

Become more specific about why you do what you do, and you become even harder to compete with. I was "Canada's leading strategic legacy planner", a speaker, author of three books, business coach, as well as portfolio manager and philanthropic advisor. Any one or two of these positioning statements elevated my positioning; the combination of all of them erected enormous barriers between me, the strategic financial advisor, and other competing investment advisors. Niche building further reduces the number of competitors you will have and thus the barriers you build will be even stronger while they will be tested less. The only way for my competitors to rise above the positioning I had worked so hard to build was to do it on their own, then add their own unique offering. They really had to do all that I did and then do more. This gave me time, space and opportunity. Once you gain such positioning, you need to go out and aggressively own that territory. Marketing, blogging, speaking, writing, etc. in your own geographic market are all ways to put distance between you and your closest competitors. Remind prospects, customers and your competition of all those bricks in the barrier. Do all these things and do them often. My competitors would review my LinkedIn profile or read my speaker bio and get exhausted just thinking of trying to catch up. You must get there too.

Leave your competitors in the dust. Do more, be more, and build more. Exhaust them…

… and as you achieve your goals, you will be able to take a breather and rethink your next move to the next level, while they are still treading water. Laziness keeps the majority at bay — there is hard work involved in all this. Have no doubt: it takes effort and determination to be exceptional. The distance between your potential and others can be expanded by simply putting in more effective work.

"No successful entrepreneur needs to build barriers to their business when their competitors perceive the effort to compete is far too great."
— Mike Skrypnek

GROW GET GIVE

27. Embrace Technology

"Technology in business is designed for the customer to deliver what they want, how they want it, when they want it. Better, faster, cheaper."

– Mike Skrypnek

Resistance to technology gutted the music industry. Music companies, distributors and producers were desperately hanging on to a dying model of music delivery to the consumer. Jeff Hoffman, former CEO and Founder of Priceline.com, highlighted this in his many talks on disruptive technologies and business. He has told the story about his days producing music with the likes of Justin Timberlake and the Backstreet Boys. The story goes like this. They were on a tour and were doing an autograph signing event in one of the world's largest brick and mortar music stores, owned by one of the largest music companies and he was speaking with the manager about CD sales.

The owner of the store was immensely proud of the ton of volume of sales of CD's that they sold. Asked why people came to the store, the manager responded, "to buy CDs" - that was why they came. Jeff responded that he didn't think so, but the manager said that's what the people wanted. Hoffman then responded that "people didn't want CD's – that little round disc the music was on. They wanted the song, right then and there. They simply wanted the <u>music</u>. CD's were just the medium." Just how LP's, and audiotape were. The response of the store owner highlighted the hubris of the entire music industry at that time and previous decades. Their deeply ingrained belief and financial commitment to it was that it was the medium of delivery that sold. The record, the 8-track, the cassette, and then the CD all became the focal point of the transaction in the minds of the industry. They believed it was the tangible sensation. Yet what the customer wanted to do was enjoy the music: to feel it. The medium didn't matter to the consumer, but it was their only option up to that point.

It took a technology player outside the entire music industry to radically change things forever. In 2001, no one would have ever believed that Apple Computers would be the company that revolutionized the entire music industry. They made billions by removing the CD (and the record and the cassette, and the brick and mortar stores!) from the picture and delivering the music directly to the consumer, digitally and on demand. In a single-handed swoop Apple literally triggered the demise of a decades-old model for the record industry. While that industry was thinking of self-preservation, hanging on to antiquated models, technology had eclipsed the past. The music industry would never be the same and many "old school" businesses would never recover.

Do not risk becoming wiped out by your hesitation to embrace technology. Admittedly, we aren't all comfortable in the realm of tech and quite frankly, most people are often a bit intimidated when it comes to technology. Early renditions of new technology are clunky and often imperfect – early adoption can be frustrating and costly for entrepreneurs. No one is suggesting that you jump on the next tech fad in your industry, let alone invent it. However, you must recognize there is always a shift coming for every industry. Be informed and be ahead of your competitors by embracing these changes. Do not put blinders on and ignore the facts. Do not allow the risk of obsolescence to be your greatest risk by hanging on to the old way of doing things. ALL things can be improved upon –

even if it is ever so slightly. Technology will ensure it. Simply accept and embrace that this is good.

GROW GET GIVE

28. Deliver More, Do More

Brian Tracy is one of the most prolific business marketers, book writers, and speakers there has ever been. In a Skype interview with a good friend of mine, entrepreneur and master marketer Chris Hamilton, Brian stated that "you must always provide a value greater than that which your customer expects."

To get into business you must attract new clients and make sales, but the way you stay in business depends on how you delight and keep clients. There are so many small things you can do that are unexpected that make all the difference. For example, simple gifts, better quality products and experiences, even attentive listening does the trick. The impact of listening (and caring) cannot be over-stated. Your customers want to know they matter. They want to be reminded they are more important to you than your products or services are to them.

You can express this to your customers in many ways. One is to making gift-giving a part of your appreciation. Gift-giving can be regular and expected, but I much prefer an element of surprise or spontaneity. Now, on my side, I schedule when I will give a gift to a client, they just don't know when I have scheduled it. While seemingly random, the gifting is planned out and implemented as a process. Therefore, I do not forget to do it and I am not scrambling to decide what to gift. There many different approaches to giving. Some entrepreneurs believe that simple trinkets do the trick and their placement – in the home, in the office or in the car - is the goal. Small and useful gifts can send strong messages. Some think that elaborate, elegant or over-the-top gifting is the key to a "wow" experience. Others will use gifting to reinforce the fact that they care enough to know the most important personal details of their customers' lives. A way that you can give a personalized gift that shows you know your client is by giving them an experience. You could buy them a t-shirt and ball cap from their favorite sports team, or you could send them to the game and get them a meet and greet with the players. Either way demonstrates that you cared enough to listen. One might be more impactful in the relationship than the other.

Lastly, the personal touch that comes with acknowledgement of personal milestones or bestowing insights that celebrate their interests is also a great gift. Listening better helps you connect deeply with people. It is something you must do to understand the importance of certain events in your clients' lives. When you acknowledge them or share your appreciation of those events, you demonstrate you care. Even being able to provide one small and simple insight or recalling a personal like or dislike or passion engages your customer in a much more meaningful way.

The gift of an interested and genuine personal connection is more powerful than any trinket.

Beyond gifts, doing more for your customers means going the extra mile to provide a memorable and enjoyable experience. This is a gift in and of itself. Consider that every Four Seasons Hotel staff member is provided a "make things right" budget. It is designed to empower the staff to immediately and unilaterally decide to act to make things right so a customer will enjoy their stay more, or have a problem solved immediately without seeking approval of a manager. In so many ways Four Seasons does more. This is their gift to their customers. They do more for their employees by giving them autonomy of decisions and responsibility of managing their own small budget and they are blowing the customer away!

Decide what types of giving you wish to use to delight your customers. People use different ways to gather information about clients to ensure they can match gifts with personal preferences – you don't want to gift a bottle of wine to a non-drinker. I use a "favorite things" questionnaire that asks several personal questions. This gives me a list of possibilities to customize my random congratulatory or personalized gifts, I then use a basic gift-giving schedule that is the same for everyone, and lastly, I take a lot of personal notes to learn important events, people and things in the lives of our clients to be able to give meaningful input or communication at the right time. Decide what works for you, combine different gifting methods and plan it out.

GROW GET GIVE

29. Give Impeccable Service

"We create properties of enduring value using superior design and finishes and support them with a deeply instilled ethic of personal service. Doing so allows Four Seasons to satisfy the needs and tastes of our discriminating customers, and to maintain our position as the world's premier luxury hospitality company."

This how Four Seasons describes its Service Culture:

"Much admired, and not easily replicated, the Four Seasons culture is firmly grounded in our people — in who we are, what we believe and how we behave. Our goals, beliefs and principles are described in the Four Seasons corporate mission statement."

The Four Seasons Hotel and Resorts chain is arguably one of the best quality hotel experiences you will ever have. Their attention to the customer and making their stay memorable and enjoyable is top priority. Not only do they place the customer first at every turn, they also empower their employees with autonomy to handle customer inquiries and concerns on the spot to "make things right".

The key is to learn and understand what your customers want and what they desire — and give it to them. Note I did not say "when". There is a fine line in customer service between doing the small things and setting a precedent of extra service that you might not be able to or even hope to continue.

It is preferable to send the message to your customer that you are available and concerned about their urgent dilemma and have a policy to ensure that they won't wait too long for a response, but setting boundaries is important. For example, responding to an email or answering the phone call late on Sunday evening might deliver the wrong message for your business. It can be as effective to set clear service expectations in advance, and then "wow" them in another way without sending the wrong message about your service relationship. Even building slightly lower expectations can give you the ability to exceed them with your service. This is not "sandbagging". Do not deliberately imply or implement a lower standard, but always give yourself a little room to impress, while holding the bar high. Start with achievement then aim for overachievement.

Do the little things and they will make big waves.

You often hear about the "wow" factor. Well this is something you want your customers to say often. When you deliver something they didn't expect, "wow" is their response. People get complacent about their expectations. Too many times, businesses let them down, so they don't expect much. Sometimes extending the effort to add a personal touch can surprise and delight.

During Christmas of 2013, one of Canada's most innovative and customer friendly airlines, WestJet, took "wow" to another level. They launched a customer appreciation event that was a surprise and a relatively small expense for a carrier during the busiest seasons of the year. On a flight from Toronto to Calgary, guests were treated to an incredible surprise. At the departure gates in Toronto guests were greeted by a kiosk with a TV monitor. On the TV monitor was a live feed with Santa Clause. Santa was asking each guest to insert their boarding pass to check in and while doing so, he asked them what they hoped for Christmas. Little did they know "Santa" was in a studio in Calgary — their destination. At the same time, he was taking their gift wishes and linking them with their personal information. Once all the passengers were on the plane, West Jet staffers in Calgary had four and a half hours to go out and buy all the things on their guests' gift list. When the passengers arrived in Calgary, each guest was greeted with their personalized gift. Everything from toys to big screen TV's were given. There were shocked, surprised and touched people who all were genuinely impressed and overwhelmed by the generosity and cleverness of the airline. This was one of the most impressive givebacks I have ever seen. WestJet launched it online as a viral video and it was a viral hit.

GROW GET GIVE

30. Create Multiple Revenue Streams From Your CORE Business

Building multiple revenue streams from multiple diverse sources has long been discussed by the so-called investment gurus and media. "Rich dads" didn't get rich with different multiple streams of revenue; they got rich doing one core thing extremely well, and then diversified their investments to protect their assets or enhance the revenue that resulted from their core competency. It is a myth that you should somehow be great at many things and somehow expect to profit from them. Engaging in multiple businesses that are not your niche or expertise is not a recipe for success. It is a recipe for mediocrity. You will end up doing several things average, add risk to your personal and financial picture and stretch yourself and your time thin.

Years ago, I was sitting in an LA hotel restaurant with a wealthy, retired anesthesiologist I know. Lynette was sharing her excitement with me as she was about to head off to the Toastmasters World Championship in Kuala Lumpur. She had taken up speaking only a couple years prior. She had retired in her late 50's from her medical practice. I was impressed by how she was able to retire and shift careers, or rather her passions, at such a young age. She told me she and her husband made a lot of money, were modest spenders and invested all their surplus income while paying down every debt over their lifetime. They had plenty to live on.

She told me the story of one of her partners, who was in his mid-seventies and still working full time. You see, her business partner had decided that even while he was a successful physician making a great income in his '60's, he would become a day trader and real estate speculator. It was clear that he made a serious departure from his expertise in medicine and decided to venture into business areas that require significant knowledge and time to become successful. Additionally, finance and investing are very different mindsets from the sciences and physiology focus of the medical profession.

As expected, the experience wasn't a good one. His day trading racked up regular and significant losses — in fact, Lynette said he would sometimes be trading from his cell phone in the operating room! We'll leave out the malpractice possibilities from this story. He also became highly leveraged on his real estate investments and they all went bust in the 2008 recession. With no savings, and no other assets, he pretty much had to work until he was eighty.

As a wealth advisor, I always recommended my clients diversify their investments, not as an income or business generating activity, but for risk management. It was not recommended they do it themselves. I was their investment specialist; their role was to focus on whatever their professional expertise was. This was especially true for entrepreneurs. Investing in your human capital, to do what you do well, is a smart plan. The returns, when successful, far outweigh any basic market investment returns you can expect. Focusing on your niche and building your core business as the expert should be your primary focus. Do one thing exceptionally, but when customer interest or demand dries up or markets shift, your family and lifestyle need security. Diversification of risk comes in other investments as well as managing your debt and cash flow.

Diversifying does not mean that you commoditize yourself or become "FedEx". They used to run a TV commercial where the office manager comes in to ask his boss if they "do that", and of course, he says, "Yes, we do that". The manager does this repeatedly. He walks into the boss' large office, while the executive is tattooing himself and beating two chess masters with one hand. The message is simple; FedEx does everything and the impression is that all the things they do are somehow different. At its core, FedEx moves stuff extremely well. They can deliver anything, anywhere, anytime. They have singular strength in logistics and a very single-minded focus and that is delivering packages. FedEx is a great example of extreme diversification around their core ability. Build on your core strength and figure out many ways to sell the services or products connected directly to that core.

When I was an advisor, my peers in the industry basically received a single traditional stream of revenue from their business in the form of trading commissions (or even fees for assets). During my last ten years as an advisor, I was determined to establish multiple revenue streams in my business doing one core thing. That was to provide excellent strategic advice and financial planning for impact-minded people considering their retirement, succession to wealth and philanthropy. I had one, clear core ability with many different facets and ways to earn revenue for my business. The results were that I did not have to rely on the fees from value of investment accounts as my sole way of recognizing revenue. By the time I retired, I was able to put at least six methods to generate revenue in place, including annual advisory fees, planning fees, insurance, hourly consulting fees, speaking fees, and even some commission fees. I even received a few dollars from book sales occasionally.

Many different streams of revenue are recommended to provide you with many opportunities to save more money, to pay your debts and bills, and to invest more in yourself. It is also a good form of risk management. When one revenue stream is low, the others might be able to carry you through. Developing these gives you the ability to pull on any lever at any time to manage your revenue or drive more. When all of them are working at the same time, it is powerful. There will be periods when everything you offer, you create, and you sell are creating cash flow for you and your family. Your peers will be amazed at how you did it, your competitors will wish they were as successful, and you will profit. It all stems from one single core ability or skill.

How you build and leverage multiple ways to sell, package and deliver your core ability will determine your long-term wealth – not how many different businesses you can get yourself into.

31. Put The Pedal To The Metal

Successful entrepreneurs make big decisions fast.

Watching Elon Musk, the late Steve Jobs, Jeff Bezos and Richard Branson, it would be reasonable to think they make huge decisions about their next business move at the speed of light. They seem to be so aggressive and committed when acting. Because of their incredible wealth and influence, their decisions also mobilize people and large sums of money. They also inspire. They are assertive and move quickly. In fact, to the outsider or even their own employees, it appears they are sometimes rash and impulsive. Be assured, they are a lot of things, but they are not rash or careless. That is evidenced most times in their success. Even with audacious and unusual goals they are often successful – take Elon Musk's "The Boring Company", for example. Musk wanted to escape the grind of overland travel in Los Angeles. He determined that air travel was not an option – due to noise, risk, lack of infrastructure, etc. He did, however, see possibility in below ground, tunneling, moving cars and other multi-passenger vehicles through tubes at high speeds below the earth's surface.

Within a very short period, he had completed and tested his first mile of tunnel. It wasn't pretty, but it provided a glimpse of what could be. In the process, they learned a lot, created a brand for the operation, developed better underground boring techniques and set the stage for more development. It wasn't a failure and it got done. Working on the premise that "done is better than perfect" and "advancement is better than stagnation", Musk puts his big ideas into action quickly. If he struggles, he at least opens the door to someone else to build on the innovation he started. When things work well, the result can mean billions of dollars.

Again, in their fast action, these men are not impulsive. What these highly visible and enormously successful people have in common is that they possess a predetermined, set criterion for making their decisions. They weigh options and quickly understand the upside and downside risk of an action. They know if they can take on a project or will be able to mobilize people to do so. They basically run down a mental checklist that either "green lights" the project or kills it.

Time is money and energy. Mastering the ability to make quick decisions is an important part of entrepreneurship. To help you be successful here's a simple list that you can use to make your own quick and critical decisions. Whenever faced with an opportunity - ask yourself:

1. Is this opportunity immediately valuable or will it be a value to my customers in the future?
2. Is this consistent with our brand?
3. Can this be done elegantly?
4. Will this be profitable?

Speed and execution matter most. Dan Sullivan, founder and creator of The Strategic Coach™ program, really focuses on this concept for entrepreneurs. My first book, my business processes, and my marketing efforts never would have happened as quickly (or at all) if I hadn't constructed a framework to make such decisions and to be comfortable with moving fast. In my second year of "Coach", this principle empowered me to drive ideas forward. Moving everything 80 percent forward leaves you with 20 percent … of which you then attack to 80 percent and so on. Successful entrepreneurs push ideas forward.

Malcolm Gladwell, in his book "*Blink: The Power of Thinking without Thinking*", investigated quick decision-making. He wanted to know how success can come from acting on something in the blink of an eye. The reality was that those who act fast have a skill for "thin-slicing" information and have already established a strong understanding of the decision at hand and the underlying variables. They have a process. They are just able to filter all this better than most people. Some people have developed this more than others, but it is a skill that can be learned and is a huge advantage for those who can do it well. Make decisions quickly, get stuff done fast, and close sales rapidly. Beyond your own actions, it is also a good idea to "train" your customers or marketplace to get better at making quick decisions when it comes to buying what you offer. Develop your own repeatable process to allow people to construct their own system to move them from uninterested, to interested, to buyer. If you can give someone the framework to act, they will apply them readily when considering your business.

Lastly, Musk, Bezos, Branson and Jobs are business visionaries. Their decisions reflected their passions and advanced their business and often indulged their own curiosity. In your business decisions, ensure that all your timely actions are directed toward your ultimate business goals: more engagement, more sales, more freedom, and more impact. Develop this skill and it will drive everything to a point where people buy you, your ideas, your services and your products. If you can refine this, you will make a huge positive dent in this world.

GROW GET GIVE

BOOK TWO

GET MORE FREEDOM

GROW GET GIVE

Introduction

William Wallace:

"I am William Wallace. And I see a whole army of my countrymen, here in defiance of tyranny! You have come to fight as free men. And free man you are! What will you do with that freedom? Will you fight?"

Reluctant army:

"No! No...."

Reluctant soldier:

"Against that? No! We will run, and we will live!"

William Wallace:

"Aye! Fight and you may die. Run and you will live, at least a while. And dying in your beds many years from now, would you be willing to trade all the days from this day to that for one chance, just one chance, to come back here and tell our enemies that they may take our lives but they will never take our FREEDOM!"

- From the movie Braveheart, 1995

Why are you an entrepreneur? FREEDOM! Who, or rather what, is your enemy? Whatever robs us of our freedom.

The number one reason entrepreneurs do what they do is for freedom. Choosing to be an entrepreneur is not a safe decision. Leaving the comfort of a predictable schedule and regular pay-cheque to pursue your "thing", while seeking time flexibility, creativity and perceived financial gain, is a big step. Moving a vision forward and starting ventures to support it takes us into the unknown.

Growing a business from nothing is fraught with risk. Starting out, cash flow is uncertain, there is no job security, and every month, week, or day brings different challenges and opportunities.

With all its difficulties and risk of failure, entrepreneurship also has tremendous rewards — both financially and personally. One of the most important drivers for entrepreneurs is the promise of freedom offered by being your own boss.

It is true, entrepreneurs set their own hours; make decisions to balance their business ambitions with their lifestyle, and have the flexibility to move in any direction they choose. Freedom can be described as having more time.

What that means is different for everyone. For some, more time is just that, more time available away from work. For others, it might mean more time to do what they love to do — in work or leisure. Time or freedom from being "IN" your work constantly in order to work "ON" it is special. Doing what you love never consumes time, it enhances it. It is where creativity happens, where big ideas germinate, and innovation grows.

We know as entrepreneurs that an ideal balance between work and personal life is sometimes hard to achieve, although something close is possible. I have always said entrepreneurs come to me with one of two main challenges. The first is what I cover in *GROW your business*. They do incredible things and have a unique and desirable offering, but their positioning and marketing doesn't translate into more customers and, thus, revenue growth. They aren't making more money doing what they love and it is frustrating.

The second challenge is what I will deal with in this *GET more freedom* segment. That is where moderately successful entrepreneurs make money but feel stuck in their business. They are overwhelmed and overworked. They often are working 50, 60 or 80 hours per week IN their business! I used to be one of those people. Then I discovered that I didn't have to work as much to sustain and grow my business.

If you are one of those people, then your utopia hasn't been realized yet. Working deeper in your business by doing the same things over and over, are not going to improve your outcome. This is not a prison sentence and you can master strategies to gain your freedom.

The year before I decided to sell my investment management business, I was making more money while working in my business less than ever. I enjoyed three months away from work each year to spend with my family and doing the things I loved. I'm going to share what I've learned with you. People, processes and systems will set you free.

The following secrets are tips that successful entrepreneurs have used to achieve freedom, enjoy a creative and prosperous work life, and a fulfilling personal lifestyle.

GROW GET GIVE

1. Strive For Magical – Mastery Gives You Freedom

I've always been a fan of professional sports as opposed to amateur – college or otherwise (I would classify most top Olympic level or World Cup sport athletes to be "professional" as the goal of the highest possible level of success is their only pursuit – it is essentially their "job" and passion). While I understand the excitement of amateur sport and the unpredictability of fallibility combined with passion for the game in a "pure" form, unadulterated by the money of professional sports, I prefer seeing the absolute best of the best compete at their highest levels. One argument that people have in their unwavering passion for amateur sport over professional is that they perceive that many pros simply do not compete their best day in and day out – that they don't strive for that zone of mastery enough. That might be true some of the time, but often it is not.

Pro athletes constantly push the limits of what is possible and approach their work with a single-minded focus. When it matters most, the best rise to the occasion. It is in that time and place where mastery becomes magical. It is incredible to behold. You give LeBron James the ball in the last second of a game and he will make the shot more than he misses it. That is his job and he does it better than almost anyone on the planet. You will find the same is true for top-performers in any industry, like entertainment, the arts, business, surgery. When the moment counts the most and the stress level would otherwise be the highest for a "normal" person, true professionals will perform. I admire this quality immensely. To be prepared and rehearsed to deliver when it counts. Amateurs can reach these levels too, but the differentiator is the frequency and quality of top performance when required.

Whenever possible, set your sights on observing and achieving mastery. Mastery is often elusive because once achieved a new goal is set. Skill development is constant. When mastery is achieved in anything, magic can happen. We are lucky to see the result of mastery often, so pay attention when you are in its presence.

I was always curious about the roots of mastery. How it develops and where it starts. When a master is interviewed or questioned about when they became great, or where their ability came from, they would respond, "I've always known" or "ever since I was a child". It was something they always knew they would do. They don't often share their own journey. Whether it was an innate drive or passion, or simply curiosity or even fixation, it was clear more times than not, that athletes who achieved mastery were wired differently. Everything seemed easier for them.

The fundamental beginning of the journey to mastery has been something I've been lucky to observe in our son, Coen. At a very young age, he trained his focus on pursuit of mastery. His progression to mastery is still being realized through his chosen and extremely difficult sport – or rather the sport that called to him – downhill mountain bike racing.

From the very first time he pointed his bike down a slope of undulating terrain, jumps and drops, covered in rocks, dirt and roots, Coen was better than his peers. He seemed to have an innate ability and vision for riding. At nine or ten years old, he could ride harder terrain, do bigger tricks and was faster than kids two, three or even four years his senior. By age twelve he had exceeded the skills of most of his coaches. I watched with awe and wondered aloud, "What made him better? Why was he finishing a run, while others were only halfway down? Why couldn't I keep up with him anymore?" I became passionate about observing him as he quickly moved from "stumbling novice" to "magical mastery".

The essential element required to learn any sport is progression and with individual or extreme sports, it is amplified. When I observed my son and the pursuit of his World Cup racing dreams, my understanding of how mastery happens, how it develops, and how it grows expanded.

You see, people who do extreme sports reach their best through rehearsal and preparation like any other athlete. The downside risk of failure, mostly resulting in injury, is much greater and winning is reserved for one person in a category, not a team. Many athletes in these disciplines can get very good as they progress. They can master several skills and string a few together, but getting through mastery and beyond to magical, takes special talent.

Coen was always interested in biking. He had a natural tendency on his bike to be physically stable and coordinated. He was also comfortable with high speed, acceleration and being airborne. In fact, for the longest time we figured he was better on his wheels than he was on his feet. He was safer, quite frankly. He'd trip less and he didn't walk or run into anything. On his bike, he seemed to be in his natural state. Beyond basic interest, you won't become a master of anything just because you're passionate or have an inclination toward something. However, the gateway to becoming masterful is that passion and the commitment to becoming better than you were the day or the moment before.

Mastery is never achieved or realized without stumbling around, making mistakes, and suffering the consequence of it. It is also a product of repetition, persistence, commitment, and execution of fine motor skills or activities that are foundational. I describe the stages of mastery for mountain biking, in line with the "Conscious Competence Learning Model", developed by Noel Burch in the 1970's, like this:

1. Stumbling Novice (Green Run) – giving it a shot. *Unconsciously incompetent.* No conscious idea of skills or techniques, just actions. In the mountain bike vernacular – "sending it". Everything requires thought to happen, although there is no inherent grasp of the skill or technique needed for success. Some training or coaching is required here to help the rider understand the bike components, the concept of riding and the basic safety concepts and skills need to move forward. At this stage, with or without guidance, the attempt is good enough. This is where early interest might even give way to passion. Passion isn't needed to become good at the fundamentals, but it can be aroused here.

2. Routine Intermediate (Blue Run) – where repetition and skill development converge through execution. *Consciously incompetent.* Basic skills are still mostly "cognitive". All actions require thought and intention. Ride your bike over things and increase your speed over varied terrain. This is where coaching and training begin to make big differences in competence and how to *think* about riding. Equipment, fitness and nutrition are considered but not prioritized. Passion for riding emerges in some people and they move on to their next competency level. Most people will simply, and happily, stay at this level.

3. Experienced Expert (Black Diamond Run) – this is where each skill is added upon another and linked together in a series to make performance happen. *Consciously competent.* Competitive racing can happen here. Adding tricks or advanced skills to basic riding while speed

increases, and "style" improves. Coaching and mentoring are needed to provide objective input to move basic skills to more advanced ones. Rehearsal, practice through repetition and experimentation happen here. In downhill mountain biking, this is where people begin to observe that certain riders "see" things differently, in advance, that others don't. They see the "lines" in the trails where the fastest riding or easiest path lies. They envision themselves moving through the trail before it appears to them. In their mind's eye they have already ridden the trail that is immediately before them and under them. They are conscious of what they are doing and what they are about to do.

4. Magical Mastery (Double Black Diamond – Pro-Line Runs) – High speed racing occurs here. *Unconscious competence*. The required skills for action are executed mostly without thought. Decisions and adjustments happen automatically. This is a stage where athletes often describe the game or action to be happening in "slow motion" and time is perceived to stand still. Their unconscious mind is driving, while they are experiencing the rhythm or flow of the activity. This is where the freedom of creativity and improvisation occur. It seems effortless. This is the "wow!" factor. For them, there is no conscious consideration of their present. They are seeing and living their future. They can maneuver themselves through space and time in ways that amaze observers. Creativity happens here. Innovation happens here. Magic happens here.

How does this relate to business??

At a most fundamental level, business mastery starts with the dedication to first becoming proficient. That is working on the most basic skills required for the task. Let's say you were learning how to present to speak to audiences to sell. If your ultimate goal was to sell your product to thousands of people on television, then the first things you should probably master is learning the language of sales, learning the language of your customer, and finally develop a mastery of those fundamental skills. You write and rehearse scripts and marketing information.

Once you understand how to articulate your message clearly and demonstrate your product or services in a way that is pleasing to the audience, you can begin to master the skill. Once those basics in place, you begin to work on your personal appearance and presentation techniques. These would be everything from how you move and look on stage to working on the volume and intonation of your voice. Where you place emphasis on stories, words or concepts matter.

When you are ready for the "blue runs" you consciously think through everything. The basics happen and you might consider more advanced strategies. If you applied this to customer service, it would be where welcoming someone to your shop, then facilitating a transaction, thanking them and saying have a nice day happens. When you reach this level, as a habit, or routine, you become open to learning how to improve the experience. Instead of just getting through, you're now going back into that tool kit, using the tools in the way they were designed, for their maximum potential, and now you are ready to move to mastery.

Mastery is cyclical and never ending. You experience growth, achievement, and then raise the bar. It's not because those who reach mastery become bored, it is a desire or need to continually push. When your level of mastery becomes mechanical, it is time to move up to another level. This transition between conscious incompetence and competence often involves setbacks. Making the step to another level features discomfort and exhilaration. You are quickly using new techniques, or other ideas that can be added to improve your fundamentals, so that your next level is even higher. Stumbling occurs here. Some people understand this is normal and natural so they persevere, while others find the stress is too much and fall back to their "blue runs". The majority settle back into this territory. For a few, though it is a big leap forward in mastery. Because so few take this step, competition is less and opportunities abound.

Become masterful: Freedom is found in the progression to mastery. When you are no longer conscious about the fundamentals of what you do, when your basic daily activities energize you as opposed to consume energy, you are ready to go to the next level. Freedom is on the horizon when you're in that stage of experienced expert.

Think of demonstrating expert mastery through performance. This is the art of selling. I give performances where I present, train, and educate, and essentially sell for a day, two days, or three days. That's my performance. When it becomes masterful, it no longer troubles me or gives me anxiety; it is the last thing that worries me. I can perform optimally and enjoy the benefits of this state.

Moving to mastery is enjoyable. It should give you joy, happiness, fulfillment. Because of this, mastery gives you freedom. You don't get freedom immediately; you must work at it. You must build mastery, but once you're there, it gives you enormous amount of freedom because it removes the most stressful, intense part of your life, your business, your pursuits, and it makes them simple, effortless, and elegant.

GROW GET GIVE

2. Select The Right People

I meet plenty of entrepreneurs whose businesses are doing well, sales are good, and they are growing, but they are working all the time and feel they can't step away because things would grind to a halt or something would go wrong. These folks might have gotten the "GROW" part right, but they are now stuck. They can't get out of their daily grind. They haven't been able to think creatively for ages and feel they are running on a treadmill. The result is a loss of freedom and reduced happiness. Entrepreneurs experiencing this are usually challenged with a lack of processes in their lives or the wrong people.

Time is the one thing we can never replace. Once consumed, it is gone forever. We can enjoy it, waste it or simply pass it by. For entrepreneurs, more than anyone, time is freedom. More time gives you the freedom to focus on the things that matter, like your passions. It is the freedom to manage how you spend your energy and who you gain energy from, like family, with friends, for yourself. The reason this is so powerful for entrepreneurs, specifically, is that when an entrepreneur's mind is rested and stress-free, they can create big ideas and great solutions. Anyone can enjoy this, but when an entrepreneur experiences this, they put things into action right away.

The right people in your business will give you time.

If you own a business and you can't be away from it, then the business owns you. If you don't trust the people you have hired or partnered with to run the business seamlessly without you, then you have built yourself a prison. Have you ever said this? "If only I had the right person doing [fill in your biggest challenge here], I could spend more time doing the things that I love and increase revenue for my business". When working to improve this, it leads to two dilemmas for most business owners. The first, of course is developing processes to hire the right people for the right roles. The second is dealing with the people you have put into place who are not necessarily the right fit for their roles.

Learning to hire right is dependent on understanding the qualities of the person you wish to hire. Mostly intangible, the beliefs and values of people who you will rely on must be consistent with yours. These qualities make your work environment enjoyable; they improve the overall morale of your employees and the customer experience. In challenging times, when you work with people who share similar values as you do, it is easier to solve business problems because the level of negative discord is low. Everyone's compass is on the same set point.

A person's skills, knowledge and experience are objective qualities that also are important. These can be measured, tested and matched with the role you hope to fill. Anyone can hire these people for you with a clear process and criteria. In fact, it is best if the entrepreneur helps to build the process, then allows others to execute. I will discuss this further in the next section.

We all know too well what happens when we hire the wrong people. We know it intuitively and quickly, yet we tend to be slow to let them go, so our experience is costly — emotionally and financially. Considerable time and energy are spent dealing with the wrong people, while money and opportunity are lost in doing so. Just because someone has the right personal qualities and values, it doesn't make them a right fit. Hiring someone because they are "fun" or enjoyable to be around isn't the first criteria. Entrepreneurs are visionaries. They also want to sell their vision with anyone who will listen. Not everyone will buy into your vision and they won't likely be motivated by your vision. They might like it and aspire to the ideal, but they aren't driven by it. They will be motivated by their own set of priorities and life goals. We hope they are like us because we are looking to be energized, but the qualities we require to provide support for our business are not found in copies of ourselves.

The right people lift you up and allow you freedom. They do not have any need to "be like you". An entrepreneur's perception of a lack of time is really your view about the lack of time you spend doing the things that energize you. When you get right people working with you the skies will clear, and the sun will shine through. The same days you previously struggled through become simpler. The sense of unease you have about stepping away from your business will eventually go away.

There is a famous African saying quoted heavily around the world in business and that is:

"If you want to go fast, go alone. If you want to go far, go together."

While an entrepreneur is alone in many ways — unique vision, unwavering determination, and acceptance of risk - they are never truly successful on their own. Understanding how others fit, how people lift you up and support your vision is critical. The people you surround yourself with make the difference between success and excellence. People will give you freedom. This is the key difference between a stressful grind and an enjoyable and fulfilling life. Surround yourself with great people, train them, and encourage them and you will gain more freedom than you ever thought possible. Those who are not a fit will cause you to lose your energy and restrict your freedom. Remember the people you hire will allow you to operate at your best in your "zone" using your unique ability as much as possible. Gain your time back with the right people.

3. Establish A Process To Hire Great People

Freedom happens when you have the right people working with you. These people are best suited for the role you need filled and happen to share the same basic values that you and your company have. They do not have to be your best friend and do not have to be people you hang out with. It is always good when they push you and challenge you as a leader, and you should return the favor. When hiring, it is important to work with people who challenge you and have skills that complement you but do not recreate you. You are the entrepreneur. Hang out with other entrepreneurs, mastermind with them, and share ideas with them. Hire the people who are going to free up your time, make your business better and give you freedom.

We want people with certain qualities and values. We want to like them and want them to like us and believe in our vision. Hiring is easy to do poorly because we feel we must, as the entrepreneur, control the process. But this is misguided and will end badly because we can't help that we want to sell everyone our vision. Most of the people that will give you freedom aren't motivated by your vision. In selling them, you sell yourself and often make errors in hiring because you like them, and you were a good salesperson. You give them cues as to how they should answer and they oblige. You miss red flags and try to squeeze them into roles they don't fit. I recommend you always have someone else do the hiring for you, or at the very least, with you. You set the criteria and even the hiring process, but have other people implement it for you.

Repeat after me: *"An entrepreneur shall not hire one's own employees' single-handedly."*

Here's why:

You are always marketing … this will include how you conduct your job interview.

Selling the candidate on the role inserts your vision where it is not effective.

Without a process for hiring that has specific and clear criteria, we will very likely make similar wrong decisions in hiring over and over. During an eight-year period I went through seven different full-time assistants. The assistant role was a critical interface with clients and a huge support for administration duties. In the investment world sometimes your assistants are shared, sometimes they move from one advisor to another. There is a strange and overwhelming belief that they must come from the industry and should work towards becoming a fully licensed advisor as well. The compensation model is standard and overpays for average work, with rewards only linked to the advisor's success. As a result, the pool of possible assistants is limited and trained to do the same work with the same pay structure. This is faulty and dysfunctional and places huge limits on success. During that period, I lived by the old standard and hired within the "system".

I did not have a process and most hires happened when I was desperate and exhausted. A lot of the people I hired were nice people, but I couldn't stand them after the first year. They weren't the right fit and the stress it would cause me was unreal. My wife would hear about my staffing issues constantly. I couldn't handle it anymore and finally interrogated my business coach asking him how he hired his amazing assistant and some of the other amazing people who worked with him. He shared his wisdom with me, and it worked. It was an unwavering hiring process that I quickly adopted and never turned back.

How do we build our process and list of criteria we hope to have in a new employee? Well, you start at the same point any effective marketing program would…you ask the target customer what they need and want. You will learn a LOT!

When I needed to hire my last (and perfect) assistant for my wealth management business, I spent an hour interviewing another assistant whom I admired, and thought would be a great addition to my team. I wanted to learn what was important to her in her role, so I could tailor my hiring approach to the person I needed. I asked her what her ideal day looked like, what motivated her to perform, and asked her about her thoughts on fair compensation. Very much unlike me, she stated that she valued security and consistency both in her daily routine and her compensation. She preferred task-oriented bonuses rather than business growth ones. Additionally, she valued time even more than financial rewards for meeting or exceeding performance targets. Time off and flexibility to manage appointments and personal requirements throughout the week mattered a lot to her. She had a family and was a working mother. Naturally this was quite an eye opener for me. If it was up to me, I would have structured the role and my hiring process to reflect my values and the things that motivated me as an entrepreneur. A lot of those points wouldn't have been considered by me. It became clear why I was so unsuccessful at hiring in the past.

While building your ideal candidate role, clearly articulate specific skills they need to be successful in the role. Whether you end up being the one to do the hiring or someone else does, it must be unmistakable. It prevents you from selling the position to the candidate. Build the role and job description first and then hire. It is a significant error to ignore your role description and criteria only to end up hiring someone you really like and want to work with but doesn't fit the role. You are not hiring for "fun" and to have another friend around. You have friends. Hire to have the best possible person for the role in place. Avoid creating the role for the person … the role comes first the right person will follow.

Other important criteria to include in your hiring process are qualities such as experience. This will largely depend on the role and will depend on the type of business. There are degrees of experience. In one case you might need an applicant with significant industry specific experience. In others it is a skillset they need, where the type of business experience doesn't matter, as the skill is transferrable. If you offer extensive on-the-job training and prefer to hire individuals with no experience, but who have the capacity to learn, then you want to be sure you hire people with a degree of intelligence and common sense. Businesses with strong processes and systems in place need smart, energized, and qualified candidates. Everything else can be learned or followed.

Other qualities that are important to consider in the hiring process include a person's core strengths and their natural tendencies. There are many assessments or evaluation metrics available to employers these days. I highly recommend you make use of widely available personality testing protocols. They work and they prevent headaches down the road. They also provide much more objectivity for decision-making in hiring. I extensively use the Kolbe A Index™ and occasionally use Tom Rath's "Strengths Finder" to get to the heart of how a person will naturally tend to behave and act and where we might uncover their unique ability. Hiring a likeable person to do marketing, who has incredible academic skills, but is naturally shy and introverted, will not likely find success in such a role. This might be common sense, but sometimes isn't so apparent.

I interviewed a person for an executive assistant role who I liked very much, who had a great resume with a lot of experience and seemed very driven. In fact, I was blown away at how she had spent the past decade learning, advancing, and growing her resume. She was likeable and clearly a motivated person. When I reviewed her Kolbe A Index™ results, I realized I liked her because she was more similar to me in her tendencies and had the success she had because of her motivation for continuous growth and change. What the test revealed was that she did not score well on her ability to follow through or to dig for facts. These two qualities were extremely important in the role I was hiring for and to offset my high "quick start" tendencies. With the Kolbe A Index™, and other such tests, there are optimum matches for people with varying scores or profiles. Both Kolbe and Strengths Finder offer guides on how to use their findings in hiring and combining employees. If you use these, adhere to their results.

Lastly, while not every single position requires a Mensa candidate, I recommend you hire for intelligence in conjunction with the other qualities and criteria I have already mentioned. Basic qualities of intelligence (or cognitive ability) can never be underestimated. Certificates and diplomas provide some evidence of baseline intelligence but can be deceiving. Use a simple intelligence measure to set a baseline for your candidates. I have met many intelligent idiots. A high common-sense IQ reflects someone culturally connected as well. One test that is used by people I respect is called the "Wonderlic Cognitive Ability Test". It is focused on aptitude and problem-solving abilities. It is a simple, fifty questions, multiple choice test that takes less than fifteen minutes. The test will tell you whether your candidate will be able to learn and adapt to the requirements of your training and the role they are applying for.

Whatever types of assessments you decide to use, make some of them part of the pre-interview process and include some in the interview as well. Too often employers hire, and then test. I was guilty of this too. What this did was basically shine the light on the fact that I hired the wrong person…or worse, it gave me another problem to solve and I spent hours and hours trying to fit the person to the role within their test results. Setting roles, establishing criteria, and adding these types of tests bring small and important hurdles to your hiring process. A candidate who decides to complete your process will rise to the top. In fact, they will be only one of a small number who get to that point. The process helps you filter many candidates who consider your process unnecessary or unusual. Quite a few will be offended that you require them to perform these tasks. Those people are not for you. If you don't stick to your process you will allow people through who would otherwise be wasting your time – and theirs.

Here's one last word for your new hiring process. Don't allow yourself to accommodate a poor showing for any reason. When you really like a person and the same candidate believes they are well-qualified, they may show a less-than-high standard — while simply positioning it as them being more "casual" or personal. If they show up late or unprepared, do not hire them. If they do not "look" the part or act appropriately, don't write it off as quirky or amusing. They won't change for you or for your job, so don't hope that they will. Formality and achievement are measurable qualities and they are indicators of pride in work, attention to detail, and understanding of importance. When you accommodate a lower performance level and establish low expectations, the standard is set. Subsequently, you will be disappointed with the results. Raise the bar very high up front and you can always soften your stance in time with the right employee. Trying to raise your expectations after you've set the tone will not work.

GROW GET GIVE

4. Invest The Time And Energy Into Processes To Train

To be hired, your new employee successfully went through your standard process. You have invested time and energy finding the right person. Everyone is excited and ready to move forward. On the first day, you walk the new employee around your office and introduce them to the other team members, show them the kitchen and the copy room and their workstation. They turn on the phone and computer, and then you promptly head to your office or a meeting to get on with your typical busy day. Along the way, you request certain tasks to be completed and point them toward steps you hope for them to take. Later the same day, as you pass by them, you rattle off some inaudible instructions and go on to your next task.

This persists for a month and things seem to be going okay, until the day that you demand a report or task completed and it is not done right, nor on time. You then consider that maybe the new hire is not quite right for the position. Maybe you missed something when you hired them, or maybe they're just not up to the task. From that point on, failings are exaggerated, and shortcomings are glaring. They get frustrated and you want them gone. The problem is of course, your fault. You brought a quality person on to your team and left them blowing in the wind. This could have gone worse. The new employee could have miscommunicated with a customer or blown a sale.

This happens in the "new economy" as well. Where geographic flexibility is normal and work- spaces, or non-traditional offices environments are commonplace. You engaged the new employee online and exchanged all pertinent details in this way and had a phone or video call for your interview. The next step is to meet in person, and you arrange the meeting at a local coffee shop to welcome them and take care of some basic planning items. Then, later in the day, another video conference call is arranged to introduce the new person to your team. A welcome package and hyperlinks are sent to the new employee. These are links to the cloud-based central communication platform for the virtual office. There are business applications and downloads needed for HR and procedurals manuals. After that, the new employee is left on their own, by themselves, in their own personal workspace with the promise of calendar invitations to the next online meetings and a link to the deliverables calendar for the team. Next, you continue with your day, you check in occasionally and repeat the previous cycle – only virtually. Whether you operate in a virtual office or physical space does not change the way most owner/managers end up moving past the initial hire.

To avoid those two scenarios, you must care for your new hire. Nurture them and train them. Look into their eyes, listen and confirm they understand. Those eyes are the windows to freedom for you. They are your best assets and they are the face of your company or the backbone of it. Either way, you hired them to give you more time, more peace of mind and to increase your capacity to do your thing. It is critical that you spend time training them and set them up for success.

Well-run, successful businesses invest money and time in training their people well.
Don't leave anything to chance.

You will ask: who is responsible to train these new people? You own a small or medium-sized company with limited time and resources. You hired someone to improve things, not bog you down. YOUR reputation is at risk. It is your company and if this doesn't work it will cost you time, customers, money and wasted energy. While you personally might not be the right person to train the new employee, you most certainly are the one to set the tone and structure for the role, as well as ingrain the vision for the company. You, therefore, must build the scripts, design the processes and goals. You can delegate the details, such as building the training manuals or processes and procedures.

Dictate every process, audio record it and send it for transcription. Give one staff member the role to clean up the document – adding procedural improvements and practical insights - then publish it. This is a great start to giving your new hire the right tools and instructions for how to use them to achieve success in their work.

Follow up then becomes the most important step. For the first days, weeks, months and maybe even year, you will need to have regular meetings or reviews to ensure your new employee is on track to learn the processes and systems. They must feel the autonomy needed to develop a sense of ownership of their job and role within the company. Add clear measurement and evaluation, and then find opportunities to improve, re-train, or advance and repeat.

GROW GET GIVE

5. Give Authority. Get Freedom.

This GET secret crosses over to GIVE. When you give people the authority to make decisions and take responsibility, you give them ownership…and you give yourself more freedom. It goes beyond simple delegation. As owners, entrepreneurs and leaders, we tend to occasionally overstep our bounds in the delegation process. We believe that once we delegate, we let go, but often what we do is delegate and dictate. You might be smiling right now knowing that it is quite likely true for you. You have probably done that. Delegate and dictate means that you give people the sense that they have the authority as they see fit with their abilities and visions, but then in short order, you micromanage their work and decisions. This undermines their efforts. It is reasonable to inspect the work you expect because it is your business and your reputation, but there is a fine line that must be drawn.

Helpful and proactive guidance is a lot different from control. You must give them actual autonomy, not alter or dictate their every step. Invest the time to give them clear and productive guidance initially and then let them make the decisions that you need them to make. If they take big steps outside your expectations, there are two possibilities. One is that you might have the wrong person, but the second is, most likely, that you haven't provided clear enough instructions on what they must do and what you expect.

When delegating, you must advocate. You brought quality people into your business with a clear hiring process. Give them strong leadership and let them shine. If you have the right people in place and give them responsibility, you can give them leadership roles. Giving them permission to make decisions and say yes in the right circumstances allows you to free yourself of the duty. But it is more than that. By giving authority, you free yourself of the time, energy and worry. You can focus on your next thing, your creativity or just the one thing outside your business that you are doing right now. It is liberation.

In my last book, I discussed a client of mine, Michael. He was intensely focused on building his online project management software training business from $60,000 to $600,000 revenue a year. In 2014 when I wrote about this, it was just a goal. In four years, he achieved it! As a one-owner operation, with one full time employee, he accomplished a lot. He added a second employee and outsourced or contracted many jobs, collaborated and delegated a lot. For the first few years, he was consumed by his business. He felt stressed and worried about his main assistant, Julie, and how she was going to move to that next level. She had been with him a long time, but when it came to the vision of the business, he never felt that she was completely onside, and most certainly, she was not an entrepreneur. Julie liked consistency, simplicity and predictability. The kind of thing everyone who is not an entrepreneur enjoys. But given they were the only two key players in his company, he was constantly reminded of this and it troubled him daily. He didn't embrace her natural skillset and wanted a partner.

Then he was offered a chance to work with one of his long-term customers on a contract consulting basis and go in-house for almost two months. It would be a great opportunity to enhance his knowledge and build an important ally in the marketplace. We discussed this at length and decided on one of our coaching calls that it would be a good idea for him to proceed with the gig. The wisdom he could gain combined with good compensation, would help him build another training course. At the same time, it would be a test of his own business to see how it would run without him – and by his assistant. He was nervous and anxious and excited. Prior to this situation arising, we discussed Julie's compensation in detail and made adjustments that significantly increased it. He gave her the raise, and then told her about running the company on her own.

Six weeks into his consulting role, we spoke about the experience working away from his company day-to-day. He responded the experience was great, and he was amazed that his business worked so well without him. In fact, things went so smoothly that he was considering dedicating most of his energy in the following summer months to building a new course that he was passionate about and taking a few weeks off to travel and vacation with his family. He did this too. His business continued growing, clients were pleased and things functioned well. He realized he didn't need to be involved daily. He achieved FREEDOM!

Delegating responsibility improved Julie's skills as a manager and boosted her confidence, not-to-mention her job satisfaction. She was able to put her own stamp on things too, creating an "ownership effect" that Michael had always hoped for. The freedom Michael realized in this delegation of responsibility was priceless. Not only was it effective for that period, but it emboldened him to take bigger steps and commit more energy to larger projects. He could look at more impactful initiatives that he always wanted to pursue. It was amazing. When you get to that point, it doesn't happen because you have automated stuff, it happens because you have incredible people. Michael took the time and energy to train, educate and bring Julie along. But best of all, he gave her authority to do it.

GROW GET GIVE

6. Surround yourself with a dream team

The infomercial and "As Seen On TV™" were part of the birth of an entire industry inspired by Kevin Harrington. This made him very wealthy. When he looked to rebuild, or redefine the next industry that he considered tackling, he set out to build a dream team of people that he would work with, partner with, get mentorship from, and joint venture with. When building this dream team, he would satisfy all the aspects that he could possibly think of in the business who could support and improve on the things he saw as necessities in that business. When he looked at his old business, he noticed that it had become woefully overstaffed with too many people who didn't fill roles efficiently, and many positions he hired for just in case there was growth in an area. These were great people with their own lives and personal needs, but they simply didn't fit in Kevin's vision of what he should be doing…versus what he had "always done". He had to make the extremely difficult decision to fire them (there is no nice way to say it). He released 80% of his staff to effectively start over and do it right.

Once he had this "clean slate", he partnered with and created a dream team of finance and investment people, salespeople, marketers, public relations and product development people. His mantra was to find the absolute best and build a dream team. Put key pieces in place and use them efficiently. You don't have to hire them all. Kevin had a bigger budget and was be able to hire full time people that we can't hire. However, you can assemble your dream team using advisory boards, board of directors, or with mentors. Hire only those people who are the most critical for your success and are needed on "staff". Contract and hire others when needed. Naturally you will need to build relationships with the nonemployee team as well as incentivize some of them to remain connected. If these people add value to you, then they will have value to others and have their own activities going on. Your issues are not theirs; they will not and do not have to adopt your vision to support you. Be courteous, respectful and efficient when asking for their time and their expertise...but please ASK!

To get your dream team in place you might have to scour the ranks of your already staffed business. If people are not part of the dream team, they shouldn't be there at all. As I explained above, Harrington mentioned that he hired too many people at one point - he looked around and there was nothing getting done, too many people and too many costs, so he fired everybody. He subsequently only assembled the dream team that could help him leverage, systematize and grow the business.

This was also evident at Tesla in the spring of 2018. Elon Musk was in the growth phase of his business with Tesla. He started out with the bare minimum of people who he thought were his dream team and went for it. He was re-inventing the car industry with Tesla, but when orders began to roll in and the pressure to mass produce his cars hit, against his own judgement, he suddenly reverted to what the past producers had done. In a panic, he staffed up like crazy in order to get things done. He thought he could do it differently than others before him, but he did it anyway. To his dismay, Tesla grew from 8,000 to nearly 40,000 employees quickly.

During that spring there was immense pressure to build and deliver cars quickly and profitably. Musk realized that his staffing effort was inappropriate and that he shouldn't have doubted his instincts. To get more cars produced, profitably and quickly, he decided to cut 10%, or 4,000 of his workforce. In making that decision he was forced to consider what he really needed from his personnel, versus all the people that weren't contributing to reaching the company's goals. Those who were not part of the future and were an expense without purpose had to go. Just a few months later, in the fall of 2018, Tesla had met its production commitments and delivered a profit – much to the amazement of the financial industry and the doubters.

Be sure to surround yourself with your dream team and build it with only the people and tools required to get the job done in the best way possible. No more. Don't add people for a rainy day. Don't add people because there might be something down the road that you can't quantify or if you're preparing for some future that hasn't materialized. Plan for it, but don't implement it. If your vision is realized, and that ideal future materializes, then you can easily define the role of new team members and hire them. There are a lot of very talented high-quality people who might enjoy what you do and what you offer. It can be exciting thinking about "staffing-up" for perceived growth, but until you must do it, don't over-prepare. Put the right people, the perfect people, in place. Build your dream team as you need.

GROW GET GIVE

7. Mastermind: Surround Yourself With Like-Minded People And Positive Influences

Hiring the right people is an important investment in your business. They will be those who support you and the business. They will not be the people who are the same as you and often won't be the ones to motivate and inspire you. If you are a good leader you will help raise them up and they will challenge you and stimulate you as a business owner. They are there to help you run your business more effectively. You will develop relationships with your employees in different ways, but you won't likely be getting together for Sunday dinner, or in a social setting. Do not confuse great morale for deep friendship.

In your personal life and professional life, hang out and seek guidance and collaboration with people and peers who energize you and challenge you. Do this to increase your energy and personal growth.

People who can inspire you, push you and motivate you will raise you up.
Surround yourself with them.

You can build your circle of like-minded entrepreneurs by joining Masterminds, building advisory committees and participating in roundtables. Napoleon Hill (author of "Think and Grow Rich") introduced the idea of Mastermind groups over fifty years ago. I have participated in many similar groups for years. I also lead them for my own coaching clients. For me, they are one of the most exciting ways to grow as a business owner. It is incredible to experience it firsthand. Think of it like cloud-computing: using the collective power of many independent servers to focus and work on your biggest challenge or opportunity with a myriad of inputs from different perspectives and wisdom. A Mastermind group is a collection of like-minded people meeting regularly with the intent to help each other achieve success by sharing insights and knowledge. It is an environment where a break-through can be made for business growth or help resolve a challenge presented by a fellow member of your group. The collective wisdom of the group raises the level of problem-solving and brainstorming. The benefits received from mastermind groups range from sharing accountability to gaining invaluable ideas to building a sense of community. Smart, enthusiastic people and positive, driven entrepreneurs bring everything to the table. Input from like-minded leaders who do different things than you give great insight and problem solving for your business.

Why do we become entrepreneurs? To get more freedom.

What is the meaning of freedom? It means spending more time and energy working in your zone and developing your personal and interpersonal relationships. Mastermind groups give you this and more. They allow you incredible freedom to expand your thinking. They improve your sense of community. The energy that comes from such brainstorming is amazing. Knowing that others think like you and can help you, as well as realizing that you can help them, is stimulating. Your Mastermind group takes you away from the naysayers, the doubters and the negative mindsets we experience daily. When you are energized and confident, you are happier. When you're happier and inspired, you improve the life of those around you and you will have more meaningful interactions with friends and family.

How do you Mastermind? The first option is work with me as your coach and your Mastermind group will always be there for you. You can join already established groups or you establish your own. Many business coaching programs will also organize groups within their coaching members. Before you go throwing the idea around spontaneously, please know that this is an investment. It is an investment in your business and your personal growth. You must invest your time, attention and money. This is something you must do frequently. Two to four times per year is what you should expect as a schedule for your group. There will be a financial investment if travel is required to meet as well as criteria for membership. There are often educational opportunities offered by the organizer or coaching group. The ideas, the personal joy, friendships and the financial benefits you gain from participating regularly in a mastermind will be exponentially more than what you put in.

GROW GET GIVE

8. Read To Succeed

"Read at every wait; read at all hours, read within leisure, read in times of labor. The task of the educated mind is simply put."

– Cicero

Dave (aka "Famous Dave") Anderson, a Native American, grew up poor in inner city Chicago. Dave is a living testament to why "readers" succeed. In elementary school, Dave's teacher asked for students to approach the front of the class to answer a question at the blackboard. Dave raised his hand to answer, but the teacher stopped him and cruelly stated, "You're too dumb to answer the question, David. Let someone else who is smarter answer it." This hurt him deeply and stuck with him for his entire life. When he was growing up, his family ran a food concession stand at Powwows on the nearby Indian reserve. Dave's thing was barbeque. He loved it and loved cooking it and selling it. This is where his vision for Famous Dave's BBQ was born — and now there are over 170 Famous Dave's restaurants across the USA. He also knew that he would need an education to succeed in business — an area where he was completely naïve.

Because of his negative experiences in school at a young age, he did not excel at school. But when he realized his life's ambition to make and sell great BBQ to millions of Americans, he needed to build his knowledge. So, he read. He read and read and read. His wisdom expanded, and his business did too … in turn, so did his wealth. While there have been many ups and downs in his life, Dave said that one of the biggest financial shocks he ever had was "losing" $80 million in a week when the stock market tanked in 2008. To be so successful that this was even possible was amazing to him. This was the experience of that dumb kid in the back of the class.

Years prior to that, his other, more personal shock was the day his family staged an intervention to help bring him out of his spiraling addiction. In short order, but not without serious hard work and commitment, Dave recovered from those hardships. He said he owed it to his passion for BBQ and his passion for learning. When I heard Dave tell his story, what I found astounding was the picture he showed the audience of his library ... or rather the new "wing" of his library. It was his garage — stacked with crates of books and shelves reaching to the ceiling. He had to move his library out to the garage after the one in his house was packed to the rafters! In his mid-thirties, Dave achieved his master's degree from Harvard. With NO undergraduate degree, it was a testament to his mantra of read, read, read. Dave connected his success to reading.

Reading gives the entrepreneur freedom by opening the world to unrestrained information and opportunity.

All you know is what you learn; what you learn is what you experience, hear and read. I know that all the wealth and knowledge there is available can be found in books. Whenever I need to learn something new, I turn to books. Dedication to reading will expand your mind and increase your wealth.

Here's a list you might want to consider:

Think and Grow Rich – Napoleon Hill

Tipping Point – Malcom Gladwell

Money Well Spent – Paul Brest & Hal Harvey

7 Habits of Highly Effective People – Stephen R. Covey

Purple Cow – Seth Godin

Good to Great – Jim Collins

Open – Andre Agassi

Onward – Howard Schultz

To Sell is Human – Daniel Pink

Influence: The Psychology of Persuasion – Robert Cialdini

The Ultimate Sales Machine – Chet Holmes

Start with Why – Simon Sinek

Shoe Dog – Phil Knight

E-Myth – Michael E. Gerber

GROW GET GIVE

9. Read To Learn HOW TO DO Things and What TO AVOID

"Within the wisdom of books lie answers to almost anything you hope to know or wish you could master." –Mike Skrypnek

Success can be found in the wisdom of the written word. Not only is reading inspiring, it can provide you the most fundamental step-by-step learning there is. While reading has expanded my thinking and enriched my life, what I have learned from reading is HOW to do things. Whenever I needed to learn about or how to do anything, I sought out books. Walt Disney once said, *"There is more treasure in books than in all the pirates' loot on Treasure Island."* Within books, there are secrets or signs and clear, detailed instructions on how to do everything. Just like this book, the steps are all there on the pages!

The greatest minds of history and the most successful people there ever were read voraciously, have written books or had books written about them. Their wisdom is shared for all to learn. Bill Gates is arguably one of the most successful entrepreneurs and subsequently one of the richest men that ever lived. He said reading enhanced his dreams for achievement. *"I really had a lot of dreams when I was a kid, and I think a great deal of that grew out of the fact that I had a chance to read a lot."*

Buy the books written by successful and interesting people, download their audio book, or simply go to the library and read them. My books are often compilations of knowledge gleaned from successful people, what they've said and what they've written, as well as wisdom learned from my firsthand experiences. Most books I read or write are non-fiction and either self-improvement or business and marketing books. There is plenty of room for fiction and novels as well. Great stories allow us to become lost in other worlds, meet people (in the pages) we might never get the chance to meet and have experiences out of our normal lives. Pay attention to how those stories draw you in. There is a lot to learn about how to connect in a good novel.

Business books can be conceptual, like Simon Sinek's "Start with Why", or they can be quite specific, from "How to Win Friends and Influence People" to "How to Build Great Hiring Processes for IT professionals". The "Chicken Soup for the Soul" or "For Dummies" series are perfect examples of the specific "how to" manuals for everything.

Reading to learn "how to" will give you the freedom of knowledge. Wisdom obtained from reading is knowledge you have forever. Once learned, you can move on to the next thing. Each book you read is fundamental to the next. Reading allows an entrepreneur to learn how to do things before they learn the hard way in the real world. Experienced knowledge becomes a part of you. When you read, you have a chance to experience the right way to do things without the risk. The biggest piles of stinking stuff have been simply, thankfully, mapped out for you by those who have stepped in it before. Naturally there are experiences that are worth enduring and you are going to make your very own personalized mistakes, but the worst lessons are not worth experiencing if you can read to learn how to avoid them in the first place. The biggest time and money wasters have been written about by the most successful people. Read their words and take heed!

It is not a pre-requisite of success to make all the mistakes yourself. Nor is it a badge of honour. You will undoubtedly make a lot of bad decisions as you move forward as an entrepreneur, but there are smarter, more successful people than you who have made bigger, dumber, and costlier mistakes than you will ever make — and you can read about them to learn how to avoid them. For everyone there will be an investment in learning on your own and from others. Reading is inexpensive tuition. It is part of a lifelong learning process. The freedom of learning before you act will bring priceless time and wisdom to your life and business.

GROW GET GIVE

10. Establish Processes For EVERYTHING

Processes give you freedom. They help you get time, get health and get creativity. While processes are for you, they are also for others. They give those who support you a road map to success. Your partners and employees require clear guidance and repeatable processes to guide them in delivering services and support. When they are confident about what they must do to make your business work, you gain freedom.

Well-defined processes for executing everything in your business take the guesswork out of your business and build consistency.

They free you up from ad hoc actions and give you a path to learning along the way. The freedom you gain from having processes will be realized in many ways. You will gain time as you extricate yourself from activities in your business that should be performed by others. They allow you to step away knowing that everything is clearly laid out for you and your staff. This builds confidence for your employees and your customers. Additionally, the discipline that process brings is comforting for everyone. As W. Edward Deming once said, "If you cannot describe what you do as a process, you don't know what you are doing." The importance of having processes cannot be understated.

When I was repositioning myself as a Legacy Wealth Advisor for the impact-minded baby boomer millionaire next door, while serving charities and their donors, I uncovered an amazing program that would allow me to do everything better. It was a thorough process that combined marketing, selling and serving. I decided to move forward with it and my wife, Sherri, who was already my business partner, was going to support me in the process. As I committed $20,000 to the program for year one and a monthly fee for as long as I was in the program, I explained everything to Sherri. I was excited about the possibilities, so I rambled on about all the things we needed to do, such as: marketing presentations, invitation processes, client presentations, follow-ups and a variety of other important tasks. We would have to teach our charity customers how to run their own programs and Sherri was going to be the liaison for all questions and inquiries from customers. She wasn't impressed. In fact, she immediately expressed great apprehension.

Now, what makes Sherri an excellent partner in life and work is that she processes things very differently than me. She really is the yin to my yang. Ready to leap forward, I was so excited about embarking on the program that I forgot just how overwhelming the project could be for her. While I saw the big picture and possibilities, I didn't really spend much time considering the minutiae. As I was describing all the aspects, she just stared at me and looked down to review her text messages. It was clear that as I spoke, she got more anxious and soon she was suggesting that maybe she wasn't the right person to handle this with me. I suddenly realized I needed to start speaking her language, and fast.

I quickly told her that the program was a step by step program and there would be people to support her and provide answers to all the questions she might have. While that helped, it didn't quite do the trick. It wasn't until the entire program package arrived and I stacked four stuffed program binders onto her desk that her comfort grew. When I saw those binders and all the pages and details and materials, I got overwhelmed and started to question my sanity.

When Sherri started leafing through the binders, she quickly realized every single step and every last detail were carefully outlined — down to the seating arrangements and placement of materials for our client presentations…even how to fold the brochures (things I really didn't want to be bothered with). She loved it! She breathed an enormous sigh of relief and immediately became engaged. When she learned that everything, even the scripts for client conversations, as well as the precise timing of steps were provided, she was elated. In fact, I found it rather confining and too detailed for my liking. I became uncertain that I wanted to proceed, but because Sherri was onside and found the whole thing liberating, I was confident we could do it together.

You see, your employees and partners don't always think like you. If you hired them correctly, they will especially appreciate any process that gives them structure and makes their lives more predictable. Give them process and allow them to focus on the details. Process gives you time and freedom. When you have processes in place to handle your business, others can carry the load and you become free to pursue more of what you uniquely bring to the business and you can do it better. When you stay in the thick of daily activities, and everyone in your organization scrambles to find solutions and making things up as they go, a lot of time is wasted. Their capacity to handle more volume is diminished. When they are limited, you are limited. Processes give you freedom.

First, you will be able to escape the day-to-day operations of the business. Next, you can relax, knowing your employees will all follow the guidelines and that all customers and situations will be dealt with in a standardized manner. You become free to think about bigger picture things, or free to step away without worry for your personal time. Time you will need for life enjoyment and to stay energized.

Lastly, I would remind you that you must be the one who builds the outline of your process for how things should be done. It is your business, your vision, and your reputation. Don't leave anything to chance. This means spending time initially establishing your processes including scripting of communications with clients, marketing messaging, and sequential activities. After you develop the outline and important details, hand the process document to your employees to add their input and insights. They will know the details you likely don't. When they improve your document, they take ownership while giving your freedom.

HERE'S A HELPFUL TIP: Make an audio recording of all that you do. From the specific sequence for marketing, customer service, or communications and have it transcribed. Send it to a transcription service like Rev.com and in 24 hours, you will have it back in written form. Edit it, hand it to your staff for their input and presto … you have your process manual(s). Do this for every area in your business.

11. Create A "Hate Doing" List

Create a hate doing list. Itemize, in writing, the things that you hate doing.

The goal is to raise your awareness of these things and to work to never do them again. This is not intended to be a negative experience. Consider it cathartic. Build a list of things you won't do in your business, the type of business you won't do (or offer) for others, the people you won't work with and the actions you won't tolerate. While building this list, identify the things you do now that you acknowledge you "hate" but for some reason you still do them. Too often, an entrepreneur will tell me they are doing some chore or task that they absolutely can't stand, but that it must get done and they do it because "someone has to do it". My gut reaction is to ask, "Why does anyone have to do it in the first place?" Will your business somehow be better off because it was done by you?

Will the tedious activities in your business make it better? These tasks can be things that you do to serve customers – often the wrong ones - or even the simple act of working through holidays or into evenings when you could be doing something else you love with your family or for yourself.

This IS NOT intended to be a "bitch-fest" or process of wallowing in the bad stuff. Simply write these "things you hate to do" down and build the list. Do not get emotional; do not allow frustration to build up. When you list these things, your next step will be eliminating them from your life. This is a happy day…and effectively, a happy list.

Once your list is created, act quickly to cross each item off the list. Once removed from your list, never add them to your life or the list again! It might take a while to remove all things you hate, because they might appear on a rare occasion – lucky you. Don't do them anymore.

Once your list is written, the next step is to decide how to deal with them. It is about delegating, eliminating, automating, or choosing to do them yourself. Here are the tools you will need to make these decisions. Follow this progression and you will set yourself free.

DO IT…

…yourself. What are the things that you enjoy the most, have the strongest ability to do and would be best served to have them done by you? You are an expert in what you do. When it comes to performing there is no alternative. Sometimes it is not so clear what exactly you should be doing or what you should relinquish but consider whatever it is that you uniquely do that defines your business. Review your own Kolbe score, or Strengths Finder measurements to remind you of what you must maintain steadfast focus on.

For example, if you are an 8 on the Kolbe "Quick Start" and a 3 "Fact Finder" – then you should not spend time on the compilation and entry of data or list management or administrative details. This should be delegated. Stick with advancing ideas and your business. Selling and presenting is a good idea - marketing, too.

AUTOMATE…

…what gives you scale and leverage, or what is mundane and arduous. Can you automate a task by doing it better with a machine or computer? Some examples of this could be mailing and online marketing, database, list management, or communications. It could be payment processing or order fulfilment. Here's a word of caution. We are mostly dealing with "behind the curtain" things. When you are customer facing and using automation, be certain it enhances the customer experience. In an era when companies all over the globe, large and small, are trying to use technology to streamline the delivery of services the customer is often forgotten. Don't allow your automation to turn into customer "DIY". Think of instances where automation has enhanced experience. I think we could all agree booking travel is an activity where automation greatly improved the user experience. Selecting and booking flights, hotels, cars online is a far easier, cost-effective way to plan trips for business, for personal trips, and for your family. This isn't the best idea when booking for large groups, or trips to exotic and unfamiliar locales. When it comes to experiences, a more customized human centric approach is warranted.

Consider dentistry. We all must see our dentists regularly. Booking your appointment and even paying your bill online is convenient and enhances our patient experience. However, nothing about the delivery of technical services is improved by handing it over to the customer. No dentist or patient would prefer the drill in the customer's hands. Financial services are like this as well. The emergence of "FinTech" is overtaking the traditional model of delivering financial services. Banking, basic insurance needs and investing are done extremely well using online, automated processes and applications. Even some in-depth planning can be done with more customized solutions but understanding and managing the emotional side of finance isn't so easily done with automation.

When you look at investing, the most opportune time to act, if at all, is when perceived risk is the highest or when it is extremely limited. Buying low, successfully, happens when markets are in turmoil when people are fearful and when the headline news is at its most pessimistic. It goes against human nature to buy into the fear, yet it is almost always the best decision. Unless an app or DIY approach is pre-programmed to buy or sell without your interference, you are the weakest part of the decision-making process. Emotions won't help you here because the one element of risk is you. Overconfidence in exceptional markets or fear in bad ones will create bias that often is incorrect and leads people to make the wrong decision at the worst time.

Apply automation to things that enhance your business and the customer experience, but before you ask your most important source of revenue (your customer) to do-it-themselves, be sure you consider doing if for them first. It often makes more sense to deliver this directly.

DELEGATE...

...**the tasks others do so much better than you**. This does not need much explanation. When you created your "hate to do" list, you will have easily identified the things that you should never be doing. If you're like me, you likely hate paperwork or administrative tasks. The financial industry, even with advanced technology, drowns itself in paperwork. I considered it a soul-sucking part of the work that stole my attention from attracting and delighting clients. To my astonishment, I found people who loved doing paperwork. They would happily go to work, complete forms, follow up and file all day long. They enjoyed the simplicity and the sense of accomplishment when things got done. They also did not care to consider work during their free time or on weekends. They didn't want any of that. Working was only a way to pay their bills so they could live their lives. They liked the consistency and predictability of their role. Paperwork and administrative tasks are predictable. One of my help wanted ads used the phrase "must love paperwork". When I found the right people and delegated those tasks, my business and life immediately improved.

ELIMINATE…

…if you're doing something you hate, there's never a day that you should be doing it yourself. If, for some reason you're still doing it, then it must be invaluable to your business to continue. If you can't delegate or automate, you must eliminate. Nothing you hate is so important that you can't let it go.

If you are having a hard time taking that last step to eliminate something, use the old sweater test. We all have those articles of clothing that are in our closet that we rarely wear, but we hesitate to throw them out or give them away. We liked wearing that sweater at some point. We even wear it occasionally because we feel bad about neglecting it. However, if you haven't put that sweater on in a year, then you really should be getting rid of it. Try not doing certain things at work for a long time. If you haven't missed them or your customers didn't notice, then eliminate that activity.

Your "hate to do" list will often reach beyond your business. In fact, there might a large quantity of things in day-to-day life that you could give up. Many successful people delegate housecleaning and yard work, some stop cooking and either automate it by having prepared meals delivered or hire a personal chef or nanny. A lot of our personal activities are habits that might be better off avoided. Delegate or hire others to do the things you can't stand doing. This, of course, does not apply to things that you take personal joy in. Some people love cooking, some love yard work. It is about energy. If you get energy doing these things, keep doing them. There are even a lot of things I like to do in my business and personal life but shouldn't do. The "hate to do" list is black and white. The "probably shouldn't do" list is a bit tougher.

Important to making the decision on doing, automating, delegating or eliminating is setting criteria for each. Again, your "hate to do" list is simple, while those "shouldn't do" items are not as clear. Just as you are certain of those things you know you must do it is equally important to build criteria for how to deal with the things you must not. This will help you allocate to each of the other three "buckets".

12. Make Everything A Campaign

Every marketing effort you make should revolve around some form of campaign - no matter how big or small. How do you effectively invite someone to an event? You could simply send an invitation and hope for the best. If you send to a large enough number of people, you will likely get someone to show up. With direct mail or email, results are predictable. You pick the audience size you are hoping for, and then multiply by the number of mail pieces needed to reach industry response standards. Direct mail can be costly and provide varied results in terms of the quality of attendee. Quantity is a numbers game. Quality is in your marketing content. If your message doesn't attract the right people, direct mail often results in a lowest common denominator attendee. This is a "fingers-crossed" approach.

What do I mean when I say "campaign"? Well, the easiest thing to compare this to is a political campaign. Just think of how a candidate's campaign unfolds. There is the "buzz" around the person who might seek candidacy, as "whispered" intention is leaked. Then there is the announcement of their decision to run and official entry into a race for office. Once the information is out there, many things begin to happen. Signs and advertisements begin to go out. They have simple messages and remind the public who the candidate is by name and slogan. At the same time, the candidate arranges to get their message out there. They take a three-fold approach: 1) identifying and highlighting the public's biggest concerns, 2) detailing solutions to address those concerns and 3) informing the public of the candidate's values and credentials that make them the right person to execute the solution - the right person to elect.

Once the campaign is in motion, there are other actions that occur, such as constant reminders of the candidate's core message and regular rebuttal of the competition. Finally, when the deadline for voting is nearing, there is a the massive "get-out-the-vote" effort to ensure people are aware of the necessary date and times to vote and that they affirm their commitment to the candidate by voting.

Political campaigns are magical when you think about it. Overall, they are the most effective sales and marketing campaigns there are. All business owners should study how they work and apply them to their own efforts. Maybe it is because my mother taught me right, but I believe the one aspect that should not be emphasized is the negative messaging or attack on competitors that has become commonplace. However, it is important to identify and highlight how you differentiate from your competition and how you are a better solution for your audience.

Campaigns use every tool in the toolkit. Social media, print media, television, face-to-face presence, door knocking, cold (now "robo") calling, and a ton of people on the ground making it all happen. The candidate's desire is to become ubiquitous in name, message and image. Yours should be too. It is the effective use of many types of sales material and endorsements interwoven into a marketing campaign that is designed to educate future potential customers why and how they can buy products or services from you.

EVERY marketing effort is a campaign.

I use what I call the "Campaign Cycle". This is a repeatable, predictable, and logical sequence of marketing messages that drive a customer to a decision whether to buy you or not. It is also used to filter out those who are not a good fit and attract those who are seeking you. Through a simple, multiple message process using a variety of mediums (from email, to blogging, video, to direct mail, print media, phone calls, and in-person marketing) that serves to inform, educate, highlight concerns, inform, offer solutions, inform, make an offer, inform, make an offer again, close, follow up … and repeat.

Try this approach next time you are trying to build an audience for an event.

Inform: this could be a "save the date" notice or announcement. It is not a formal invitation. It is a notice of things to come.

Educate: this communication will remind your target audience what the landscape is for the message you are trying to convey. You can use a special report, white paper, book and many messages that position the challenge or opportunity you hope to be the solution for. Such as *"studies have shown"* or *"we interviewed 20 professionals in this market, and this is what we found."*

Highlight Concerns: this communication will shine a light on the futility of your target prospects' current path of action. It will uncover their pain for their own discovery. Pain is the best motivator…pleasure comes second.

Inform: this is your solution to the prospects' greatest pain. You identify the simplest path to the quickest way to alleviate or remove the discomfort.

Offer (can be combined with above "inform"): this is your formal invitation to attend, purchase or subscribe, along with the pricing and commitment required by the attendee.

Close: ACT NOW! Provide explicit incentive to move fast and be first to register, to buy, or to pay. You can do this by creating urgency or scarcity. You can even offer special gifts or rewards as an enticement to buy.

Follow Up: confirm attendance or purchase decision before event/sale. Follow up again afterward to reduce or head off any sense of "buyer's remorse". Connect their buying decisions with their goal to relieve their pain and achieve a pleasurable outcome. Consider gifting as a show of gratitude for the customer's commitment.

There are many steps to this, but in combination they are very effective. These can be laid out in a clear and repeatable process and systemized for ease of use. Setting up an effective campaign takes time and energy, but once you have built the chassis, the car can be outfitted however you like and tuned up for top performance.

13. Outsourcing: Buyer Beware, Buyer Take Care.

I recommended a time management decision-making process that encourages you to eliminate, automate or delegate. It enhances efficiency. Applying this to your business and life is both important and challenging. Using the internet and the limitless online world of educated people and capable resources available today, you can expand your capacity exponentially. There is a downside to all this. If you do not know what you are doing, you can end up investing time and money while learning a lot of costly lessons, including who not to hire or what not to pay for. Many services and applications are inadequate or too simplistic. The internet frequently allows people and businesses to artistically enhance their appearance and lead you to be persuaded by their veneer, versus their abilities. I see it all the time in well-crafted websites, fronting for pathetically lacking freelancers, consultants or shoddily crafted products. The internet has removed our ability to "experience" our prospective purchases in advance.

Online services like Upwork or Fiver have thousands of writers, graphic artists, web designers, consultants, etc. They all compete in a global online marketplace for your business. It is often cost-effective and simple. However, a major drawback can be lost in translation — quite literally. Sometimes the good quality, low cost professionals are from all over the globe. It is amazing to see all the incredibly talented people who exist and are there to serve. When it works, it is magical, but if your project requires conveying your vision or a message to a specific and local demographic, you might find the cultural nuances can be lost when you see the finished project. It will very likely be on time and on budget … but in some ways, you'll find it might not be quite right.

How do you sort through these platforms, and more, to hire who you need? Well, you should apply similar processes to hiring online freelancers as you would employees and contractors. Define the role and your needs before identifying the person. These platforms give you the ability to do this in detail if you wish. You should. Use the scalable online workforce to leverage and identify high quality resources, without placing them on staff, and focus on what you do best.

14. Use Tools Others Don't

You want to sell something or have people come to an event, so you send out a hundred emails, or thousands of emails, then you send out more and repeat. That's all. It is your full messaging, invitation or prospecting campaign. One hit wonder. Of course, you have your website and the SEO that is part of it, with your Facebook page, Instagram and even LinkedIn. You post here and there and even add a keyword or two and hashtag a few things. This whole process seems to have become the "lazy" person's way of marketing. It used to be effective, too. To some extent, it still is. But now it seems everybody's doing it. It has become average and a common way of getting average or no business. You are joining everybody else on the internet, saying similar things about similar topics, and sending it out to thousands of people who won't pay attention, won't connect, and won't buy. There is nothing novel to this any longer.

There are finite mediums to reach out to people and basically, they have all been done before. The differentiator is how you use each medium. Just think. In a broad sense, there is conventional mail, email, phone calls and text, face-to-face meeting and TV/social media. Deep into an age of email and internet marketing tools there is little interest in the "old-school" ways to reach people. The ease and scalability of the internet and social media has made marketers and entrepreneurs lazy – and sneaky. It is too easy to send out an email "blast" then sit and wait. Cookies, tracking, tags and meta-tags all add to this. You reach a ton more people quicker and more directly, yet open rates are usually in the 15-20% range at best and click-through rates exponentially lower than that. Capturing the attention of people in their inboxes or on their smart phones is a battle that rages between you, other businesses and "*kittens doing funny things*". Due to the volume of marketing messages and the global reach you might be able to generate, you might still win over prospects eventually.

What has become lost in the age of internet marketing, even with video marketing, YouTube, Instagram, Twitter, FB Live, TikTok and on and on, is direct human connection. Hard wired into our requirement for survival and self-preservation, is the need for direct personal contact. We want to consciously and subconsciously read the cues that others send to us through their body language, tone and volume of voice, their smell and the subtle mannerisms that allows other humans to make judgements on safety, trust, security, potential happiness and relationships. These are natural instincts. They are critical to our survival. Physical connections are part of how we cement relationships and decisions.

I use all forms of marketing mediums. I write reasonably well and enjoy it, so email and social media posting works for me. I enjoy and have success through video marketing. I have found some success in traditional direct mail marketing too. However, when it comes to closing sales and connecting with people, it is direct personal contact that works best for me. In fact, I have found there is no better way to move people to a sale than to face them and connect.

How do you get the best possible one-to-many results that the internet offers you in scale? Networking groups (some) as well as public speaking and hosting events are powerful tools in my sales arsenal. I had this vision of working without geographic limits. "If only I could master internet marketing and online sales funnels", I thought. I could build a store, produce content from anywhere on the planet, create marketing funnels, place ads in the right places and voila! I would start to see the money just rolling in as people who didn't know me and didn't understand my value to them would start clicking and buying.

I knew that it wasn't really going to be that easy. I would have to put some serious effort into learning how it worked, as well as refining the marketing and ad messages. Then I began. Crickets. Adjust, refine, and repost, crickets still. Messages and campaigns and ads went out into the ether. A few sign ups and a handful of book sales. I didn't sell a course, a workshop or a webinar. Don't get me wrong, just like the P90X fitness program is a long term commitment for results, I certainly didn't believe that a one and done approach would get me sales, but there was something missing and I couldn't put my finger on it...until a client of mine shared her thoughts with me.

I was sitting with my client Dianna and we were discussing how I was really trying to get this internet marketing going so I could get the geographic freedom I was seeking. Then she said something that kind of took the wind out of my sails. She said that when she read the messages I had been sending out in these clearly "canned" campaigns, they simply didn't sound like me. Not only that, but they sounded rote and "salesy". She went on to say that it made me sound like a bit of a "shyster". "Holy shit!" I thought. I had been modelling others who did this who were incredible successful. I thought the way they messaged and marketed was effective, but Dianna was telling me that I sounded like someone else. That I sounded like I couldn't be trusted. Yikes. I clearly had lost my "voice" in the process. This had a profound effect on how I would move forward to market online as well as offline.

To provide me with a bit of good news, she said that I was better in person and I should "do more of that". As well, I should use more content from my live events and video marketing in the writing for email marketing. That wisdom was helpful. In fact, I have likely told every single coaching client of mine to do that to.

How would I get more "me" into my marketing for the benefit of others? I knew it didn't need to be me talking about me. It could be me talking about clients and prospects in my unique way. I got that. What I needed was the platform(s). I would keep marketing with email, and even using old school mail. But I would do some traditional things to be "live". I decided to seek out networking groups to build leads and do market research into the wants and needs of entrepreneurs, so I signed up for a lunch club. I went and was asked to refer 10-15 people I just met and didn't know to my own network. I knew nothing about how they help others, or the services or products they provide. Immediately I knew that it was not for me but I learned what I wanted in such a club. I started my own lunch for entrepreneurs and called it my "One Thing" Lunch. It would be a free session, with limited seating and conversations without selling or asking for referrals. It allowed business owners to get to know each other and maybe help one another with an idea or two. Out of the time spent, and a good lunch eaten, there would always be "one thing" that the participants could take away. It was a small success.

Another thing I decided to attend was a speaker's club. I had never taken part in Toastmasters, nor had I done any speakers club type of thing before, but I had spoken publicly for years paid and unpaid as a keynote, breakout session speaker, trainer, workshop coach, etc. I drove across town on a ridiculously cold and snowy December evening in Calgary. I almost didn't leave the house that night due the imminent "snowmageddon". But when I got there, it was magic! The format, the diversity of business owners, entrepreneurs and speakers in the room, the positive vibe and the platform all worked. I signed up and became a member. I invested my money right there and then. Every month I could have a stage.

Over the holidays, I discussed the prospect of me running my very own club with my wife Sherri. She saw how keen I was and thought it was a great idea. When I showed up for my next club meeting in January, I asked the leader, how I could get one of my own. She directed me to the founder. I called her and told her I wanted to start my own club right away. She responded by telling me I needed to go through some training, so I asked when and where. She told me to be in San Diego in 60 days. I signed up, booked my flights and hotel and got down there. I was trained, started my own speaker's club and held my first session five months after attending that initial event back in December. The club was a success, the attendees loved it and I did too. Over time, I realized that the clubs attracted a lot of people who weren't my ideal client, so I made some changes to attract entrepreneurs and added message coaching. I called it "Speak 2 Sell" and brought it into my own business. Entrepreneurs are my kind of people and I like hanging out with those who enjoy public speaking. I love to hear their stories or pitches.

Another platform that I used was Facebook Live. It became a "gateway" to further my confidence and skills as a speaker – even after years of paid public speaking. I was sitting at the VIP lunch in LA at my coach's annual boot camp talking to my peers at the table. I shared that I shifted 100% of my time to coaching and I suddenly realized I had a very limited and shallow pool of ideal prospects on my contact lists. You see, I had been serving baby boomer millionaires next door for a decade. They were at the other side of wealth creation and business growth, planning for succession and philanthropy. They were amazing people from whom I learned many, many important business tips, tricks and secrets from, but they were not my ideal customer for coaching. I was seeking the growing entrepreneur and business owner seeking wealth creation. Not preservation or transition. I was basically starting at ground zero in list building.

One of the women at my table heard this and immediately offered her input. I was all ears. She asked if I did "Facebook Live". I said I did not. I never had, because in the investment community I lived and worked in for 22 years, there were simply too many rules and compliance issues associated with "live" online speaking about topics that interested my clients. But I was open to the idea now. She said that she knew a guy who started doing FB Live every single day and in one year he grew his contacts ("friends") list from zero to 5,000! That seemed like a good thing to me, so I committed to do two per week every week…and started a day after I returned home. The direct personal contact I needed happened almost worked immediately. I started out with a measly 100 or so "Friends" on Facebook and began adding 200 per month for five straight months. When I held a live event thirty or so people would watch, with double that amount watching the recording. By the end of a year, over 120 people would tune in to watch live or the recorded version and my contacts grew dramatically. When you find things that work for you to build your audience, your following, your tribe, stick with it and then do them more.

I now use a blend of live events that provide me a platform to further my positioning as a thought leader in the business community and someone who might be sought after as a business advisor, coach, or mentor. I market daily, layering email marketing, online advertising, word-of-mouth campaigns and telephone marketing to raise awareness for my events, as well as free and paid public speaking to engage people and increase their interest to come to my next event.

Too often marketers will use current trending methods and stay away from those perceived as old school tools. They discount past approaches as passé or ineffective (without trying them) or even as too costly. However, I can tell you that direct mail or a face-to-face meeting might seem inefficient but realizing that your shitty Facebook boost or ad ended up with a cost of two-dollars-per-click and getting almost no clicks is worse. At least with direct mail or in person you can make immediate and qualitative adjustments. With online ads, you can feel like you're simply shooting at targets in a dark room. There are a number of "double blind" attempts you can make, but without clear feedback, it is still guesswork. Online, you know the people are out there, but you are just blasting away in hope that you hit your mark. Too often you are simply wasting ammo. There are a handful of things that would be considered as the top goals of marketing, but one of the most important is to stand out. If you are doing the same thing everyone else is doing, then you disappear into the crowd. Standing out means doing things others won't or using tools others don't. Be the "Purple Cow" as Seth Godin would encourage all marketers to be.

A costlier solution and decades old practice is direct mail. It is expensive to print copy, and buy envelopes and stamps. However, if done right the "open rate" and "conversion rates" can be predictable. The mailbox is not crowded these days and unique mail will stand out. Two of my coaches have used mail as one of their primary tools. If done right, there is staying power in your materials. For events it is one of the best ways to ensure people show up. RSVP's and then "no-shows" are HUGE problems with email marketing. Their commitment is about as valuable as the cost to send the email. But with direct mail, people who RSVP tend to show up! There is something more personal that connects them to their commitment when they handle a piece of mail and take the time to RSVP. Direct mail works, and the math is simple. The expectations are that 1% or the intended people invited to something through direct mail will RSVP. This can be higher if your prospects/contact list/customers are more engaged, better served and fit your ideal customer profile. I add personalized notes or requests in writing on my direct mail pieces and it works extremely well. Often up to 25% of the seats of my events are occupied by people I added handwritten notes to on a mailed invitation. Never underestimate the value of a personal touch.

People are more apt to open something interesting, entertaining or engaging when they get it in the mail. It's almost a surprise when they don't get a flyer for pizza, fast food, a bill, or a real estate flyer. When the next piece that comes that is offering interesting, helpful, and educational advice or insight they might decide to open it and engage with. Why not try direct mail?

Of course, there's never anything wrong with direct personal contact by phone. I personally think that **cold calling the unqualified** is a waste of time. But you can find success in approaching the right prospect, the right way. In 1995, I started my career in the investment management business; I knew nothing about investing, and even less about wealth management. Eager to make the best of the opportunity and transition from personal training agency owner to advisor, I energetically and enthusiastically wanted to prove a point that I could sell anything to anyone.

My full training consisted of being given a manual that described a system on how to cold call. I filled my index card container, found a corporate directory list and began calling. The list had about 2000 names of owners, executives and directors. At the end of 90 days, I had called 1,200 people! I got 1,080 "No's", but I signed up 120 clients. They fell into place exactly like the cold calling manual said - I just followed the procedure. Remember, I knew NOTHING about the investment industry. That sounds decent for cold calling, doesn't it? If I could earn $1,000 from each new client in the next year, that would be pretty good math. In fact, if I had been in the asset gathering business at the time, and not the "deal" business, those 120 could be worth $2,000 to $10,000 in revenue each year! Just 90 days. WOW! But there was a hitch.

You see, the problem was that I sold them on the sizzle. We only offered access to deals not portfolio management. You are right, it sounds a bit like a boiler room. It wasn't quite, because the investments were very real, and my intention was truly to help people make money. I didn't know any different, either. This was not "Wolf of Wall Street" but it was close. Lessons were learned.

You see, the new clients were simply transactional relationships and they were only as good as the next deal or stock pick. If things worked out, people stayed with me. At that early stage in my career, they never brought their real money to me. In retrospect, that was a good thing. I had new clients, and the relationships were predicated on performance only so they weren't very meaningful. You can imagine the stress that this carried. When things didn't work out the clients would stop trading with us or leave and they had to be replaced. The worst was that too often the reason things didn't work out was way beyond my control. It was a poor sales model, poor marketing, and a bad understanding of the relationship model that I needed to learn. But it certainly worked once.

My thoughts on cold calling to sell are that I would never want to do it that way again. It is difficult to become of value to people you don't know ambushing them on the phone when they least expected it. The connections are shallow and you're constantly treading water.

Qualifying new prospects is not cold calling at all. Warm calling people that may not know much about you or may not be interested in your service, can open doors if you've done the homework to properly qualify them or were introduced to them. They've either qualified themselves via your marketing, or they may have qualified themselves through a referral from someone else. They might be the specific professional or person in that area or niche that you're looking to connect with. You can serve them and have something valuable to offer.

If you've done all that prior work, then direct market to them, calling, meeting, or engaging them reaches beyond cold calling. Instead of calling 2,000 people, you spend the equivalent time and energy of a thousand calls doing the homework first, so you're only calling a few hundred people (or less), and maybe getting one hundred higher quality clients.

You can't get more freedom if you continually waste time and money and energy on things that either aren't working or have a low percentage chance relative to the cost. You'll need to constantly adapt, engage and use other mechanisms and tools that may work. Find the things that other people are not doing and put the extra energy into them up front. Whatever works, keep doing it. Then layer on something else.

Technology has given us a ton of leverage with marketing tools and a reach to prospect audiences that we have never been able to do with such ease. But, like everything, once everyone is using the same tools, your scale to sales is lost or diminished. Build a repeatable and effective process to execute marketing with those tools then focus your energy there.

You can build a process around any methodology to market. The process becomes transferable and can be applied to any new or additional tool that emerges. The result is time gained.

15. Hire Coaches & Mentors

How much can you accomplish when you are inspired? If you receive advice that is helpful and works for you in life or in business, do you stop listening and carry on, or do you seek more? Unsuccessful people simply listen and ignore most advice. Average is a road paved on self-counsel. "Askholes" keep asking for help and advice, but never do anything with it. Top performers, however, view this information and its source as a fountain of knowledge and vitality! You see, what separates success from failure or "average" is not hubris, but humility.

The understanding that there are great things to be learned from people who have gone before seems like simple common knowledge. Checking one's ego at the door to gain wisdom is a trait of success. Being coachable is a sign of champions. The top athletes know this, the best singers and actors know this. The top CEOs and entrepreneurs in North America will tell you they have mentors and coaches. The highest performing business professionals work in mastermind groups. They share big ideas with others like them. They network and learn firsthand from others' experiences.

Consider what happens when a golfer wants a few strokes off her game. She hires a coach, takes instruction and practices. They don't work harder they work smarter and it is smart to hire someone who can help them. The coach can see things the golfer does not. They have a working expertise in connecting the dots. Their objective eye can identify areas for improvement as well as push for further growth in places where a little support can be the big difference in moving to another level. Through observation they also know when to pull back, rest and regroup. The training coaches have received, under the tutelage of other successful coaches, provided them firsthand knowledge of their craft. Good coaches can synthesize ideas and apply objectivity. Great coaches can motivate and inspire.

What is the value of a business breakthrough to you? How much would you invest to learn how to predictably attract a steady stream of ideal clients? If you could get advice that allowed you to free up a day per week for yourself and your creativity, what would that be worth? How would you like to learn about the things that you do all the time that might be holding you back? Who can help you?

Great coaches collapse time.

Your employees won't give you strong constructive critical feedback, but a coach will be straight with you when you need it. You invest in them to guide you. A good or great coach can be a fountain of ideas and information that you can implement right away. A skilled coach will give you only what you can handle. When you get the right idea or recommendation at the right time, your mind races to incorporate your experiences and vision. Sometimes it can seem overwhelming – like drinking from a firehose. I recommend applying knowledge you gain from time spent with your coaches in the way that you would eat an elephant … one small bite at a time.

One good idea from a coach can make all the difference. For a pro basketball player working on free throws and worried that they are aiming at the wrong place on the back board, or worse yet, worrying about their shooting percentage, it could be simply keeping their elbow in or a shift in their stance or even a word that always brings them into focus. For a singer wondering why her voice tapers off when they are on a high octave run, it could be a small adjustment in posture that helps them breath to improve their tone. For an entrepreneur focused on pricing their services for sales, it could be directing their attention to scripting communications not the price point. Whatever it is, the coach sees it when you can't. It is that one thing that makes all the difference.

I was working with a coach years ago. When visited him for an intensive one-on-one session, I was brimming with all kinds of ideas and goals. There were new initiatives to discuss and ideas I had for future projects. But there was one key problem. I was overworked and couldn't focus on business building because I was carrying the freight in my business. I hadn't done well to hire quality employees who I could trust to mind the store while I was away working on rapid growth. I was also trying to skimp on paying a newly hired employee in the process, as I was constantly reinvesting my cash flow into the business.

My coach stopped my grandiose ideas in their tracks and brought me back to the present moment and helped me focus on two key things — stabilizing my cash flow and hiring the "right fit" employee. The decision to concentrate on my hiring process to get the exact right person in place was powerful. He showed me a road map to get that done. Within six months, I had two "right fit" employees working with me, both of whom were excellent. The investment in doing it right the first time paid huge dividends. They gave me time and energy to focus on the things that energize me and grow my business. Within a year I was on the way to making even more money and working substantially less.

The wisdom of coaches and mentors will SAVE YOU TIME! They will save you years in development or they might encourage you to focus on a specific goal that could grow your business exponentially. The freedom you get from crucial time-saving help is a key benefit.

Another way a coach helps you is by raising the bar for higher achievement. This is one thing I have directly experienced years ago with my first coaching customer. When I began working with Michael, he was struggling to figure out ways to increase his membership model for online training. He did plenty of work on building his platform and recording online tutorials and courses. The product was good, but he wasn't focused on the marketing and sales. He had about $60,000 in sales the prior year and had only been attracting four or five new members per month. He concentrated on building more and more products for those users; he was working on programming, website development, and bookkeeping over 70% of his time and only focusing on marketing for about 15% to 20% of his time. His number one requirement was to maintain his lifestyle for his family - but he was lacking sales. I quickly set to work with him restructuring his membership model and re-focusing his time on marketing and sales. He was moving outside his comfort zone and I knew it, but he had no choice. In order to grow we needed to give him the tools to make selling more natural and have it stay top of mind. Within three months, he was tracking at twice the number of registrations as before and was on track to double his annual sales.

Michael and I worked together for years. We spoke twice per month and his business grew ten times larger to be exact. We tackled every challenge, from sales to staffing, joint ventures, marketing and administration. The business evolved to provide multiple sources of revenue that became predictable and reliable.

It is exciting what can happen when you take people beyond their own mental constructs to a place where they can have great success that they didn't fathom. Being coached and being coachable are necessities for success. My coaches and so many others do this regularly. Their objectivity expands your mind. This unrestrained thinking gives you freedom to be more and achieve more than you thought possible.

GROW GET GIVE

16. Accomplish Three Things Per Day

Did you know your business can survive and thrive by accomplishing just one thing per day? That means moving one thing forward, applying one idea, getting one more thing done and selling one more product. I suggest you try three things each day in three areas. In fact, your business would flourish:

- If every day of the year, you did one thing to grow that furthered your business, your relationships, and your success.
- If you did one thing that helped you get freedom and time for creativity.
- If you could give by doing one thing to focus energy on yourself, your family and causes that matter.

If you did just one thing to advance yourself, three hundred times per year, you'd be massively ahead of all your competitors. We are hardwired to work for short, sustained periods every day. If we are not working, we have been brainwashed to think we are being lazy or wasting time, and we believe it! A sense of guilt weighs on us. Our peer group even frowns upon our time away from working as though we're negligent in our duties. But we aren't working optimally every hour of every single day, or at least we shouldn't be, and we shouldn't think that we must every day. We should not feel obligated to put our head down and blinders on to work incessantly, while ignoring the rest of the world, our lives, and our families in single-minded pursuit of perceived business success.

We can construct a life that gives us the right blend of time and freedom that we want and one that we idealize. There is no work-life balance. There is only life. We have only one chance at it. In time, your regrets for pushing your life aside to pursue business success will be many and they will loom over your days as you age. There is no question that business owners and entrepreneurs are driven by their passion to excel at whatever it is they do. I am not suggesting you should hold back. Earn a living and as much money that is right for you in your life. The key is to do it in a manner that doesn't sacrifice everything along the way. Never live with deathbed regrets. There is yet to be a reported case of someone lamenting as they were about to die that they felt unfulfilled without spending more time at the office.

How can we build our lives around a philosophy of grow, get and give that positions us for the most success we want to enjoy professionally and personally? I suggest something I have built into my life that has alleviated my "worker guilt", opened my mind, reduced my stress and increased my creative effectiveness. I suggest that you pursue NO MORE than three things each day. Simply try to accomplish a single thing to grow, get and give that move your business and life forward every day. Imagine the results in one year! You might accomplish a few hundred or even a thousand important things for your work and your life.

If you could do a thousand things in a year that moved your business forward, a thousand incremental steps forward, they would have an exponentially large effect. The leverage on your business and your life would be powerful.

Achievement accumulates over time and this approach also gives you many other rewards. By allowing yourself to focus your days and your life in this way, you are also giving yourself the freedom to be "done".

That is, if you have achieved your three "one things" in the first hour of the day, you can step away from the list and leave the rest of the day open to whatever comes along. If it takes all day, then it's because you have made that choice as well – maybe you're on a roll, or your creativity is at level ten. If you are a painter, you might think the one thing is to paint a shadow along the edge of your subject, but you might become inspired and devoted enough to painstakingly paint the most detailed parts of the image. Whether your list of "one things" takes no time, or all day, the next day you begin fresh. What's done is done and either closes a loop or opens one. Layer upon layer, your business is built, and the foundation of your life broadens. You will never have the guilt or remorse that you haven't done enough because you have done what you have done and then done more.

The result is that you allow yourself to have pure focus on only a handful of things that you can do well. You'll be far more productive and able to give the attention and energy needed to get things done.

I aim to accomplish fewer and fewer, yet important, things each day that help me grow my business, help me get more freedom and one thing that allows me to give back. Staying on track each day takes commitment. It can be frustrating sometimes, as patience for settling on just one thing as opposed to as many as you can fit into your day is a learned behavior and not something that comes naturally. When you are effectively doing one thing that moves you forward, you must recognize the accomplishment and gain satisfaction in your progress.

You see, no different than an actor or singer or surgeon, I perform. I prepare for and promote my performances as part of my daily one thing list. I get paid when I perform, so it is my number one goal to attract an audience (of one or many) and deliver the best possible performance. Since the performance is my focus, I don't worry daily about selling or sending an email or closing loops. (Don't mistake this for <u>not </u>doing it. I build processes for how to do this. All these things matter in a business, but how you prioritize them is what is important.) The busy things don't really matter anymore. Do you think it matters to Lady Gaga on the day that she has a performance whether she personally returned a phone call or email, or scheduled her next dentist appointment? No, she hired people to schedule things and return calls. She simplified her life decisions and doesn't let anything distract her from the most important part of her business. What matters is that she performs at her best. That's when the money is earned. That's when the magic happens and when the mastery is exhibited.

Simplifying and doing just three things a day will improve the quality of your life in so many ways. Why would you create a life that is so complex that you feel inundated with things to do, a constant belief that you haven't done enough or checked enough off your list, and have guilt for not doing all those things well or at all?

The compound effect of small things makes a big difference. In fact, incremental steps make exponential impacts. As they say, little hinges swing big doors.

17. Protect Your Time

Dan S. Kennedy is a master at this. In fact, you could say he wrote the book on it. One of his many "No B.S." books focuses on time management. He suggests you start by measuring what your time is worth to you, and then fiercely protect it. When you spend time on things that are not productive, take an inventory and value them against your worth. This can be thought of simply as your hourly rate or, but more importantly, your time value. You will soon realize how much time you waste in unproductive pursuits and distractions.

You alone, can't protect your time. It requires gatekeepers and people, processes and systems to manage effectively. You must adopt methods to train others to assist you. Start with time blocking strategies.

On the first day of Strategic Coach™, you are taught the basic principles of time blocking. How to segment your time into money making (focus days), business building (buffer days), and personal regeneration (free days). This is not the perfect system, but it is a pretty good one. If anything, you pay more attention to segmenting time to better handle the needs of an entrepreneur. To perform at your best when you are "on stage" earning money requires preparation, confidence and energy. The buffer and free days give you this so you can deliver your best. Too often we are working "in" our businesses, not on them.

In order to grow and thrive, you must spend more time thinking about your business and planning for the next big opportunity.

Warren Buffet, one of the richest men in the world was quoted as saying:

"I insist on a lot of time being spent, almost every day, to just sit and think. That is very uncommon in American business. I read and think. So, I do more reading and thinking, and make fewer impulse decisions than most people in business. I do it because I like this kind of life."

This is obviously beneficial, and it is often time that entrepreneurs never invest. Driving forward with single-mindedness and few sidetracks or contemplation leaves less to be achieved.

Without time for great thinking, there are no great ideas.

Not investing time in this cheats you and those around you. Work, thought, and personal time are equally important. You must also make time for you, your family and leisure or learning pursuits. If you let your personal time slide, then you are risking the most important things in life. We all have the same, finite amount of time each day. Protect it fiercely and enjoy it.

18. Schedule Your Work Time And All Your Appointments

Time is freedom. It is precious for you, your family and your business. If you are losing time throughout your day attending to busyness and wasteful activities that extend your workday, or diminish your effectiveness, then you are allowing an intrusion into your personal or family time. You must protect your time unapologetically. This section is about managing and maximizing your time and limiting wastefulness.

Scheduling everything for business in your days is the first place to start. Create a schedule for each week to focus on making money, to think, and to rejuvenate. In order to do this, you must block your time. You might ask how you can do this when your customers or staff want and need you desperately. Well, the first thing you need to understand is that they'll be fine without you for a while. The second thing is that they will be much better off with you completely focused on them during a set appointment or focus time that you will be attentive to their needs or concerns exclusively. Contrary to your hard-wired belief, or rather, "always on" compulsion,

limiting access and scheduling appointments show respect for customers and your employees as opposed to sending a dismissive message.

In my investment business it took me the first thirteen years to figure this out. Ironically, it took a long while to gain my own time. I had to look outside my industry for examples of taking back my time. In fact, I learned great things about scheduling my days from my dentist. Have you ever tried to reach your dentist for an unscheduled phone call during the day? What about stopping by for a coffee? How about in the evening? Would you call them then? No, you wouldn't. They build their days to focus on their patients. That is their money-making activity. They hire reception professionals to schedule, answer questions, as well as process patients and their billing. They have hygienists to do the cleaning, x-rays, prepping and patient support work. The result is that when the dentist is working with you, they are 100% focused on your issues at that time. You get the very best of them when you are with them. There was a time, my clients felt they could drop by during business hours, reach me unannounced or call at any time of the day. I thought to myself, "Why can't I do what my dentist does in my business?" So, I did.

I'll admit I was nervous to make the shift. I operated in an "always on" mode for a long time. I knew some people would not like it, while others would be indifferent. I thought I would lose clients. But I implemented it anyway. I scheduled all my client reviews on a quarterly basis, dealt with email at certain times of the day and had my assistant take all my calls. We even scheduled urgent ones for some time in the same day. Even if it were five minutes later.

This was a monumental shift for me and my business. In the past, all the customers I worked with were used to unscheduled calls and ad hoc meetings; I was always available, and anything could happen at any time. I felt like a slave to my work and began to feel contempt for my clients who were barging into my day. I took every call because I was concerned they would think that somehow by being unavailable I might be ignoring them or their phone calls or emails. I didn't get much productive work done and the best I could do was react. To my detriment, it was such a habit to behave this way that some days, all I would do is wait for the calls to come in. It was too exhausting to build a plan for the day and have it constantly interrupted so I would simply react to everything. Guess what? It became so frustrating I began to hate most of those days. My customers weren't getting the best of me; they were merely getting my reactions. I was doing nothing strategic to help them.

When I changed this and began to schedule my time, some of my customers didn't like it. In fact, I lost a few clients. They were looking for something different and I wasn't going to compromise any longer. It took a while for me to stay committed to it, despite the push back by some. To be honest, there were still a few people who always had unobstructed access, but I was even reducing that list as well. That access was for top customers, people who energized me, and my immediate family.

By setting a quarterly review schedule process, my primary goal was to standardize my customer portfolio review and contact. Several positive side effects resulted. The first was that my year was broken into four, three-month segments with consistent themes. Month one was client reviews, month two was follow up and implementation, and month three was business development and education or training. Early on, the hardest thing for me was to get used to my own perception of a lack of activity during the business development month. I had grown wrongly conditioned to believe that the only time I was working effectively was when I was on the phone speaking with customers. When committed to scheduling and appointments, I was able to work on bigger projects and strategic marketing. Those strategic efforts took longer to create meaningful results.

Second, with structured scheduling, the goal of standardization was achieved. It also gave me the incredible power of connectedness that improved my customer relationships. The predictable, consistent scheduling process instilled confidence and even anticipation for my customers. They became responsive to our program for scheduling and were more prepared when we spoke. Our planned, undistracted conversations became more productive and meaningful.

Third, due to the nature of our structured appointment agenda, we covered more details about their life and financial situation than in the past. Some conversations enhanced our relationships, while other conversations lead to revenue generation, planning, and implementation opportunities.

Finally, because conversations were more in-depth, there was less need to connect between quarters. I became free to work on marketing, strategic planning and think more often. That was almost impossible when I was running a reactionary business.

How do you put this into action? To begin, you must assign the role of gatekeeper to someone you trust implicitly. They oversee protecting you and your time. Ideally, you will have them answer all your incoming phone calls, review and filter your email, and most definitely stop all unscheduled walk-in meetings. This person will also schedule every appointment, call, or meeting. While this can be done using online calendar apps, I believe strongly that the direct phone call for scheduling is a great personal touch. It can often be used to gather important personal information about the customer.

Your gatekeeper will be the voice of reason when you feel compelled to throw out the process and revert to your old ways. They should be empowered to question your time use and decisions and remind you that certain things are wasteful of your time. You will quickly learn to appreciate the intervention. I would suggest giving them the veto on some of your time-wasting endeavours.

Entrepreneurs take on tasks or roles that might be interesting to us yet drain us of time and energy. These things are disguised as favors, requests to "pick your brain", and invitations such as "let me buy you coffee". If you hear the following, run! "I was wondering if I could get your opinion on something." Your gatekeeper will sometimes recognize these time-wasters better than you and they are in a good position to gently remind you that maybe your time is better spent focusing on your core business. They will help you say "No".

Again, DO NOT take ad hoc calls, meetings, or conversations during your working hours. These will burn your time faster than polyester pants near a blazing campfire. Poof! Just watch your day go up in smoke. Here's another thing: attending office meetings, unless they are customer facing or for strategic planning and implementation, is a complete waste of time. You must avoid them at all costs. How many meetings have you sat through and wondered to yourself why you accepted the invitation in the first place? Exactly! Stop going to them at once and do not organize them without a clear agenda and a defined time frame. They smash a two-hour hole into your previously productive day. Again, avoid staff meetings at all cost.

GROW GET GIVE

19. Maximize Your Time

This is more about your mental health and energy than client management. If you have effectively scheduled everything and have your gatekeeper in place, next focus on making the most of the time you have now blocked for yourself. View this in a bigger context than just your working days, include your personal life. Consider that during a typical day, there are the same twenty-four hours for everyone. We sleep for roughly eight hours, we might work for about eight hours, and the other eight hours are spent in personal time: eating, grooming and enjoying personal pursuits and family time. That means over two thirds of our days are exclusively for us. We must ensure this time is healthy and enriching. We must leave work and stress out of our minds while being fully present with ourselves and our family and friends.

When was the last time you were able to completely disconnect from your work? Not too often, right? This is because entrepreneurs have a nagging sense that they didn't get enough accomplished in their day, that somehow you must carry on until you are done everything. But we know that never happens because once one project is done, we're on to the next. There is always some work left to do.

Here are some ideas on how to manage your work time to improve your personal time. We can reduce the stress of bringing our work home with us by ensuring we maximize our time productively during our work hours. That is the roughly one third of our day in which we devote to building our business, realizing our vision, and making money. There are many ways to become more efficient and more productive — in fact, I am sure most of you who are reading this book already accomplish more in a few focused hours than most people would in an entire week of work. Eight hours of work is a societal construct rather than a practical, energy-based approach to work. Quality trumps quantity every time.

When you are freed from the chaos of random conversations, ad hoc meetings, phone calls and email distractions, you can focus and be more productive. When your mind lets go of the need to take on everything and solve every problem as it comes along, you become free to think strategically and create.

The first suggestion is to get up early and set a daily ritual or routine. This is the series of things you do every day that clear your mind, reduce anxiety, and energize you. Everyone has a different bio rhythm, so how this unfolds each morning is up to you. An hour spent each morning in a healthy, predictable, and personal regimen will set you up for increased productivity. Wake up early and rested. A good breakfast to fuel you is a must.

Another key component is to partake in some form of physical activity — from a short vigorous workout to yoga, walking, or simply focused breathing and stretching. You will find you become wakened and alert as a result — the lifelong benefits of regular exercise are immeasurable. Showering and taking time for personal grooming prepares you for the day. Also, reading inspiring or motivating information, quotes, or blogs will set your mind to a strategic course.

Finally, tackling something complex that requires your full attention will allow you a big accomplishment at the outset of your day. Your mind is active and ready to function in the morning. You will notice I did not recommend reading the news, sleeping in, lounging around or reviewing your email. These habits will slow you down, fill your mind with negativity and distract or force you to work on someone else's schedule.

Your day will not move forward in a productive manner if you allow these behaviors to creep into your daily routine.

The next key to daily productivity is something I call energy blocking. We all only have so much energy to focus on a project for any given amount of time. Some of us work well in 30 to 40 minute bursts; others can constructively sustain focus for up to 90 minutes. Whatever your focus zone is, you must understand this and work within it, taking healthy breaks of 10 to 15 minutes in between those periods.

When I work, I take frequent, short "walkabouts" for breaks. I liken it to coming up for air, then diving back down to work again. I require these little releases of energy to maintain my productivity. I am very capable of working vigorously for long stretches, but when I am in that frame of mind, I ignore everything else, including food, hydration, and even hygiene. Clearly that is not healthy, so I take short walks and get back to work. These breaks will allow you to pause, restore, and refocus. For some it might be making a personal call or doing a personal task or catching up on the day's events. You will find that moving through your day in this manner truly allows you to be more productive and more focused in the work you are doing. As I mentioned before, none of this will be possible unless you protect and schedule your time.

How you react when things go off track is also important. We must also accept that this might happen at any time. While I strongly recommend a very structured approach to your workdays to maximize productivity, it is also critical that if, and when, things out of your control occur, you can refocus and get back on track without creating stress for you. It is never the action that is disruptive; it is your reaction to the disruption that must adapt. Developing a simple ritual to refocus is helpful. Think of an actor going through a dramatic and emotional scene. They might have to do twenty takes to get it just right. In between takes, when things go wrong, there are many distractions. There are make-up people, lighting, sound and other technicians working around them. There could be other actors creating challenges, there can be elements of the set that are distractions too, but a top quality actor will have very specific ways to center themselves and refocus. This might be breathing techniques, or mind clearing actions. It might include a verbal ritual or physical movement. They do this every time, then reset and begin their acting again.

I recommend this simple technique. Take three minutes to do this and you'll be focused and ready to go after a disruption. Simply, stand up (slowly) out of your chair, placing one hand on your desk or chair for support so not to fall over during this exercise. Close your eyes and breathe. Use a four count to breath in through you nose, hold for two counts, and then breathe out through your mouth for a five count. Doing this for two or three minutes will calm and center you. Open your eyes and get back to work.

20. Limit, Reduce, Or Outsource Email Handling

In the socially connected, yet non-verbal world of communications we are evolving into, there are very few ways to avoid email, text messages, instant messenger, Twitter, Instagram, etc. There are many extremely good things about using email and other messenger apps. The obvious benefit is it helps us communicate directly with the recipient in a written context and allows us to share documents and images efficiently.

Email is a powerful tool to use to provide scheduling and supporting information for live phone calls or meetings. There are many supported apps for this as well. It also helps expedite business driven requests that do not need the usual banter that phone communications bring. Remember, I schedule all my appointments, phone calls and meetings, so when we need to simply communicate updates or confirm a recommendation or request that has a yes or no answer, email is a far more efficient use of time than a phone call.

One thing we never do though is expect that the recipient will always be on and at the ready to reply. If we want immediate confirmation, we must indicate so, or make a direct call. Outside of the utilitarian use of email, there is an inordinate amount of junk and wasteful data flowing in every day. When I was working as a portfolio manager, I got to a point where I was simply reviewing email so it wouldn't pile up every day. Between 5pm at the end of every day and 6am the next day, my mailbox would amazingly fill up with no less than 150 emails. I always wondered why this occurred. Most reasonable people or businesses wouldn't expect a response, call you, or come to your office unannounced during those hours, so why should my inbox be so stuffed during off hours? I'm not talking about the basic flyers or spam that appeared in my junk mail, I am talking about requests or comments or inquiries that were written in a manner expecting an immediate response. I would get messages that were written between 11pm to 2am that had a sense of urgency and were conversational, as if I was awake reading them. Are you kidding me?

I deleted hundreds of emails daily. For example, I would delete 150 emails, with less than ten percent being somewhat useful. When reviewing the ten percent, some were forwarded and delegated to others, with a few being left for me to deal with. While I became efficient at dealing with this, it was time consuming. The daily ritual was a compulsion for a while, to log on and get to the email pile. If this had come in the form of a stack of mail, I know I would never have sifted through the mountain of paper. I would have allowed it to grow and grow. Determining what percentage of your email is important and what is junk is up to you. If you engage in reviewing your email first thing each day, you have already set your energy on a reactionary course, as opposed to a productive proactive one.

Responding habitually to email places your time on "their" time. You are gradually drained of your freedom.

What do you do? Start by getting out of the habit of reviewing the first fifty emails of your day. They won't help you focus on the things that are important to you to achieve. Set a time to review them and delete 90%+ of those emails. Then schedule time to deal with the ones that might be important. Don't respond on command, be in demand! Responding like a dog to a dinner bell when email arrives sets a precedent of expectation, turns your actions into reactions and distracts you from completion of important tasks in hand.

You could even outsource or in-source email management. Hire or assign someone to review your email. To ensure that you deal with the important communications included in your email avalanche, you must take the time upfront to teach or train those you assign the responsibility to identify important information for you. Design a process to have them bring the important things to your attention and use systems which can handle the processing and communications needs for this. I prefer scheduling time to deal with these things myself. I have become effective at filtering unimportant email, as well as allocating time to deal with important email. I have criteria that quickly determine whether to act on the email or simply defer it for later. I never feel compelled to respond immediately without applying my filter.

Believe it or not, some of the greatest marketing gurus of all time have important email printed and then reviewed on a specific day or specific times. I'd consider this prehistoric thinking, but it is probably very effective at filtering out all irrelevant info. While a time-waster for the person doing the reviewing and printing, it forces them to make better decisions on what is truly important for the business. They aren't going to print everything; otherwise it is a colossal waste of paper. How you deal with this is up to you, but you must deal with it. If you devoted only an hour per day scrolling through your long list of email messages, you are losing an hour that could be spent planning your next initiative, doing marketing, or furthering your sales.

GROW GET GIVE

21. Use Systems To Leverage Your Time And Resources To Give You Freedom

"The amount of stress you feel in your life is in direct correlation to the lack of systems in your life."

Systems are applied to processes and make your business scalable. Processes give you time, systems give you leverage.

Examples range from using Outlook and Gmail to hold contacts and manage email to more complex CRM systems. Systems like Infusionsoft, A-Webber, Click Funnels, Office Auto Pilot, Salesforce, or Mail Chimp (along with so many more) will help you manage marketing and communication with your customers and prospects. There are extensive project management systems for building, tracking, and monitoring. Entrepreneurs can rely on technology and people. Two things must be done before you integrate systems into your life and business. The first is to identify where your business processes would be improved with more efficient ways of doing things. Second, hire or contract people who know how to maximize the use of such systems, so you can increase your time spent on marketing and sales. Don't attempt to learn the intricacies of using all these tools yourself. You must be great at your core business and identify what you might need before you find the right people to help.

Gain a rudimentary understanding of how systems work so you know how to hire or how to integrate them into your business.

Systems and software today are accessible, but sophisticated tools. They allow you to learn about marketing your business as well. You can learn who is reading your information, how they found you, and track where they go afterward. You can experiment with multiple marketing messages simultaneously to determine which are the most effective.

Few companies are fully leveraging technology. Outsourcing and freelancers are available everywhere. You no longer need waste time and money on menial activities that consume your employees' days. Something as simple as data entry or market research can be outsourced through the internet inexpensively. In turn this will free up funds (and time) that you can then direct staff to delighting customers or attracting new ones.

Cloud technology has expanded on-line outsourcing and data management systems. When working with a small business owner who ran an anti-snoring product company, a colleague of mine learned the owner was having staff members enter data in multiple software programs, and then reconciling it all manually. They were using QuickBooks, Google Docs, and Amazon for tracking orders, another software program for tracking sales, and then taking time to combine all the information into usable data and statistics with minimal success.

She investigated cloud applications which would accept all that information as it was realized, then reconciled all of it, in one central platform using the multiple streams of data. This freed up an enormous amount of time for her staff that were always busy in data entry. She decided instead of letting them go, she would train them to improve the sales and customer service side of her business. She was saving money on her employees' time and, by re-directing her staff to revenue producing activities, increased her sales and profits. When your organization is not constrained by data entry or administrative tasks, the inputs become helpful outputs and you are able to focus on growing your business exponentially versus incrementally.

Systematize everything

Another example would be how Amazon's CreateSpace which was re-branded as KDP (Kindle Direct Publishing) developed a process for people to self-publish. Many others have followed, as well. The step-by-step model is very clear and allows you to fully publish a book. It's a very simple, automated program. Anyone can do it. Create processes for what you do and systems for how to do everything. Find the things in your business you can create processes for and then systematize those which can give you leverage that will free up your time and get you more freedom.

GROW GET GIVE

22. Model Everything

Model everything. I used to use the phrase "copy great" but copying gave people too much latitude. I don't recommend people copy, steal or replicate. I've been plagiarized by one of my coaching clients and I won't have that happen again. It's never okay. They say mimicry is one of the highest forms of flattery, but there is a line that should not be crossed where no self-respecting entrepreneur should steal or copy another person's proprietary content.

Therefore: "model great". There are many excellent ideas yet to be realized and brilliant ones at that. There are also centuries of great ones that have already manifested. In fact, what you believe is unique to you, has likely already been done. This is true in music, sports, art and business. Science might be the only field where all that has been done before gets renewed and improved, as new frontiers are always opening. Who you are, is how you differentiate yourself from all those who have gone before you.

Modeling great is how you use the best of what others have done, saving time and energy, but build it into your thing. The framework is there - enhance it and share.

Learn how to participate, compete, grow and serve clients in a specific area, track prospects by finding the people, businesses, or products that are doing it today the best and model them. Invest in their products, processes and services. Learn how things work, follow their lead, and make it yours. Don't reinvent what has been done. Make unique improvements that reflect your business. No one can be you, so your take on what has been done is as good as having created it.

While there is an advantage to be the first mover in any market, it is tough sledding. What the first movers know, and the lessons they learned, can benefit you. By modelling great, you can refine and improve. I'll be the first to say that there are many things in life that are more enjoyable when you've been through a struggle to get them, but that doesn't mean it is necessary. It isn't even virtuous. You are going to make your share of mistakes. You will step in your very own potholes, but they won't cost your business. That's the great thing about being the second (or third, or fourth) mover - you don't have to risk everything to know what not to do, you just watch, listen and learn.

Think of siblings. Life can be easier for the second born. I don't remember my sister, Cheryl, ever getting in serious trouble with my parents. It was as though I wore them down for her. I did everything first and in a big way. I made the mistakes, had the spotlight on what I did and often was the one who got the attention. I created a big wake behind me, so my sister was able to cruise in it. She didn't have to contend with breaking new headway all the time and I was often pushing or pulling her in some way. The standard was set, and she almost always rose to the occasion, invented her own successes and stayed out of trouble.

Cheryl was able to get better marks in school because of the high standard in our house, and she excelled at sports because she had to constantly keep up with me and my friends. She was a "walk-on" goalkeeper for the university soccer team mostly because while growing up, we always stuck her in net so we could practice shooting for hockey, soccer - whatever we could throw or kick into a goal. She stopped anything the older boys could hurl at her. My sister was able to have some successes that maybe would have been harder if she was spending a lot of time challenging our parents and butting heads in life. I did all that and she could focus on her strengths. I was the first mover and she jumped on her opportunities and made the most of them for herself. She didn't shrink in the face of the challenge; she rose to it.

The first movers in business endure the big challenges. Look back at the emergence of the dot com era. The biggest names that don't exist anymore were first movers and others copied, refined, modeled, bought, improved the technology, changed one thing here, repositioned, and had more success. Model everything; don't be obsessed with being the first mover. It is often the second mover who rises to the top and sometimes becomes the only surviving business in the space.

GROW GET GIVE

23. Seek Points Of Leverage In Marketing Your Business

If you work or serve customers directly in a business to consumer ("B2C") business, there are likely ways that you can tap into business to business ("B2B") strategies to build your customer base. These strategies might be directly related to building a relationship with a business customer by providing access to their many employees, or it can be through working with a credibility partner, as I explained earlier in this book. Be positioned as the subject matter authority serving the partner. Whichever business customer you identify, they can leverage your reach and ability to get more sales, as opposed to simply going after one-on-one sales. Strategic partnering, joint ventures and systems to support such activities can help you achieve the goal of building a reliable, repeatable pipeline of prospects or sales opportunities.

Establish leverage wherever possible in marketing.
Your overall reach is much bigger than you think.

One of my longest standing coaching customers ran an online training enterprise. His customers were individuals who were upgrading or learning a specific type of project management software. His primary revenue stream was a B2C membership model. He would use SEO, email marketing and other online marketing tools, as well as an occasional classroom session, to market to individual users that he offered this training. This was a slow process that had some traction but worked to build his membership.

Once we were able to refine some processes and his marketing message, we were able to ramp his new member registrations up quite a bit using his prospect pipelines, but we were not being as efficient as we could be. We had moved from three to six new members per month to eight to ten and higher, but we both agreed it would be much better if we could accelerate that. We decided to build marketing positioning for him to take on corporate RFPs. A successful RFP with the one best fit corporate partner could mean up to three hundred employees signing up for online training at once! Obviously, there would be a discount price for the volume, but such a strategy could exponentially increase his membership base. We would blow his short-term membership targets out of the water if we could simply engage the right single corporate partner. The leverage that would provide would be huge.

He would continue marketing to individual customers, using all methods possible, but would add this new marketing leverage as well. Eventually he was adding up to one hundred new members each month. A well-developed corporate relationship is like a credibility partner. Successful engagement with these partners can provide your business scalable growth but can add risk if you become too reliant on them. The big opportunity is the scale such a partner brings. To do this, you might have to enter the RFP process. The effort to successfully apply, complete and submit a proposal in an RFP can be daunting. Remember, you will differentiate yourself by how you serve your partner. You often do not know who else is competing and how they are positioning their business case. A by-product of participating in this process is that it forces you, the entrepreneur, to hone your marketing and positioning skills. You will sharpen your understanding of why you do what you do and how you become a resource to serve your individual customer. The success of such a process for my client resulted in significant growth from a single effort; while the improvements to his marketing message for individual users also increased his overall memberships. The experience expanded his knowledge and he was able to establish himself as a resource for large corporations seeking his services. As a result, he gained leverage by positioning his marketing for the business customer. His competitors were desperate to get the same access, while he was being sought out by the corporate client.

In my own experience, I have used the concept of leverage to further my own marketing efforts. You can call this joint venturing, "spider-webbing", whatever. As a simple example, I enlisted the help of credibility partners to extend my reach and gain leverage. I decided to arrange a book signing a few years ago at a local Indigo bookstore and was thinking of ways to get the message out about the event. The intent was to spread the marketing message I had to share. I wanted something to use to build credibility for other initiatives I was undertaking about six weeks later. The premise was to remind as many people in my market that I was a local author with a recognized bookstore, Indigo, hosting the event. My list in my new target market was small. I only had a few hundred contacts to send my information out to. I had to figure out how I could leverage my reach beyond my 300 or so contacts.

Again, my primary goal was not to have a large audience at the event, nor was it to sell books. The goal was to establish more credibility in the marketplace as an authority on philanthropy. It wasn't about the actual event.

I constructed a press release and an email letter to three key charities that I wished to support. I offered to donate all proceeds from any sales on the book signing day to those charities and asked them if they would spread the word. They agreed. Before the event my marketing message went out to my small list of 300 contacts and the three charities' additional 3,000+ contacts! My reach was ten times larger. I ran a simple press release with a newswire service the day before the event and my reach expanded further. The book signing was on a sunny, beautiful Saturday morning - never good for a book signing. Naturally, not many people showed up. I was not the least bit concerned. Even though I had hoped to sell more books so I could give money to the charities, I was able to stay top of mind with my audience, capture images of the event in Indigo with people lined up to buy my book, have credible organizations promote the event to their contacts, and now my news release was parked on Google for years to follow. How can you serve your contacts to help them and generate leverage for your marketing and theirs?

24. Done Is Better Than Perfect – But A Little Better Is Even Better

The Pareto principle was coined by management consultant, Joseph Juran, but attributed to Italian economist, Vilfredo Pareto. We understand this as the 80:20 rule - that 80% of the effects come from 20% of the causes. This power law has been applied to economics, wealth, business and health. Time after time, evidence shows that something close to the 80:20 principle seems to be pervasive. When considered in a business context, it is often referenced as a process of constant improvement. By spending concentrated time in effort and focus, you get the biggest results. Extrapolation of this suggests that 80% of your success comes from 20% of your work. Again, work less…make more.

Too often entrepreneurs pursue perfection, but true success is found when progress is made. My message to clients is that done is always better than perfect. Most time perfection has no place in business advancement unless you are in the surgery or rocket science business. So, tackle your first 80%, leave the 20% alone for a while, and then carve into that 20% later. Do another 80% of that 20%, and so on and so forth.

I met one of the most successful fitness business owners consulting others in their gyms across North America, India and the world - John Spencer Ellis. Now one of North America's top entrepreneur coaches, John asked, "If you're good with 80/20, why not 95/5?" I agree.

Why can't we put 5% of our maximum effort, our supreme elegance, our sublime skillset or mastery into something that gives us 95% benefit? Why can't we pursue that factor as entrepreneurs? Get more time and get more freedom by being more focused, more skillful, more masterful at those smaller things that move mountains and have huge impact. Work to find where 95% of your business success comes from 5% of your activity.

Not perfection, but close. Be great. Then apply the principle toward progress, where you reach 95% by advancing, then backing off and advancing and so on. Do the final 5% or not. Few things in life must be perfect and even those which we believe are near perfect are imperfect at the tiniest levels. I would suggest that in medicine and machining, the tools used for the work must be made near perfect. For most everything else, things don't have to be perfect; less than perfect often works well. Most people can't tell the difference between near perfect and perfect. They can sure tell the difference between average and perfect and maybe 80% isn't quite the mark to strive for. Stick to 80:20 as a goal for achievement; make it work and stop being so hard on you for not being perfect. If possible, 95:5 would be a wonderful thing to aspire for, so we can put 5% effort in to get 95% of the reward. Let's aim for that.

25. Invest For Growth

Invest in experience and knowledge — it is ALWAYS worth it.

I have had coaches and mentors all my life. I had them in sports, in music, and business. There have been good coaches and not so good, but I have learned something from all of them. The best teachers I have ever had often succeeded in some way in their field. It isn't a pre-requisite that your coach was an all-star in the sport, the music or business field that you are in, but their direct and personal experience both in success and failure is. The fundamentals of business are universal; a plumber does not need a plumber to coach them on running their business. It always helps if your coach understands the language, challenges and nuances of your industry, but they did not have to prove themselves there. In fact, insights from outside your industry are often very helpful. New ideas help differentiate.

Phil Jackson, one of the most successful basketball coaches in NBA history, was a specialist in basketball, but he could easily have taken his skills to pretty much any sport or industry and applied them as a coach with stellar results. His passion was basketball and that matters. Beyond their experience and wisdom, where your coaches' passion is will determine their effectiveness.

Who do you believe would be the best to coach you? Someone who gets paid for what they coach, or someone who has never been paid? I had coaches offer to train me in building my investment business that never made a living at the financial service industry or their coaching business. It is important that your business coach built and ran some business successfully. They could then demonstrate understanding of how industry worked and what key concerns and challenge you face. I want to learn from coaches who experienced success and whose coaching is not their Plan B.

When you consider the industry specialist for a coach, you want someone who has succeeded in the industry. However, it is sometimes the case that they stopped mid-way through whatever their profession to become a coach. They realized their unique ability and it drove them to coaching. They have hands-on experience and that's what gives them insight and allows them to relate.

I can relate. After two decades in the investment industry, I left to pursue my calling. I had some failures and some big successes throughout my career. I know what went wrong to hasten future failures and I understood with detail what had to happen to give me the success I enjoyed in my last decade as an advisor. For those in the financial services industry, I make a great coach given my intimate knowledge, understanding exactly the challenges faced and their language. I prefer working with entrepreneurs who are free to move in any direction, unencumbered, and earn income in any way they see fit thus only a handful of advisors fit this profile. Many are confined by regulation, compliance and an industry wide lack of innovation.

Beyond the fact that I ran my own business successfully, managed money and understand finance and financial statements. I am a five time author, paid speaker and expert in my field. But what really makes me an asset to business owners in any industry, is that I spent twenty two years analyzing and investing in a myriad of companies. I understood the merits of the companies in their industries, learned the challenges they faced and see their future economic potential. I witnessed the birth of some great companies, as well as the death of some and occasionally took part in the autopsies. That information flowed daily to me for two decades.

I have participated at top levels in many industries. In turn, I have been a coach in those areas, including sports, education, financial planning, and business. My involvement as a coach or mentor originated with others asking me to help them or share my experience and knowledge. I invested over $180,000 working with coaches, participating in mastermind groups, training and education. This was hard earned money that I invested in furthering my knowledge and my own success. I have invested so others don't have to and as a result, my clients benefit.

I can comfortably say that the return on an investment in me has outstripped any investment I could have made in the stock market or real estate. It created the foundation for a lifetime of success and opportunity. The time and wasted energy you save from learning from others who have gone before you is immeasurable. You might gain freedom from going it alone and getting it wrong, but the hours and dollars spent pursuing strategies and tactics that don't work are a heavy price to pay and they can also be emotionally draining. Entrepreneurs operate optimally when they are confident and energized, not demoralized by an ignorant or naïve mistake.

There is no glory in learning from a school of hard knocks when the collective wisdom of coaches and mentors can spare you a lot of the heartache.

Coaches have prevented me from doing damaging things to my business (and life); they have streamlined processes for me and shared wisdom that would have taken me years to learn on my own. The freedom I gained from coaching was priceless. My coaches collapsed time for me.

Continue to invest in coaching and training every year for you. Invest in the people around you so they can receive coaching and training too. Consider what the value of one customer or one idea is for you. You might find the three-year value of one perfect customer is $30,000. If that is the case, how much would you invest to attract that single customer and then learn how to do it predictably and repeatedly? I know I'd invest $10,000 or even $20,000 for that one customer because not only is that a good return, but I would be able to replicate all I learned to attract more. If you could learn an idea that would save your business $30,000 of wasted time or investment what would that be worth to you? How about hiring the right person or people? What is that worth?

It is important to understand the return on investment when you are considering working with a coach. If you invest money into a time saving process that teaches you how to grow quickly, and increase sales to your ideal customer, what ratio of investment to return is reasonable for you? Compare it to your investment return expectations or normal business growth expectations. How much money do you invest and risk do you take with a goal to earn 10% returns? Even if you could do this every year for a decade, how does that compare to investing in learning how to save yourself eight hours per week for the rest of your life for leisure? Or what about that lifetime value of working with multiples of your ideal customer? Are you pleased with $1 invested and $1.10 returned … or do you need $2 or $20? Deciding what coaching is worth to you requires investigation. It really is about leveraging time, money and energy. Once you establish what those measures are for your success, you can make a commitment to coaching.

GROW GET GIVE

26. Unplug The Drain

There is likely more than one person in your life, work or personal, who constantly complains about their circumstances. They have drama all the time and suck the life right out of you. You find yourself drawn into their chaos somehow and become distracted or pulled down with them for the moments you are together or beyond. Their lives are stuck in a never-ending pattern of conflict or complaint. They are like a "floater" that just won't be flushed. They want to pull you into their misery and need to drain your energy to charge them. People who matter in your life benefit from you when you are energized and positive, so today is the day to retake your energy and allow the "drainers" to swirl in the bowl and disappear. It is time to let them go. Pull the plug and allow them to swirl about the drain, disappearing out of your life.

Life is too short, and your time is too precious,
to allow others to hold you back or drain your energy.

This does not have to be done harshly or hastily. You can reduce the time you spend with them progressively. First, reduce your time with them. Next, if you are not able to avoid being in the same place as them, when you interact, don't engage with them in their misery. This will prevent them from gaining energy in the exchange. They will lose interest and eventually stop connecting because they can't suck any more energy out of you. They will move on to someone who they can. If you remove your own feelings from the equation, you will find they weren't that interested in you anyway. They were only interested in themselves and the energy they needed. At first they'll act hurt in order to further drain you, but they won't really be offended that you no longer give them that space. Remove the drama and the "drainers" from your life.

It is easy to replace your "drainers" by adding or including only those people who energize you and want the best for you. This will enhance your life and bring your energy up. Your creativity will soar when you share your thoughts and time with people who are positive and share your passions for success. Be conscious of your own behaviors as well by reflecting who you wish to energize you. Engaging in gossip or drama will reflect poorly on you. We are all prone to a little bit of this, be sure to catch yourself, acknowledge the behavior and move on to ideas.

"Great minds discuss ideas. Average minds discuss events. Small minds discuss people."
— Eleanor Roosevelt

27. Dump The Meetings

Avoid unnecessary meetings at all costs. They are a big waste of time. I am not talking about client meetings or strategic planning meetings integral to your business; I am talking about all other business focused gatherings of staff or personnel in a company. This includes the newest version of time-wasting meetings – the corporate "video conference call" (i.e. "Zoom" or "GoTo Meeting").

When I was in the financial services industry, we would attend meetings all the time. Meetings for the staff, meetings with other advisors, meetings to listen to product sellers, wholesalers, company pitches, analyst commentary, and so on. The longer I used to sit in a meeting, the more and more aggravated I would get. Most of my time in those meetings was spent thinking of the more productive things I could be doing while I tuned out the uninspiring conversation. I would analyze the presenter's technique, their sales pitch, or their PowerPoint, wondering how they even got the opportunity to be there. For me, the best thing I ever did was to stop attending meetings altogether.

There is nothing so important discussed in a meeting that you need to be there.

If it is that critical, there will be someone who can provide you the "Coles notes" version. You can then review and absorb the information at your own pace, right after you accomplish work that is important to you and your business. Taking a walk to clear your head and refresh is better than time spent wasted in a meaningless meeting.

Attending a meeting is not a break, it is an interruption. I liked setting up customer facing appointments or calls during the exact time of a meeting so I could make productive use of my time and not be questioned for missing. Client facing activity was the best way to gently decline any meeting. Sometimes, I would close my office door and carry on working with no explanation at all.

As for you (the boss), don't call meetings. They are a platform for you or someone else to project your idea of what is important onto people who do not share that opinion. Send a memo, use emails or have a scheduled, short one-on-one (or small group) meeting to get your point across and end the meeting quickly. It is not a forum for complaints or a stage for you to pontificate. If you must hold or attend a meeting, do not ask or encourage questions that are not specific to the topic at hand. Have an agenda, hand it out well ahead of the meeting and stick to the agenda. Set expectations, demand accountability, and increase communication, but don't waste everyone's time with meetings.

28. Don't Serve The Wrong Customer

Accepting customers who do not fit your ideal customer profile will only lead to future stress. It might seem reasonable to get a short-term sale and add another possible contact and referral source, but if they are not a fit, there is a strong possibility they will cost you dearly in the long run. It might not be money, but they will drain your energy and time. The stress you feel will increase and your support staff will be exhausted. They will pull you outside your unique ability and distract you from bigger things. The wrong customer is like an insidious disease. They will eat away at your productivity and your energy. You cannot allow this to happen.

In the financial service industry (no different than the insurance, legal, accounting, real estate, extended health care, or most other service-based industries) we were taught early on in our careers that anyone with a pulse and a pocketbook are a potential client. When you are starting out, you only focus on growth as fast as possible, so you can keep your job, increase your revenue, pay your bills and gain acceptance with your managers and your peers. Build your numbers and the revenue will come. And you know what? It is true. Your revenue grows, your wrong fit customer list grows and so do your headaches. Early on in my career in the nineties, I worked with a senior partner and the two of us had over 1,200 investment clients! Most of them were poorly fit clients. The goal he set for me was to build a massive book of clients with as many investors as possible. The nature of the business was deal-driven, so he needed more clients to spread out the risks of funding new companies. As you can guess, people were only happy and engaged when things went well. When investments performed poorly, it became a nightmare.

It was insanity. We had six phone lines ringing constantly. Email was not established yet, but I can only imagine what kind of electronic avalanche that would have been. There was absolutely no planning for the future nor any staffing or systems in place. It was impossible. We were running as fast as we could to keep up with the influx of demand. When things inevitably went poorly, we lost a lot of clients … who we had to go out and replace. It was a horrendous treadmill we were on. I lasted three years in that mess and when I jumped off, I vowed never to jump back on. Clearly, we did not have 1,200 ideal customers. There were probably just 10% of them who were a good fit.

When you work with the wrong clients, they assume their pleasures or challenges will be your only focus. They don't respect your time and they don't respect your value.

Understand this was not their fault. You are the one who determines who you let in and how you will serve them. In the last decade of running my investment business I raised the bar very high on the commitment I demanded of my new clients. By design, the hurdle kept a lot of people from working with me and sometimes it was tempting to be more flexible. The result was that I engaged with fewer families who were more committed, more enjoyable, and had a strong understanding of the value I provided them. By the time I sold my business, its value was high, and less than 75 client families made up all our investment management households.

In my coaching business I only accept a maximum of twenty new ideal candidates per year on an ongoing basis. I might work with up to forty new and returning clients at any given time. It is because of the commitment I demand, both financially and personally. When putting up barriers to filter out the wrong clients, you need to get comfortable with the phrase, "It's not right for everyone." It must become part of your vocabulary. Placing the onus on the prospect to achieve a higher standing to become a customer either repels them or attracts them to you. Either way both of you wins. Wrong fit customers are not an opportunity for you. You won't change their behaviors or mindset; they will drain you. Remember, "It's not right for everyone." This mantra will free you.

Not accepting the wrong customer is one thing. The next is to dismiss the people you are working with today who are not an ideal customer. This will often be a relief for both you and them. These are typically people who you have already "quiet-filed". The relationship has been over for a while, yet neither of you wants to take the next step to end it formally. Plan and set the date, then end those relationships. The result of no longer working with the wrong customer is that you look forward to everyone you do work with who is right for your business. You will be energized, and your time will be respected.

GROW GET GIVE

BOOK THREE

GIVE BACK

GROW GET GIVE

Introduction

During my career as an advisor and portfolio manager in the investment industry, I worked with hundreds of families guiding them on their wealth, their succession and planning their legacies. Most of my clients were Canadian Baby Boomers. The experiences I gained working with this amazing demographic were the best, and most distressing, lessons in *"if I only knew then what I know now."* Those were the lamentations of those who discovered all the best things for the planning they never did, but should have. The strategies they should have considered and the tactics and tools that were no longer available, or affordable, to them. They were transitioning from their working lifetimes to some form of retirement. They were concerned about their financial future, taxes, their kids and passing along their legacy.

I can comfortably say that seven out of ten people I met simply did not have their affairs in order. They were mostly without wills – or at least, those wills were outdated. They were lacking in proper financial planning and their assets were at huge risk of being taxed heavily – up to 50% of their net worth in some cases. These were the challenges I helped them solve. All too often the biggest risk for these families was inaction, or rather, procrastination. The delays in taking the necessary steps to protect themselves were sometimes catastrophic.

The examples of how things could (and did) go wrong were plentiful and most of them were health related. That excludes the untimely passing of people that I would inevitably witness each year. There was the client who put off his will and estate planning and extended his retirement by six months – only to have a heart attack the week before he left work. This was before he updated his will and added insurance intended to protect his family in case of his passing, his estate from taxes, and his wife against the event where a critical illness became financially debilitating for them.

There was a fifty-year-old client who amassed a large portfolio of real estate working his fingers to the bone, balancing his cash flows, spending more time working than with his family, and stressing daily about the immense and tangled financial dealings he had been juggling for years. He joined an integrated health clinic and went for a thorough toes-to-teeth check-up. In the screening, a large tumor on his pancreas was identified and complications from subsequent surgery arose, nearly killing him. All he worked for began to slip away. The added stress must have been terrible. Prior to this incident, he told me when I saw him on his 50th birthday that his biggest fear of aging was that he would reach the milestone, get sick and die. A few months later this nearly played out. His fear unfortunately wasn't enough to get him to act in advance to protect his family or his wealth.

There was another client who had built a considerable amount of wealth through his various businesses over his lifetime. We would meet once a year for a coffee to review his investments and financial picture. One Friday years ago, we were sitting at a cafe with our various papers laid on the table, and our coffee cups placed on top of them. As always, our conversation focused on the Calgary Flames and a variety of topical news stories of the day. In a break of tradition, the man spoke up and told me he was concerned that he hadn't planned whom or what he would leave his wealth to. I was a bit surprised at the change in topic, but engaged him and asked what he meant.

"Well," he continued, "as you know, my wife passed a few years ago and my children are living successful lives with their own families. I am proud of their accomplishments and they are independently wealthy. They don't need my money." I prompted him forward.

"Yes, I know this." He continued, "It is just that in my 84 years, I haven't ever really considered how I might pass on any kind of legacy beyond my family. There is a lot of money to consider and I want it to have the biggest impact. As well, I'd rather not give to the government either if possible."

Naturally, I was really beginning to wonder where this was headed. We hadn't gotten into these things in the past, as he was a pretty private person. I asked him, "This is not our usual chit chat -why has this become so important to you?" he replied, "I saw my doctor last month to go through a battery of tests. I hadn't been feeling very well and I was hoping to learn why. Well, the reason was that I have been diagnosed with pancreatic cancer and it is spreading. My doctor says I only have weeks to live."

It was as though I'd been hit by a truck. The shock to hear such a thing from a wonderful man and friend was too much. I had a hard time expressing my emotions, so I simply moved to my advisor mode and asked him if he wanted to come by my office on Monday morning and we could begin working on some planning and maybe sort things out for him quickly. He agreed. We attempted to make progress in the planning, but within weeks, he succumbed to his cancer and died. There was no planning in place and his legacy remained unwritten. Beyond his loss, the financial loss to his estate and legacy, out of the hands of his known beneficiaries and the ones yet to be chosen was immeasurable. I still wonder the impact he could have made if he had planned for it.

If anything, our lives are dreadfully short. We move through life trying to do our best to live well and with prosperity. Some of us accomplish a lot in business and become wealthy and successful. This is hard work and for most, it is all-consuming. Sometimes our families take a back seat, and a lot of times we barely impact the world around us and our communities the way we had hoped. But when all the effort is expended on our business, and we have aged and we look back on our lives and accomplishments, it is normal to want to give back. If we are lucky, we are healthy and capable of doing this. In a lot of cases, some of the possibilities to have the greatest impact have slipped away because we simply waited too long. There are tools or strategies that just don't work at certain ages or in certain circumstances. Many things can still be done, but the biggest opportunities may have disappeared along with our potential impact.

You are reading this because you want to learn to grow your business and get more freedom to enjoy your life and family even more, but you also have a sense of commitment to a bigger impact. Through my current work with entrepreneurs and business owners we focus on creating wealth. This is different than when I worked with baby boomers planning for their financial transition. Because of this, there is an opportunity to share wisdom. I have the privilege to share the exact experiences of those who have gone before you, unaware of their options, or even dismissive of them, while they were focused on only one thing: making their business work. It is also my honor to be able to pass on this wisdom in your language, in terms you can relate to and with a deep practical understanding of not only the strategies for impact, but the tactics to make it happen.

You know as well as I do that we're on this dance floor of life just once and if we want to bust a move, shine and do great things, we must start today. In this next segment I will help you connect with your philanthropic side and teach how to implement strategies that will help you enjoy big impact giving.

The secrets to **GIVE back** focus on giving back to ourselves, our families, our communities and the causes that matter most to us.

GROW GET GIVE

1. Be Kind

To You, Your Family, To Your Community, And The Causes That Matter Most To You

"Work hard, care more," said Leeza Gibbons, Emmy award-winning TV host, incredible product spokesperson, and winner of the Celebrity Apprentice. She is arguably one of the highest profile "nice ones" in business and TV. She is a humanitarian who owes her success to being kind and decent in life and business. Her belief about work comes from her upbringing and her mother who lead by example, teaching Leeza principles like, "show up and do your best and let go of the rest". Doing good and doing right by people is a powerful way to win over, persuade and enjoy fulfillment. Of course, this is persuasion by genuine service and caring.

Leeza certainly understands that nice people can finish first by being kind. It is a recipe for success. Make no mistake, she is not a pushover and is a shrewd businessperson. It is possible that having business savvy and a no BS approach is consistent with treating people honestly and decently.

Kindness is simple. It takes altruism, compassion and vulnerability. Too often people want to belittle or find fault. They are inclined to disparage those who are successful. Wealth need not come as a result of sacrificing others or your goodness.

To be influential one must be genuine. When you are genuine, you are honest. Honesty allows others not to simply trust you, but to trust in your word and your intentions. Market economies thrive when the participants trust the agreements they make and are clear about the intentions of counter parties.

Entrepreneurs live with risk all the time. The risk of new ideas, big investments, or new marketing is uncertain enough. If you throw in the risk that people won't be true to their word, or they will mislead you, then simple business risks are amplified and often become too great. Entrepreneurs are susceptible to people with bad intentions, as we are optimistic, visionary and hopeful that we might be able to achieve bigger success.

If someone is skilled at convincing you with lies or half-truths, or is simply disingenuous, agreements break down and the exchange of energy, money or services is risked.

Kindness eliminates an important risk of dealing and as such, people and businesses will be more inclined to work with you and you will be more likely to have or impact that you seek.

"Work hard, care more." It's a great motto, it's a great way to be, and when push comes to shove, when you're put into a situation of struggle and challenge, then be kind in how you deal with it and how you deal with people. Make Leeza's motto yours.

2. Profit Through Kindness

When I teach entrepreneurs, I cover the six "P-s" of business success.

1. Passion,
2. Purpose,
3. People,
4. Positioning,
5. Process,

The last "P" at the summit of **Grow. Get. Give.** Success is...

6. Profit

In my universe, PROFIT = IMPACT. If you live this life well, you can top if off with a profit of kindness. This represents winning nice, serving others, and profiting through attraction. My good friend and author Jill Lublin, four-time best-selling author, in her book "Profit of Kindness" discussed how it's not mutually exclusive to be kind and to have business success at the same time.

When I met Leeza Gibbons she said that *"kindness is the currency of influence"*. I thought that sentiment was poignant and inspiring for entrepreneurs who can look at profit as influence. We are clearly in business to make money and a profit. Business can be done for the benefit of others, as well as make a positive impact, but it is NOT charity work. In charity there is a social impact and often intangible impacts that are not the result of the pursuit of financial gain. Money is donated or granted and the return on investment is often difficult to measure. Profit is not the primary driver. Funding is found through gifts. Products or services are not created to sell. Beneficiaries receive funding or resources to serve the cause. I often argue that charities should have financial sustainability and that they must not become the charitable cause while supporting a cause. This could be construed as pursuit of profit, yet the inflows of capital come in many ways and aren't always monetary (i.e. volunteerism, advocacy, etc.).

Let's get back to business. Profit is the primary motive of any business. It provides growth, sustainability, improvement and expansion. Stakeholders benefit financially. A business might do well, but having a benevolent impact is not a prerequisite. I understand not every business is formed to make a positive impact or change the world. Some exist purely to attract money and create wealth for the owners. However deep or shallow a business is, my preference is impact. I work with those owners who choose to make their bigger impact through what they do.

Kindness is easy. It takes far less energy to deliver and sticks to our natural tendencies to be nice. We learn early in life to say please and thank you. It is not ingrained in us to be aggressive, mean-spirited or ruthless. Putting kindness first should be natural for us.

Lasting profit or impact certainly requires a solid foundation. That foundation is constructed on decency, integrity, trust and kindness. When you build your business with a base of genuineness and are honest about why you do what you do, you will attract others who share these values. When you deal with decency and respect, you can serve people better and lead them more effectively. This always shines through in the positioning of your company, product or brand. Peter Shankman, in his 2014 book, "Nice Companies Finish First", reviewed effective leadership with the premise that it pays to be kind. The hallmark qualities of loyalty, optimism, and humility and quality customer service noted in research done by CEB Inc. found that employees are less likely (87% less) to leave when these values are prevalent, and when they are committed, they perform 20% better. Clearly this has a profit-margin widening effect. Kindness drives profit.

Lastly, when you install processes of kindness in your business that respects stakeholders, you will find less problems, complaints and challenges. You gain entrepreneurial freedom. It is reflected in how you interact with people one-on-one, how you connect with them in your business, how your staff and stakeholders approach others, and how you approach your family and the world around you.

Being kind improves the bottom line.

GROW GET GIVE

3. Break Up With Yourself

"You are the average of the five people you spend the most time with," said Jim Rohn. This statement intends to highlight several things. The first, of course, is the obvious. Who you hang out with will determine where you can expect to be financially. Hang out with motivated high income earners and you'll likely be one of them.

The intention of Jim Rohn's quote is to get you to consider the company you keep and focus your thinking on living as the person you wish to become personally and professionally. Surround yourself with the people who will get you there.

The second, message is that in order to change, grow and succeed, you must shift your thinking and your friends. These are difficult decisions. Be assured, it becomes less difficult as you grow, because the people you attract and learn from and serve will change as you succeed. This is a concept I wish I understood in my late teens and early adulthood - something my parents, mentors or teachers never highlighted. I had great friends who were very bright in terms of their academic achievement, but their personal decision-making and actions weren't focused on success. So much time was wasted on useless activities and foolish behavior. Goals weren't discussed or established, and the concept of future accomplishment didn't hold their attention. They didn't see themselves as successful or on a path to achievement. We had some pretty fun times, for sure, but I could have benefited immensely from a change of scenery. This is not a personal or character judgement. It was not clear to me at the time, but looking back it seems so obvious. Today, I do not intentionally spend time people who don't challenge me, provide insights that I don't already possess, or aren't willing to engage in intellectual rapport. If I can't find those people in person, I look for inspiration through reading. Hanging out with smart people in a literary sense can be just as powerful.

When you break through and grow as a person, and as a business owner, you will see fewer and fewer of your "old" peers. When you look at the mental programming you've done in your life, the types of business decisions you've made, and sometimes you may even need to break up with yourself. That is, break up with your old self.

Often you must change the person you <u>were</u> completely. Replace all old habits with new habits. It's much easier said than done. The whole idea that it takes 28 days to build a new habit is, in my opinion, bullshit. It's not that simple to build new habits that have staying power. Although, I have found that 28 days is a good time frame to break a bad habit. Once deprogrammed, the next step is to replace that old habit with a new better habit. It usually takes six months, a whole year, or even multiple years to establish a resilient new habit.

In the early nineties, I worked as a personal fitness trainer. I served all kinds of people with their fitness, and the overweight, middle-aged clients expected results quickly. This was something I could deliver, but small, quick improvements were easy. Bigger changes tended to take time. They were often disappointed that after six to eight weeks of habit breaking and building fitness behaviour patterns, they weren't achieving the results they had hoped. I would remind them that we were constructing life-long changes. We'd discuss that they were unwinding the effects of twenty, thirty or even fifty years of bad habits that put their bodies in the shape they were. It was entirely unreasonable to believe they could change those deeply ingrained habits in only weeks or even months. Change can be hard, but positive change is always worth the investment.

It might be discouraging to think that new habits are not formed as quickly as old ones are broken. Have hope, because old habits are able to be broken down, rewired, or "un-wired" in a shorter period.

The habit of not doing the old habit is really the new habit.

A great strategy is to institute a habit of replacing actions. If you woke up and smoked first thing in the morning, what you would do as a replacement would be to wake up and go walk or wake up and read, or eat, or meditate, or have a coffee. Maybe smoking isn't a great example because there's truly a physiological addiction factor to it, it goes beyond a habit. However, simple habits like waking up and looking at the world stock markets and then your finances might focus your energy and attention on unconstructive things that are largely beyond your control. Replace the habit, change the routine. Do that for a month, and the likelihood of you resetting that is high. You strip out the old habit and then in time, you can replace it with something more productive or meaningful.

Break up with your old self by changing your past lifestyle, the uninspiring friends that you have, and the types of things you spend your time doing. If it's your habit to only meet with certain people over drinks, but you realize the only things you ultimately have in common are the drinks, then maybe those friends aren't people that you need to reach out to. It doesn't mean you cut them off completely, but try changing that habit and pursuing something else. Read a book, go out to a movie. Find some new friends. Do not get lulled into the comfort and simplicity of the familiar, if the familiar is holding you back.

Being your future successful self requires that you make the change today. If you want to achieve more, and you have a vision for your future self that is better, different, and more accomplished than your current self, then you need to reprogram to be that person today. Behave like the ideal you. Strip away the things from your past and what you're doing today that limit your success. Break up with yourself. Sometimes that's important.

4. Connect People With Your Passion And Purpose

Happiness in life and business occurs when we are operating in a harmonious balance. The earth and nature, as well as our bodies, minds and emotions seek "homeostasis". Such balance consciously arises for us when we live and move with purpose, based on the passion that drives us. It extends to our interactions with others found in family, community and our social and business networks. Ideally, we enjoy the continuity of connections throughout. These are our tribes and some of them have deeper linkages than others. When building your business tribe, you will find people who not only buy your products or services, but share your values. In fact, when your passion is clear and your purpose is understood by everyone around you, the people who share your values will be attracted to you.

When your passion is clear and your purpose is an obvious extension of it, the right people will connect.

At the outset of this book, I discussed moving forward with passion in your business, and reminded you that being passionate about something is not enough. Sharing an ideal with people, customers, and partners is a start. But where do you go next? There is a need to put passion behind purpose and then push forward to achieve your vision or goals. The two are interconnected. Your WHY and your HOW work together.

Victor Frankl, in his bestselling book, "Man's Search for Meaning", described a harrowing recollection of his survival in the Nazi concentration camps during the Holocaust. He made important observations as to why some people survived and others simply did not. Beyond the randomness of the indiscriminate killings, each day, week, month, and year, there was a grueling battle for survival. Some people succumbed and died, while others lived. Seemingly, against all odds, Frankl survived. He summarized that it was due to his will to survive, which came from his life's purpose. He had a strong commitment to a personal, immensely important goal on which to focus upon. The first was to be with his beloved wife and family (not knowing that most of his family had perished), and the next was to share with and teach the world his observations about purposeful existence and survival. When describing the meaning of life, he said, "Everyone has his own vocation or mission in life to carry out a concrete assignment which demands fulfillment. Therein he cannot be replaced, nor can his life be repeated …"

While obviously far removed from the gravity of the life or death struggle faced by Frankl, connecting your passion with your true purpose moves your life and your business to an important result. A purposeful existence drives us daily to have an impact. It allows us to reach for higher goals. Your purpose is not required to carry the weight of a concentration camp existence on its shoulders; however, it should hold you up in times of great stress and give you direction when you need a compass. A life without purpose is a rudderless life. People and customers who share a similar purpose will want to become part of your efforts to make a difference. Share your vision with them openly and often. Start by identifying your purpose and describing your passion to achieve your goals.

5. Connect To A Cause Through Your Experience

Connecting your purpose and future actions to a greater cause will help build a bigger goal to move you forward. It will help you identify with your community. Make an announcement as part of your overall mission and connect it to your business. Doing so will help you to attract customers, who share the same ideals and goals. A common cause important to both you and your ideal customer will bind you together, with the knowledge that your business might help them achieve their own personal goals to give back.

Relationships with customers are strengthened by supporting a common cause.

We are not restricted to singular causes to support. You can decide to back multiple causes as you define your personal giving strategy. Review your life experiences and identify those which changed the course of your life. The ones that were integral in forming who you are today and how you view the world will point you in the right direction. I have written much about this in my prior books on philanthropy. I found in my research that philanthropic people, in their most important altruistic efforts, support causes which they were directly affected by in some way in their lives.

It might be extremely specific, like finding a cure or treatment for pancreatic cancer or more general, such as supporting research for all forms of cancer. The experience might have been one's own journey with the disease, or a world view of the impact of illness on the population. Whichever it is, the deep-rooted connection is personal. It might be a result of something, good or bad, that happened to them. It could have also been an event they witnessed or something that occurred to someone else. Their experience might have been the result of a revelation or decision to join a movement, such as choosing to support climate change initiatives.

For me, a life experience that focused me on giving was growing up in a poor neighborhood where my peer group of friends did not experience the same life opportunities I did. I benefited from a stable home life, with intense love and support from my parents. Even while we lived in a home with occasional financial uncertainty and the dynamics of mental illness, my sister and I were nurtured and supported in our personal development. I experienced advantages that others did not. Some of my neighbourhood friends were lost to their circumstances from the day they were born. As I aged and my social circles and business networks developed, fewer of my childhood peers were in my social circles. Many never had the opportunity to succeed like I did. There are things that impacted my life positively and negatively. My connection to various causes has become clear as a result of my own experiences and those I witnessed.

In order to connect giving with a clear mission, we established our own "Fit Family Fund" in 2008 to provide financial support for three key pillars of family support:

1. Funding family physical health and nutrition,

2. Funding for education,

3. Funding for protection of children.

With a desire to give, we also had a goal to bring our family closer to a singular effort to help other families realize some of the opportunities we enjoyed. There was a chance to instill the concept and the habit of giving with our kids. Each year, we gather to review our three pillars and make decisions about giving based on the charities that we have learned do the most to make an impact in those areas. This is something we do directly that impacts our family as much as it does the beneficiaries of our giving.

On a larger scale, through twenty-two years in the financial service profession, I developed expertise which allowed me to do more by helping others realize their philanthropic goals. This allowed me to make an exponentially bigger impact than anything I could have ever hoped to do alone. Building a business model which helped direct over $12.5 million to charitable causes while saving families almost $5 million in taxes and allowing them to pass on their wealth and legacy to their children and grandchildren, was one of my proudest accomplishments. It would never have been possible without understanding my life experiences and how they connected me to the causes I support.

GROW GET GIVE

6. Select Your Giving Organization Or Start Your Own?

With your sights set on the causes you're motivated to support, you are ready to act. This begins with the need to understand who or what the beneficiaries of your actions will be and exactly what outcomes you seek. Over a decade of serving people with philanthropic intentions, I identified three key steps to making a big impact through giving that I'll share with you.

The first requirement is to select the cause with which you connect on the most profound level. In order to commit to make a long term difference, you need to find what resonates within you to ensure you'll give it the utmost care and attention.

Ask yourself a few questions,

"What would it look like if I were able to make a tangible difference for this cause?

What would I need an organization to do to help me achieve my philanthropic goals?

What are their values and are they effective?"

How do you find a charity that fits the cause you connect to? You can start by leveraging the internet's search engines by plugging in the relevant search terms, and then take the time to sift through the organizations and websites that result. I suggest some caution here. Building an attractive, user-friendly website that sums up that charity's core message in a few paragraphs and pages is easier than building and running an effective charity that consistently delivers measurable results to the cause in question. Therefore, you must look under the surface.

Investigate larger philanthropic organizations and you will see that some of them operate much like big businesses. They might be incredibly well run, but that's not a given. There could be plenty of waste and bureaucracy. Therefore, you must exercise due diligence before you hand over a dime. Let's look at homelessness as an example and start with the big picture. If you decide that you want to "end homelessness", you need to recognize that this is a real stretch goal. It's huge and far-reaching because homelessness exists on both a local and global level.

Start by narrowing things down with a few questions. Do you want to tackle homelessness in your own city? Do you want to reach across the country or around the world? Is putting a roof over a family enough or do you want to address the root cause of their homelessness? Will you dig into mental illness, unemployment or family distress? Do you focus on those who are homeless right now or do you figure out how to keep the next generation from being homeless? If you decide that affordable housing is the key, you may immediately think of Habitat for Humanity. A well-recognized brand that's lauded for the work it does, Habitat for Humanity may be a good fit, but you may also decide that you could provide a fresh approach and perspective, or strategies and actions. You might look at dealing with this on a municipal or policy level. Time and again, I've seen budding philanthropists with deep commitment and raging passion believe that they could produce better results if they started from scratch and created a new organization. I would warn you against launching your own charity out of frustration or hubris. You need to understand the philanthropic landscape and that founding and operating a charity can be even more challenging than running your own company.

For charities, financial accountability is a major issue and impeccable financial reporting must be the standard if you want to maintain your charitable status. It also is something your donors will demand as stewards of their social capital. Are you really interested in acquiring <u>both</u> the philanthropic and financial expertise required to run your new charity? Can you accept and deal with the fact your actions, personally and professionally, will likely be subject to intense public and media scrutiny whether they have anything to do with your charity? Making the shift from a for-profit landscape to a non-profit one is more challenging than it seems. Social impact and (social) returns on investment are notoriously difficult to quantify and as such, scrutiny from the vantage point of a purely for-profit model does not suffice.

Attracting and raising the capital needed to develop and fund the necessary infrastructure and/or grow a charitable organization requires a different approach. It is invariably a much harder pitch when investors will realize only social and other intangible benefits. Gaining a sense of wellbeing or impact is quite different than monetary returns. Differently, the emotional connection and altruism of donors overrides the focus on "returns". However, demands for operational efficiency, as well as evidence of impact when it is sometimes difficult to demonstrate, inevitably increases, not decreases, scrutiny.

If you are still determined to start your own philanthropic initiative, you should start by asking yourself certain tough questions:

"Why do I think I can do a better job than existing charities?

Why do I really want to start my own charity?

Will my charity achieve better results?

What is the real cost of creating another (redundant) organization to support the cause?

Is this about my need for control and/or recognition?"

In Canada alone, there are over 86,000 registered charities. If you look, you will undoubtedly find one, or likely more, that is as committed to your cause as you are.

The second secret to making a big impact through giving is to choose a charity that takes the actions required to produce <u>sustainable</u> results for the cause you want to impact. Should you decide to work with one of the thousands of existing philanthropic organizations, you want to be sure it directly supports the very goals that are important to you. Importantly, you will need tangible proof that they take the actions required to produce their specified results. If you wanted to help reduce or eliminate homelessness in Vancouver or a city like it, what would you do? How would you choose to help? While your focus might be housing, you may want to dive deeper to address its root causes for prevention rather than address the obvious symptom of homelessness.

My third recommendation to making a big impact through organization selection is to invest the time and energy required to thoroughly research and assess the charity that you have identified. Learn how the organization takes the actions required to produce sustainable results for the cause you want to support. If you think about your last donation to charity, could you say you invested more energy in learning about where your money goes and how it will be used than the last time you bought a computer, or a microwave? If we desire bigger impact, we must be willing to invest in the process.

Once you've found the organization and determined that it takes the actions that deliver the results, you're ready for the next steps. Do you feel good about choosing that charity? Don't answer that question until you can show me that you've done your due diligence. Committing to any charity before thoroughly investigating it is, at best, naïve and, at worst, irresponsible. It could be akin to pitching your money out the proverbial window. You'll need to consider and assess their management team, infrastructure, fundraising costs versus funds raised, financial reporting and status, tangible and measurable results and much more.

Do the homework and invest in the process.

GROW GET GIVE

7. Commit

Having made your decision about your cause and what organization you will support is a great start. Projecting your positive energy through the decision isn't going to accomplish much, but it will get you to the next step. In this case, the "decision" is action. In 1988, Nike launched their "Just Do It" campaign and it immediately became synonymous with success and action. Deciding to do something commits you to big impact giving. The first step was when you identified your life experiences and how you connect this to giving actions. Then you identified which cause(s) you will support and reviewed how you might become involved. Either you will support charities which serve the cause, or you might even begin your own charity or foundation to have a more direct impact. There are many deserving charities which exist and would make tremendous use of what you can give. Doing more homework to uncover the organizations that align with your goals will be more rewarding than starting something from scratch. But, inevitably, the most important step is to act. By identifying what you bring to the table with your own strengths you will learn how you will have the biggest impact. You will be giving with time, money, and influence.

Once you understand what your greatest strength is you can commit to give.

We give money through direct financial donations, but we can also give money in more strategic ways. Investing in areas which clear the way or enable your charity to execute their mission more effectively is one way.

Providing goods or services is another. For example, a home builder who wishes to help provide affordable housing could offer supplies or labor to Habitat for Humanity or other groups in their efforts to construct new affordable homes.

We give our time in so many ways, from coaching kids' sports, to volunteering at the local food bank. Filling a needed and important volunteer role brings us closer to the cause and often the beneficiaries of our efforts. Another way volunteering can have a big impact is through participation on committees or boards of directors and even in outside advisor roles. This type of volunteerism can be a tremendous way to connect your specific skills with impactful giving.

Lastly, there is the gift of influence. This is often realized through advocacy. Our role in the community as entrepreneurs, businesspeople, and community leaders offers us a platform to vocalize our commitment to a cause and encourage others to join our efforts. During interviews for my very first book, "Philanthropy; An Inspired Process", one of Calgary's most identifiable philanthropists graciously invested his time with me to share his thoughts and own experiences of giving. One of his many contributions to the community, arguably his most important, had been the establishment of a cardiovascular research center that had ostensibly developed treatments for heart disease and unquestionably saved the lives of hundreds (or thousands) of patients. This was something I was certain he would claim as one of his most important rewards in giving, but when asked what his greatest enjoyment in philanthropy was, he stated it was influencing his wealthy (or wealthier) friends to write larger and larger cheques to fund the charities he supported. One of his greatest strengths in giving was his ability to attract more and more funding to a cause in need.

He was clear on where he would have the biggest impact and that was through his ability to influence others.

I have written about how philanthropy can be defined as the "love of mankind". Well, that love is beautiful, but if you simply exist to enjoy the feeling, then not much gets accomplished, does it? It is the decision to act that does. Making the commitment to shift philanthropy from your personal experience and an idea to action requires motivation. Commit to move forward.

GROW GET GIVE

8. Devise A Strategy To Give Which Plays Into Your Strengths

The first steps in your journey to give back are to bring your personal experiences and motivations to the table and then see how the cause which you wish to support might connect to your business and your customers. In my two books about philanthropy, as well as the previous segments of this book I revealed that taking the time to know how a cause is served by a charity matters. Solving homelessness happens in a variety of ways. It can be through building homes (i.e. Habitat for Humanity), subsidizing rents, employment creation initiatives, or family services. You must decide which cause is sensible for you to fund and align with an organization that is best suited to make an impact.

Now consider what you might be able to do as an entrepreneur. Let's say your business is in the homebuilding industry and you have identified that the cause you wish to support is fighting homelessness. When you did your research, you found that among the many solutions that are out there for this cause, you found that it was the ownership and permanency of a home which gave new owners a sense of pride and belonging. They had a mailing address. The new homeowner instantly became more connected with their community and confident in their place in the world. This translated to better behaviors and achievement in other areas, such as their employment and the education of their children. In order to develop your giving strategy, you identified that your company had excess materials and reduced pricing for materials due to your relationship with suppliers. For a reasonable investment and productive use of your overstock you could provide Habitat for Humanity with enough building materials to complete three homes. As a result, you launched a public awareness campaign through your company that rewarded your customers by connecting them to successful giving simply by selecting your organization over others. A portion of your profits would be used to fund additional materials, while the simple act of building a home created "leftover" materials that were also donated. By making this a corporate initiative, you attract more like-minded customers and do more to further your goals to make an impact.

Another example of giving through your business was how the builders of our home connected their philanthropy to the promotion of their business and community activities. They had been giving back to the community and directing their efforts to cancer research by donating their show homes each year to the various home lottery campaigns to raise funds for Alberta's two main cancer charities. This initiative generated hundreds of thousands of dollars for the charities and provided a strong connection for the company to share their desired giving goals with the community and their prospective customers. Additionally, as people became aware of the home that was being given away, more and more people viewed the home. The entire effort provided an incredible experiential marketing opportunity for the builder to showcase their craft to new potential buyers. Not to mention the fact that the donation would garner a significant tax receipt which would be used to help offset the builder's own gains from the development. How you build your strategy to give back while incorporating your personal and/or business strengths is up to you. I urge you to…

…consider innovative and effective ways that bring the most impact to the cause.

Focus on projects that help you and your customers connect in a manner that is purposefully collaborative. But consider that it might contribute to your bottom line — naturally allowing you to have more and more impact over time. **Profit equals impact for the mission hearted.** If you choose to make a personal contribution, you will need to review the same general principles of selecting the cause and the organization that will help before you invest your own resources for impact. You can give anonymously or publicly; it is up to you. I prefer disclosing philanthropy in order to be a role model and an agent of influence in giving. In my own view, sharing your philanthropy in a public manner is not intended to gain public acceptance or accolades, but to lead others by example. As a corporate leader you can extend your social leadership through sharing.

Another important consideration for giving personally requires that you seek guidance from specialists in the area of planned giving. These individuals might be your financial advisors, accountant, lawyer, or a planned giving professional working with a charity. For precisely the same reasons customers seek you out for your specialized products or services, you too should seek the strategic counsel of professionals who are experts in planned giving. By working with the right people, you will be astounded at the possibilities for impact they uncover for you, and that you never knew you had.

GROW GET GIVE

9. Bring Your Unique Thing To The Effort

In the first section of this book I encouraged you to identify your unique ability in order to grow a strong and profitable niche business. Those attributes are what you should leverage when deciding how you can make a big impact. Understanding what you can offer that is different than others is important. You might find you are better at strategic thinking and planning. Maybe mobilizing and influencing people is something you do better than most, or possibly managing financial resources is what you do well. Could your biggest asset be business building? Whatever the case might be, you should investigate this for yourself to ensure you are making the right contribution with the right organization in the best way possible. Simply because you are passionate about a cause and have a strong desire to experience your impact firsthand doesn't mean you would be best suited or most impactful to serve food at the homeless shelter. Maybe your big impact giving would be better realized by using your contacts to help source or transport the food that will be served daily. It is possible you would be better positioned in an advisory capacity, helping guide strategic or logistical actions.

As in any successful business, you need to ask yourself how you or your organization will create leverage. If you are going to step up and bring a non-profit social enterprise to life, how would you help it to grow and thrive the same as you would in a for-profit setting? There have been many companies over the years which have added unique social enterprise to their for-profit offering. There are many examples such as Starbucks and their Fair Trade Certified™ coffee, CIBC's Run for the Cure ongoing support for the Canadian Breast Cancer Foundation. Even when the show

Survivor auctions off its props from each season to raise funds for the Elisabeth Glaser Pediatric AIDS Foundation there is a clear connection to social impact through the enterprise. Finally, West Jet, Canada's most innovative airline, has focused their efforts on families and children's health to donate flights and raise awareness to help Ronald McDonald House Charities, Make-A-Wish Canada and Boys and Girls Clubs.

When entrepreneurs are acknowledging their strongest attributes, unique and creative social enterprise initiatives emerge.

10. Build Your SROI

Build a social return on investment (SROI). Connecting your business directly to the support of a charitable cause will require you to review the potential for any such pursuit. In a market economy, business exists to produce profit for the goods and/or services it provides in order to reinvest, grow the business, and pay its shareholders. That is the definition of a for-profit business.

In the not-for-profit world, the so-called profit is redirected to social good and/or designated beneficiaries. The direct benefit to the cause is the profit. Revenues, or in this case donations, are collected with the intention of flowing them through to the beneficiaries after administrative, operational and fundraising costs. The evidence of an investment return in non-profit work is sometimes hard to identify and even harder to measure when dealing with social or environmental impact. Donors do not expect financial return other than the intrinsic rewards of giving, their affiliation with the cause, and the tax credit that might come for the gift or advertising expense. Although I strongly believe they should, most donors rarely hold the organization accountable to measuring or reporting some form of SROI.

As an entrepreneur deploying a charitable giving or social enterprise strategy, it would be very important for you to be able to measure your SROI to learn whether you are making an impact or whether the initiative is worth continuing. While the goal would be to create a sustainable financial model to allow for the enterprise to continue, it will be likely that this entity will require fundraising on an ongoing basis. Money will be raised by you, your business, and other external donors or stakeholders of the enterprise. Economists would argue that you can quantify anything, and thus measure the success or effectiveness of it. I agree. In fact, economics can guide or change behaviors. You will need to be astute to truly understand the economic impact of your efforts.

If you were to develop a social enterprise that funds building affordable homes, what would the economic impact be for the beneficiary family? What can you measure? For starters, with a permanent address, they could be more employable, thus employment income and taxes are measurable over time. The family, in twenty years, might earn a lifetime income of a million dollars, paying three hundred thousand in taxes and investing in local businesses by consuming products in their community. Their children would be more secure and comfortable and likely able to focus more in school, thus improving their opportunity for success or employment in their adulthood. The residual effect of this stability could also be that they interrupt the pattern of poverty and raise their own productive family. The list goes on. There are many other measurable economic benefits including the reduction of social, health and economic costs. However, if you were not successful in sheltering just one family, even more taxpayers could be affected in the resulting burden on our social, health and maybe even justice systems. SROI is measurable and you must identify the meaningful data — either in the positive impacts, or the societal costs.

How you engage in implementing a charitable strategy that results in a positive SROI will fall back on what your strengths are personally and as a business. It seems natural for a company in the homebuilding business to engage in a homeless initiative or a grocery chain to actively be involved with the local food bank. But what does your technology company do? Finding the right fit for your corporate strengths and your philanthropic interests takes intentional thought. You can direct money, time, or influence on a cause. The choice is yours.

GROW GET GIVE

11. Redefine Giving

There are a multitude of charitable organizations doing so many different things, but fundamentally their causes remain pretty much the same. For example, caring for and protecting animals is a regular theme of a cause. Achieving impact, though, occurs in a variety of ways. Traditional approaches to animal causes range from rescue, to providing homes for animals, to advocating for animal rights and protection of entire species. Community outreach and advocacy of animal care and welfare are preventative measures that reduce abuse or neglect. Not all methods will be or should be conventional. Innovative methods have been applied to screening for families rescuing pets. Some organizations have multi-step animal adoption processes, where the initial introduction is made at the kennel. The next is an interview process, then a brief introduction at the family's home, then approval and a gradual move to make it a permanent home and adoption.

You are an innovator in business, so extend that creativity for your big impact giving by becoming an innovator in social good.

Entrepreneurs can change how we give in many ways. You are doing it all the time. Everything from micro-loan programs to work share to social enterprise requires the innovative thinking that entrepreneurs are known for. I enjoyed spending time with two amazing young Canadian philanthropists/activists, Craig and Marc Kielburger. They redefined giving with an entrepreneurial spirit and vision that created the inspiring

WE Day phenomenon to bring attention and support to their Free the Children charity.

They believe "in a world where all children are free to achieve their fullest potential as agents of change."

Their mission is "to empower youth to remove barriers that prevent them from being active local and global citizens."

The Kielburgers understood the power of influencing change through grassroots levels with the youth of our society. The energy that children bring, combined with the future influence they will gain, gives their WE Day events immense impact, as they are used to reward teens for their own selfless and creative acts of giving.

Held in cities across North America and the United Kingdom, these one-of-a-kind experiences are in demand across the world. They have attracted some of the most important key note speakers of our time, such as Martin Luther King III, Magic Johnson, Malala, Mikhail Gorbachev, Larry King, Archbishop Desmond Tutu, some of the most exciting contemporary music acts, such as Nelly Furtado, Hedley, Down With Webster, Selena Gomez and Macklemore, as well as celebrities ranging from Demi Lovato to Natalie Portman, Diane Keaton and Henry Winkler. Attendance for school children is earned by their community service and the events are the reward. Major corporations have realized the potential and now are providing significant funding for the events. The Kielburgers' vision and entrepreneurial spirit has redefined the way teens are moved to connect with charity. They raise funds for Free the Children and WE Day from individuals and corporate donors.

Over the years, they have attracted a substantial amount of sponsorship from major corporations who understand the impact WE Day has. Major companies, such as Microsoft, Allstate, DHL, Unilever, Royal

Bank of Canada (RBC), Potash Corp, Virgin Atlantic, and Barclays, to name a few, have made considerable financial commitments. Their Free the Children WE-Charity raised over $66 million worldwide in 2017 and a couple hundred thousand screaming and cheering teen ambassadors across the continent now carry the WE Day message to their peers, their communities, and home to their parents. Some of the first high school participants are now young adults working and making their own impact.

The Kielburgers combined traditional charity work, social enterprise, social networks, grassroots programs, volunteerism, and a strong celebrity connection to change the way giving is supported and implemented. They made global impact cool among the toughest demographic to inspire – young teens. Their platform is unique, and they've turned giving on its head. You don't have to emulate Craig and Marc in your efforts to have a big impact, however, you are a leader in your market for a reason … most likely because you had a unique vision for an opportunity that no one else saw. Challenge your innovative side to find the connection between your vision and making impactful change.

GROW GET GIVE

12. Serve Others

Robert Cialdini beautifully illustrated the law of reciprocity in sales with his example of the practices of the Hare Krishnas in the 1970's and their gifts of flowers in the airports. As humans, we are almost irresistibly and unconsciously compelled to reciprocate generosity. When they gifted you their flowers and handed them to you, placing them in your possession before you could decline them, there was an immediate and undeniable response that you felt you should somehow give them money or something in return, even if you were going to simply throw the flowers away. They understood this "law" and capitalized on it. Where most people viewed this as a nuisance, and even knew what was coming when the Hare Krishnas were around, the effect was still there.

The law of reciprocity is so strong that we cannot resist it even though we try. Even by acknowledging it's there, we are weak to defend against it. The rudimentary primal instinct to participate in a symbiotic social group in order to secure safety, affirmation and ultimately genetic success was wired long ago. Giving to get and understanding the law of reciprocity is crucial to selling success in order to move people from an idea or perspective to your side of the table or to some common position. Those things require you to sell and reciprocity is one of the most powerful laws out there regarding giving to receive.

Let's be clear. Giving, in my life, is founded on altruism and impact. But there is nothing wrong with the plain fact that giving comes back to you in many ways, some of them monetary. In fact, if you are working with and serving your ideal customer, this powerful force will reflect your shared values, your shared objectives and good intentions. The result is always win-win-win-win: your client, you, your client's impact goals and your impact goals. There is a cascading effect to your actions. When you succeed in giving in this way, the result is immeasurable.

12b. Give Before You Get

I have one more piece of wisdom to share from Kevin Eastman, former Assistant coach of the NBA's world champion Boston Celtics and former VP of Operations for the LA Clippers. He has assembled decades of leadership ideas, thoughts and concepts, along with incredible anecdotes and stories he learned firsthand from some of the best coaches, leaders and professional and elite amateur basketball players. Coaching athletes for so long and being surrounded by some of the absolute best coaches on the planet during his career allowed him to focus on how relationships matter. He says, "Get into the mind space through the heart space." Be productive, caring and connecting, and you'll find success in your business by earning a position in the minds of your prospects and customers. When you give of yourself to people emotionally, connect with their hearts, and find a common mission, you become well-positioned to serve them. Live by a goal to serve and give before you ask for anything.

Shark Tank celebrity, creator of the infomercial, billion-dollar empire builder and master pitchman, Kevin Harrington once said that before he even considers joint venturing or working with a serious partner or prospect, he will serve them for a year before he even asks for anything. That is before he even presents the idea of a sale or a deal together. Let that sink in. He works to build the relationship for a year!

Now, Harrington has a far different budget and cash flow for his life than we do, which might give him the luxury of time. It is something I observed about the ultra-rich when I worked in the investment industry. One of the secrets to wealth and the rich-getting-richer phenomenon was that they had time. They were in no rush, rarely acted in haste and could be patient to allow relationships, markets, investments and businesses to work. When you are bootstrapping entrepreneur you might feel a little more sense of urgency, so waiting for a year builds a sense of discomfort in us. But wait you must. An entire year might be a lot to ask, but exhibiting the patience is paramount. Financially, we might need to close business more quickly, but don't rush. You'll never know if they're a high-quality relationship if you skip serving and don't commit to the process. You might also miss the important signals that a relationship might be a poor quality one. Rushing to meet your personal motivations or your own result is disingenuous. It's selfish to give with an expectation of reciprocity in that way. No one is indebted to you because you served them, so serve selflessly.

Serve not knowing what lies in the future but work to find common wins. What can it hurt to give your mind and your heart to someone in a serving role before you ask them to engage or participate with you in a business capacity? Give before you get. As Kevin Eastman says, "Get into the mind space through the heart space."

13. Give Yourself Permission To Take Time For You

The most successful entrepreneurs take time for themselves. They make it a priority. In fact, it is something that I encourage my clients to build their lives around. Decide what is important to you and gives you happiness, then build your work around that. Determine what you want your business to fund and support, then construct it. The outputs will be a combination of time, money and energy. The North American business culture puts the emphasis on work first and reward later. Somehow hard work, long hours and a grinding schedule have become admirable pursuits, when it really is a recipe for illness, poor relationships and a shortened life span.

Years ago, as I was taking definitive steps toward making the transition from the investment business to coaching full time, I had a conversation with my coach, James. I shared my frustration that I felt I didn't have enough time in my week to write, create and build a clientele around my advisory business. In fact, I couldn't even find time to exercise. He asked why this was a challenge. I had an associate, hired consultants and had well-constructed processes for my business. I said I worked from 6am to 5pm each day. I spent the last few hours of my day trying to work on my new initiative but was always interrupted. Then he said something that I won't forget. He said, "If you're done at 1:30pm or 2pm…leave." I pushed back saying that I needed to set an example for my employee, that I had peers who would think I was skipping out on my responsibilities and clients who might think less of me. He was adamant. "Leave," he told me. "You hired the right assistant to give you freedom and you don't take it. He is your employee. You are not there to show him how long you can stay in the office or please him with your attendance. Quite the opposite. Show him how a well-run business operates. Being a business owner means freedom. If he doesn't like it, he might leave, but you have a process to hire the right person and there are always people who will want the work." That was all I needed – permission. From that day forward, I left the office at 2pm and started working from my home office Monday mornings. I even worked on my other pursuits all-day Friday most weeks. It was one of the best decisions I ever made about my time. I made it a habit to give myself permission to take time for me. Giving yourself permission to step away from work can be hard for the wired entrepreneur. It means resetting your mindset by focusing on the time away from work.

From 2005 through 2011, I was training heavily for a variety of triathlon races. My longest was a half ironman, or a 70.3 event. I trained and raced in two of them. The duration of a race was roughly five and a half hours. The training for a triathlon can be immensely taxing at times — from a physical point of view, a mental one, and even more specifically, a time management one. If you want to perform well (or even finish, and not drop out due to exhaustion), you feel you must "put in the miles" or you'll be very painfully surprised by your body's reactions late in the event. I learned mid-way through those years that often putting in <u>no</u> miles is better than putting in bad ones.

With a race looming and a need to prepare, you are constantly compelled to squeeze your workouts in. It is, however, as important to take time away to recover, rejuvenate, rest, and repair. In fact, it is more important at certain times through the training cycle. As you age, you must listen to your body (and mind) for this. The same is true in business. It is impossible to be effective and keep your foot to the pedal constantly. Without a doubt, something will break down. Taking time for yourself at regular intervals will help to extend your run. Additionally, knowing when those "bad mile days" are happening is important. When they occur, you must give yourself permission to simply step away and regroup without guilt. You'll be better for it.

Preserving your mental health is an important way to serve yourself.

You can help preserve yourself by setting personal goals. It is simple. When you write down the business goals that are most important to you, they tend to happen. There is something powerful in the act of writing. When you write down personal goals in your life that are not work related, they also tend to happen more, as opposed to never doing it. Time will escape you and life will throw you curveballs. If you haven't written down your own personal goals and taken steps to achieve them, you will find they are pushed aside. Put them on paper and plan for them. Next, share them with someone you trust. That added level of accountability helps.

Take care of your personal health. There is nothing more important in this world than our physical health. Do not drive your business objectives forward despite your mental or physical health. All the financial achievement in the world cannot buy your health back once it is compromised. Permit yourself to invest in your well-being by scheduling time for exercise, eating sensibly, and listening to your body. When listening to your body, do not ignore the physical signs that tell you things are going off track like shortness of breath or poor sleep. If you experience weight gain or pains on moving you must attend to these symptoms. Increased emotional sensitivity or short temperedness are also symptoms of stress. These are all signals that you need to listen more closely to what your body is telling you. See your physician regularly and share these signs

openly. Pamper to rejuvenate yourself. This can come in many ways —
from booking a regular massage, to personal grooming, to that quiet time
spent with a glass of wine or tea and a good book, and even cat napping.
Whatever your idea of pampering is, it is up to you to do it. These mental
getaways of indulgence can have amazing positive effects on your mind
and body.

14. Eat Well

Moderation is consistent with the universe and your body's natural tendency to find its balance. Too much of one thing always results in an action or reaction that is designed to offset it. This is true of the internal systems of your body in hormone and chemical balance, energy management and fuel. Go too far in one direction, like abstaining from food, and your body thinks you are starving and lowers its metabolism to reduce energy consumption and increase fuel storage (food) as fat. If you add too many vitamins or hormones to your system, the glands and organs that produce or process these things will lower their functioning or even cease altogether. When you stop the supplementation, your bodily systems might not even ramp back up again and damage becomes permanent.

Your body deals unconsciously with these things, while you make conscious, intentional decisions about what you do and what goes into your body. Your consciousness is often guided by emotions and that is difficult to change. Emotions release powerful chemicals in your body which create feedback loops, often for reward. Behaviors formed around emotional rewards, therefore, are difficult to modify. These behaviors are what we call habits and while they are difficult to modify, they are not impossible to change.

One way to manage the emotional is to build habitual actions to reduce the energy it takes. Think about it. We all have our vices, right? Quite frankly, eating is a pleasurable thing to do. Eating and drinking well is wonderful. Consumption is pleasure you enjoy. Exercise, sex, even smart phone use/social media engagement are habit-forming. The extreme side of excess is where imbalance occurs, though occasional indulgences are manageable. Introduce moderation to your life and you will find altering habits to be much easier. Allow yourself to consume without restriction on variety but apply limitation to quantity.

Seek moderation without extreme eating or drinking. This means quantity as well as quality. Completely cut out extreme alcohol and sugary drink consumption. Moderate your wine, alcohol, soda, red meat, chocolate, breads, pastas, etc. It's difficult because eating is driven by your pleasure centers and has a direct relationship with emotional satisfaction and gratification. You need not look further than the "Food Network" or better yet, the late Anthony Bourdain's TV series. The joy of travel, food experimentation, social experience and cultural immersion are all essential parts of eating. Endorphins are released in the enjoyment of it. All are habit forming.

We must break established bad habits and create new positive ones. Breaking habits is easier than forming long term new ones. Rewiring of your neural pathways and lasting modification of hormone or neuro chemical systems will take time. Give yourself six months of adhering to a new habit and you will find it sticks. THIS IS HARD. You will fail or falter a lot. But once a new habit is formed, you can take another step forward.

When you think of eating modification, consider the word 'd-i-e-t'. John Assaraf was featured in the blockbuster movie and book, "The Secret" and is the founder and CEO of "NeuroGym", a research and development company that creates evidence-based programs producing powerful and measurable results that work safely and effectively. One key message he offers is that the brain can be re-programmed - we can essentially "rewire" neural pathways through "innercise".

I enjoyed hearing him speak and when speaking about diet, he encouraged us to eliminate the word from our vocabulary. You do this by changing your thinking about diet. Change the word, change your thinking.

A good business plan tells you what tools and tactics you need to implement your strategy. If you want to perform better physically, sleep better and look better, there are very key things you must do to make that happen. If you want to work out more, ski, ride a bike, or golf; you must fuel your body in a way that creates the optimum energy level and regeneration needed to do it. No different from how you would approach business, this will require a bit of research to learn what types of fuel and how much of it you must put into your body. So do the homework and understand what fuel you need for your body to work at optimum levels. **Replace D-I-E-T with F-U-E-L** as your new term and embrace it as a concept or mantra for how you eat. You will never choose to diet again.

It is like one of my coaching clients and successful six-figure personal fitness professional, Geoff, says, "I don't give a shit what you weigh…your sense of success goes beyond the number on the scale." He's right. Building strength, building confidence and success requires adding to who you are and what you offer.

Think about it. 'Diet' and 'being on a diet' are restrictive terms. Diet doesn't indicate moderation or good health. It indicates restriction and limits, right? How can you live a life of abundance when your most primal needs force you to contain what is natural? How can you stay on a path of health and happiness when artificial limits are imposed? When we feel limited or restricted, we tend not to want to stick to the program. That is not a natural state. We want to exist happily, feel well and "operate" optimally. Using an approach of moderation is a way of enjoying and being part of it. Knowing what fuels are needed and how much you should or should not take in will help optimize your health. Removing the implied limits and focusing on what is good for you to eat, versus what you cannot, will enhance your happiness.

If we want to perform mentally and physically at our peak, or at least at optimum levels, then we must consider how we fuel our bodies and what we consume, because it reflects very well on our energy levels, alertness, sleep patterns, and capacity for work, pleasure or enjoyment. You know that what you consume, including alcohol or too much sugar, can disrupt sleep, the levels of hormones that go through your body, serotonin, endorphins and other hormones that we rely on for regulation of our bodies, emotional health and physical health. So, eat well. Eat with moderation, and let's cut out the concept of diet.

15. Stay Healthy

Even when you eat right and exercise, there are many things that can derail your health and, in turn, your progress. Adaptability is great to manage your stress levels, but there are still risks to your health. It doesn't what your profession is in order to enjoy the time at work and the time away from work, we must stay healthy. In other words, we must avoid getting sick or injured whenever possible. That doesn't mean living in a bubble, but it does mean making smart decisions. In this rapidly shrinking world, it means managing germ and bacteria exposure. For example, not long ago, I was in the final few weeks push for attendance at a three-day summit I was holding. The challenge was that I was starting this up in a brand-new community. It was ambitious to even try so quickly, with a shallow contact list as the "new" guy in town. My attendance numbers were low, but I was hoping to attract a few more people to attend by simply going out into the community and personally extending face-to-face invitations. Three weeks prior to the event, I got extremely ill with the flu and was bed ridden for three days, confined to my house for an entire week. I could not and did not want to face anyone; my throat was raw, and my voice was gone, so had to resort to online marketing only, abandoning the more effective direct approach. I know that this cost me a few more attendees and it put my revenue at risk by reducing the possible buyers in the audience. The flu cost me time and money. At worst, this time it was possibly $20,000. Luckily, this wasn't a bigger event with more up-front investment risk. What staggered me was the fact that a simple microscopic virus took me down. I passed on the flu shot three months earlier. A mistake.

I live in Canada and have often told adventure-seeking tourists it is the big things (animals like bears, cougars, elk, coyotes, etc.) that can kill you. However, when you travel near the equator and in the tropics, it is the small things – the insects, spiders, snakes, scorpions and other critters that will do the dirty deed. You must be aware of this. Even more threatening , while travelling through airports, buses, trains, cities, and rural areas on this planet, it is disease and illness that are the biggest threats. Bacteria, germs, and viruses are some of the most impactful risks we face. How do you protect yourself against illness? Avoidance is part of the solution, but not always possible, so building your immunity through lifestyle and vaccination is critical, as is healthy hygiene.

Milton Berle, comedian and actor for 80 years, used to say, "Good evening ladies and germs" He wasn't simply being funny by talking down the gentlemen, he meant it. He would say, "I call you ladies and gentlemen, but you know what you really are." Men aren't necessarily germs, but the premise is that they're not only people in the room. They also are carriers of potential illness. It's not good for your psyche if you go through life paranoid or worried if you touch, breathe or are exposed to other people's air. Take a measured approach, but always be vigilant.

There are very simple things you can do when managing your exposure to germs. Frequent hand washing is one of the easiest and most effective ways. If you're in large groups be sure to wash your hands pre-event and post-event, or even during a longer event. You can use a hand sanitizer, but it is more effective to thoroughly wash. Only running your hands under the water (i.e. getting them wet) isn't cleansing. You must do more than rinse your hands. You need to wash your hands with soap thoroughly. Think of it. During events, or parties, you've shaken the hands of, or at least touched, 10 or 15 other people or even more. Food is served by a server and all the hands that have come near your plate or glass before them. Before you decide it's time to eat, your first decision should be to wash your hands. This is something most people forget to do. I admit I have often missed this step.

Washing your hands regularly, but not obsessively, is prudent. We can't afford to be ill frequently. It disrupts our lives, disrupts our flow and erodes our overall health. Especially if you're working and traveling a lot, your immune system might already be suppressed or compromised. I don't know what your day to day health is like, but if you're not operating at your optimal health and you happen to be exposed to contagions, you may in fact become infected. Illness then kills your days, your week or beyond. It's the kind of time off or "stay-cation" that you don't want.

It is not productive to spend your down time recovering from illness. You want to rejuvenate and refresh. I side strongly with science that shows value in exposing oneself to various germs and bacteria. Your body builds immunity to illness and manages to ward off the bad bugs. This is a proven fact, but it does not always hold true when we encounter something our body has never experienced before. Nor does it matter much when we are exhausted or physically compromised. We will get sick. It happens, but the severity doesn't have to put us in bed for three days. Generally, you don't need to go as far as wearing a mask. But you might if there's a highly infectious airborne illness that's going through the community. Vaccinations work. Be sure yours are up to date and appropriate for the area of the world you will be in.

Eating at restaurants, food fairs, and fast food chains exposes you to germs in obvious places, but there are many things we don't normally consider when protecting ourselves from illnesses. For example, some time ago, our family was at Subway (I'm not picking on Subway as the only culprit, because it could be any organization). Our son told us not to use ice from the machines. He said he learned that the containers for the ice in the top of the beverage machines never get cleaned. He said he saw this program on it and the bacteria in there are staggering. While it feels like it would be a closed system with minimal bacteria, he said that, the fact is that they don't clean it. He said that is why he would never want to have that ice.

We must not become obsessive about hygiene, but it is hard to ignore some facts. One of the worst places for exposure is an airplane. Planes and airports are very difficult places for people to manage their risks. Not only do you have a lot of people in a confined space, but you might also have people from all over the planet, and if they're not on your plane, they were on another plane that was in the airport or seat at the gate that you might have waited in.

Traveling through airports, bus and train terminals increase the risk of exposure to illness. Here are some tips for travel:

1. Drink bottled water,
2. Wash your hands regularly,
3. Cover your own nose and mouth when sneezing or coughing, avoid visibly ill people,
4. Wipe down surfaces like table trays and armrests where possible.
5. Turn on your air vent. The air in the plane is cleaned and recirculated.
6. Get oxygen. Open those valves and get air flowing.
7. Hydrate and avoid caffeine and alcohol (they are diuretics).
8. Try to reduce the frequency you touch your face with your hands

Airports are doing well to becoming hands-free in bathrooms by not having to flush or touch the taps. They have even removed all unnecessary doors/door handles. That's helpful for general avoidance of bacteria and germs that are out there.

When you touch down and are headed away from the airport, crank open the windows on the car you are in. I love doing this right away when I pick up an Uber or a cab or even in my own car. I open the windows regardless of the temperature to get fresh air into my lungs and kind of rejuvenate my lungs from being confined to breathing manufactured and filtered air. Think about it: when you're in an airport, in a plane, and then an airport again, you could be there two to ten hours in a day. You're not getting fresh air. It is recirculated and hopefully filtered air. This is air shared with hundreds, if not thousands of other people who are in various states of health. The air system is bombarded with so much.

That's just my two cents for being well. It is for your health and illness prevention.

GROW GET GIVE

16. Get Sleep

You will notice I did not say "rest", I said sleep. Simply resting is not what your body needs to rejuvenate. <u>Restful sleep</u> is critical to good health. It's how the body mentally and physically heals itself. Sleep is a period where your brain and your mind reset. The sleep state allows your brain to processes things in your subconscious that you wouldn't otherwise be processing during the day. While awake, the conscious mind subjects itself to distraction, fixations and closed regimented thinking. Additionally, many thoughts are not processed through the day as they are not meaningful in the moment, nor are they necessarily helpful to address.

Things that you ignore or put in the back of your brain can be sorted out when your subconscious mind works optimally during sleep. They might even manifest as dreams, nightmares or concerns. If you're unsettled by needing to deal with ongoing challenges that are nagging at you, a regular sleep state works these things out. This can result in broken sleep and you wake up thinking about whatever challenge or problem that you have. It is a signal to your conscious mind from your subconscious mind that you need to deal with something. Anyone will attest to the fact that once a major issue has been reconciled and put behind you, you "sleep easier". Well, it is entirely true. Sleep is a key element to the process needed to work things out. It is not just a reflection that things are sorted, but integral to well-being.

How much do you need? Well, adults are recommended they get seven to nine hours of quality sleep per night. Ideally, this is continual. Broken sleep can be detrimental, but awakening between REM sleep cycles isn't as bad as broken REM cycles. The sleep cycle includes the stages before and after REM (rapid eye movement – this is your dream state) and is as much as two hours long for young people, as short as thirty minutes for older adults, and contains five or so REM periods through a night. Adults getting four to six cycles per night will feel rested and recharged. When you consider your physical health, think of this as recharging. For example, if you get four hours of highway driving out of your Tesla Model S and can get to a Supercharging station, you'll recharge your car in roughly one hour, maybe longer. If you don't charge fully, you'll simply fall short of your destination and embarrassingly need to be towed or rescued with a charge. The recharge rate for a Tesla is slightly better than our human recharging requirements, but sleep will recharge you in 1/3 of a 24-hour day. The other 2/3 are spent expending physical and mental energy. It is as plain as that. Without the commitment to sleep, you'll basically go nowhere. As a physical rejuvenator and refresher, sleep is important. In fact, it is as important as your fuel intake. If you're not trying to capture at least seven or nine hours of sleep a day in your life, then you're starving your body; you're robbing it of its ability to heal, to fight off illness, or to grow and develop.

If you have a fitness regimen, activity or hobby you also participate in, the energy you need to enjoy this shouldn't be depleted. Mihaly Csikszentmihalyi, author of *FLOW: The Psychology of Optimal Experience* highlighted that FLOW in a physical sense requires the ability to participate in that physical activity. Flow is important in a cathartic way. It allows us to experience absolute focus, which in turn elevates important hormones and neuro-chemicals in turn energizing us. If we can experience this in a planned and regular way, we can build confidence and enjoy more happiness. You will not be able to experience flow if you are unable to endure the needed output to get there. Without sleep, your body won't recover and respond in the same way.

Moodiness, irritability, stress, and poor emotional and cognitive behavior are symptoms of a lack of sleep. Often, sleep deprivation is indicated as a root cause of such mental signals.

Here are some tips about how to sleep more restfully. Arianna Huffington, an incredibly successful publisher, owner and entrepreneur, has now become a vocal spokesperson for quality living to work well. You could call her a sleep evangelist. She admittedly did everything wrong when it came to sleep, eating and exercise while building her empire. It aged her, whittled away her health and was sending her down the road to illness and poor health. She was determined to fix that, so she researched the benefits of sleep and applied it to her life. Huffington has become somewhat of an expert in the area of restfulness and sleep. She says to get sleep, (https://www.mindbodygreen.com/0-24490/arianna-huffingtons-12-secrets-to-your-best-sleep-ever.html) these are the most important habits to establish:

1. Create a bedroom environment that's dark, quiet, and cool (between 60 and 67 degrees).

2. Turn off electronic devices at least 30 minutes before bedtime.

3. Don't charge your phone next to your bed. Even better: Gently escort all devices completely out of your room.

4. Stop drinking caffeine after 2 p.m.

5. Use your bed for sleep and sex only—no work!

6. Keep pets off the bed (sorry, Mr. Snuffles).

7. Take a hot bath with Epsom salts in the evening to help calm your mind and body.

8. Wear pajamas, nightdresses, or even a special T-shirt—it'll send a sleep-friendly message to your body. If you wore it to the gym, don't wear it to bed.

9. Do some light stretching, deep breathing, yoga, or meditation to help your body and your mind transition to sleep.

10. Choose a real book or an e-reader that does not emit blue light, if you like to read in bed. And make sure it's not work-related: novels, poetry, philosophy—anything but work.

11. Sip chamomile or lavender tea to ease yourself into sleep mode.

12. Write down a list of what you're grateful for before bed. It's a great way to make sure your blessings get the closing scene of the night.

Good night!

17. Move To Stay Alive

In the give section of this business book, I discussed eating and sleeping. Now I'm going to share thoughts about moving. If you haven't formed the habit of exercise or physical activity it will be the one thing you inevitably regret as you age. Throughout your life you need to move, but as you age, the quality of the life you live depends on it. The rate of deterioration of your health, the length of recovery from illness or injury and your mental acuity are affected by your physical fitness. Our wonderful, but fragile shells will let us down in time, but if we maintain them and nurture them, we will create resilience. This resilience gives us a better and longer life. I am not only speaking chronologically, as genetic factors sometimes creep in and limit your life span, but I am speaking qualitatively. 'Live fast, die young,' the rebels yell. Live long, live well and when it is finally time, dying fast would be my choice.

A good friend of mine and I were talking about a guy who would ride his bike all over Calgary – in any season. Those seasons include hot sun, cold snow and temperatures that swing wildly from thirty degrees Celsius above zero to thirty below. The aging man appeared to be a bit eccentric in appearance and biking "accoutrements". Looking at him, you would think the homeless have started riding bikes for distance. He would be seen in one part of the city, then a few hours later, ten or twenty kilometers in another direction. My friend, John, was one of the owners of a successful local bike shop. I mentioned I saw the man and John said he too saw him riding all over the city for years. In fact, we both saw him on the same day in very different and separate, distant locations. We joked about his appearance and our amazement at his age. John is the kind of guy who simply strikes up conversation with anyone, anywhere, any time. He said he had spoken to the man once and asked him about his riding – the miles he rode and why he rides so much. The man, who was in his 80's, simply replied, "I ride to stay alive."

Exercise your body. This is not about attaining super physical fitness. You don't need to be incredibly fit or aspire to be on the cover of Fitness or Outdoor Adventure magazine, or whatever. That's not the goal. But be physically well and in good health so that you have stamina, you're alert, and you can ward off illness. Move. Your body responds to resistance by improving. Walk a bit further as you go each time. Park your car further away from your next appointment. Move against resistance and carry stuff, push things, walk upstairs, downstairs, or up hills. Ride a bike, swim, ski, or clean the house. The great thing about our western culture is that fitness and activity is not viewed as wasteful time. It is considered productive and useful. In fact, in some ways it reflects one's affluence. Any way you look at it, there is no penalty for movement, so there are no excuses either.

One awesome by-product of good physical fitness is improved appearance. As you age, it becomes obvious who has a habit of exercise. They are the ones who appear ready for the day. Maybe not so much that they appear younger and more vibrant (they do), but they are those who don't appear old and beleaguered (sun worshippers are the exception to this – take care of your skin, people!). Looking physically great for your age, and any age, is an attractive thing. It is an outward representation of personal success. You convey a message of success habits. When you're feeling healthy and fit, you look good. People see it on you. They're attracted to it. People love the energy that you exude. There's a glow about people who are fit and healthy.

Donny Deutsch, TV personality, marketing expert and author of *Often Wrong, Never in Doubt — Unleash the Business Rebel Within* (2005), wrote that he found fitness and weight training in mid-life and hit the gym hard. As a result, he looked great, was super strong and felt awesome. He said it was a powerful feeling that he could sit around the boardroom table full of hyper-successful businessmen who looked ten years older than their age and know that he could kick every one of their asses. Even when he was occasionally mentally out-muscled, he gained confidence through the knowledge that his physical health was that much superior to his colleagues. While there are no physical altercations (almost never) in the boardroom, that wasn't the point. The highlight was the confidence that Deutsch gained from his physical strength.

When you are physically fit, you get to live. Our lives are not a right, they are a privilege. A healthy, long journey full of wonderful experiences is a precious thing. Our family lives by the motto, "*Do epic shit*". It is not a challenge, it is a lifestyle. In order to "*Do epic shit*", you must be both willing and physically capable. You are always more willing when you <u>can</u> do it. Too many people are stuck on the sidelines looking up at the mountain, bridge, monument, river or lake from the parking lot or tourist sightseeing point of interest because they don't have the physical ability to venture further. Their pictures and social media stories look great, but that's about it. They never travel further than the length of their selfie-stick. They'll never know the full experience of hiking, biking, snowboarding, skiing, surfing or kayaking. They never see the world from a natural vantage point off the marked path, trail or road. In time, travel becomes difficult and new experiences become limited. Fear of trying something new is one thing, but self-imposed physical limitation is like a prison. Understand that I am not talking about disability, because some of the fittest people I have met have also had some form of physical disability. I am talking about getting winded during twenty meters of walking or being too frail to step down successfully from a short rock ledge to the ground.

I know fat shaming is one of the last painful "shames" and it is rampant. This is too often directed at many who, quite frankly, would never be considered fat by any measure other than appearance. Well, I'm going step right into controversy. If you have a genetic disorder, legitimate physical limitation or illness that has forced "fatness" (obesity) upon you, then I am your champion. The message in this section is for those who choose to remain overweight or even underweight/frail and inactive while you have the ability to change this. If you make unhealthy life choices, like smoking and drinking, or live a sedentary lifestyle, then it says a lot about you and the likelihood of life success for you. The effort to be physically well is the same effort it takes to be financially and spiritually well, emotionally healthy, successful and impactful. You might even have a degree of financial success that you forfeit when you retire, just as you drop dead or become ill. When I spent twenty-two years working in the financial service industry, I witnessed many who decided to forego their health in sole pursuit of money and financial wealth. For some periods it was me. Inevitably, in time, the vagaries of that choice would come to roost. Health issues, sickness, stress or early death, were those all-too-frequent holy shit(!) moments. The phone call to me, after the fact, would be "can we talk about estate planning?" Or worse, I would get a call from the spouse or family member of a person who had a heart attack, wondering what they should do next after the funeral. Those were the symptoms of fat and rich. I would say they were fucking serious symptoms! Largely preventable.

I admittedly have a bias against those who find excuses to avoid success; I also have that bias towards those who thumb their noses at their health. We reap what we sow and if you sow the seeds of poor physical health, you will pay dearly.

Sure, it might be easy for me because I have always been fit. My sister and I both grew up playing as many sports as we could fit into our days. Our parents were not physically active. They weren't raised that way and they did not do much to build or maintain their fitness. They supported us every step of the way in our pursuit of athletic success. On top of being a high performing athlete, I received my Bachelor of Kinesiology (Physical Education) from the University of Calgary and have always made fitness a part of my life. That life habit is paying dividends as I enter my fiftieth year. I even named my company Fit Family Inc. and our charitable fund is the Fit Family Fund as a testimony to my commitment to live a balanced and happy, healthy, fit life. Our life revolves around fitness, health and being well.

If you put a physical task in front of me, or any sport, because I'm healthy and fit, I'm able to tackle that with at least moderate success. I don't struggle because the fitness component wipes me out, or that I'm not strong enough or capable enough to move in a certain way. I may not know the specific skill but fitness and good health and body strength, sure give me the ability and capacity to fake it until I make it. When asked if I want to try something new, my response is always yes.

If someone wants me to golf, I can golf. I golf poorly, but I can walk eighteen holes, and feel good at the end of it. I don't rely on a cart. If I want to go skiing or snowboarding, I can do that. I have clients or prospects who want to socialize and network, and they say, "Hey, let's go skiing." Done. I can be on that hill getting that personal time. Biking is the same. Hiking is the same. Any sport. Even though I'm not a master at all sports and I am rusty at golf and tennis, being able to do them and function at a moderate skill level goes a long way.

If you have children, then beyond work and your life, they are reason enough to be physically well. Be able to play with your kids and grandkids. If you can't get down on the floor with them at their level because you aren't sure you will get back up again, then you need to re-assess your fitness. Kids want to move and being excluded from enjoying all that they offer because you're immobile or you're exhausted or physically incapable sucks. That's just no way to live.

I had 80-year-old clients that were going to yoga, golfing, walking, hiking, and cross-country skiing with their friends daily. Then I had others that really couldn't leave the house and do anything because without someone carrying them or using a wheelchair or something to get them across a park for a walk, they weren't able to do it. Their quality of life was dramatically diminished. The worst would be when you have sudden health issues that require surgery or rehabilitation. Without the habit of fitness, strong bones and strong muscles, your ability to recover once ill or injured is low. You don't want that to be the thing that leads you to your grave. Emergency surgery at any age could be the beginning of the end for you.

If you haven't already established the habit of exercise by forty or fifty years old, you better be moving. It is never too late, however, undoing decades of poor life choices takes time and any setback you experience just gets worse. You better make fitness part of your life, because if you don't, those later years are going to be so much more difficult.

18. Do Epic Shit

As I mentioned before, this is something my family tries to live by wherever and whenever possible. Admittedly, I wish we did even more, but we still do a fair amount of it. It's about living. In business, I like to scare myself - or maybe more like push myself into unknown or uncertain territory. It is daring to endeavor into things when the outcome is uncertain, but I will give it a shot. Sometimes there is real risk of peril, financially or emotionally. Other times it works out brilliantly, and all the rewards of energy, low stress, happiness, and financial gain are realized.

There is this saying, "Do something that scares you every day". For some people, their response would be, "Okay, well, it scared me to say hello to that stranger today." There is no standard as to what that thing is, so even that's a good start. Everyone has different boundaries for what scares them. While just showing up is a nice step, it isn't really the spirit of what I am talking about when it comes to doing some epic shit. Come out of your shell, get into a perceived safe (not life threatening) space and try something bigger. Granted, your epic shit might be different from mine. Our lives are very short. We live an infinitesimal existence, as minuscule parts of this whole world. We're here like a flash of light, a speck of sand on a beach. Why would you spend your life not considering the option of doing something epic occasionally?

Look at the work that we do in life. Consider how we build our lives around the belief that once we finish our work, we'll be able then to go and do epic stuff. We have it all wrong.

I suggest success in business isn't as important as success in life. What is your measure? We have one shot at this. When we consider the finite amount of time we have on earth, we want to find ourselves planning those big life events, experiencing personal joy, without regret or longing. Celebrate the milestones and experiences in this wonderful, vast universe, world, country and community wherever you are. If you are reading this, you are already one of the most successful human beings to ever walk this planet. You don't spend the days foraging for food, sheltering from the elements or shielding yourself form death at the hands of foes or predators. Don't take that for granted. Don't choose work yourself to death.

Let's reverse our intentions. Plan the life experiences you wish to have and then build everything you do for work around them. My goal was to take more days off travelling, enjoying my family, and supporting our children in their activities and pursuits than working during the summer. That is something we have been able to arrange in the past few years. We get to see amazing mountains and landscapes, new cities and new towns, and meet new people while spending important, focused time with our kids.

I am going to share a secret with you. It is about developing a reliable, predictable and repeatable process to build a business and work schedule that offers me that opportunity. Here's my example. If I want one-on-one coaching to provide my base income to support that lifestyle, I will need to work with roughly twenty to thirty entrepreneurs at any given time. Therefore, I build a business and pricing model that provides that, with opportunities to earn more in different ways. Then I construct a schedule of business building that has different periods.

Through the entire year I work on promotion, marketing and list building through speaking, networking and hosting numerous, small training and speaking-based events. There is the *marketing and building* phase, there is a *performance and selling* component, then there is a *delivery* aspect. One or two times per year I execute the *"market, build, perform and sell"* segments and we schedule a balanced *"delivery"* of services. When I do sales right at two events, plus regularly attract new clients through the smaller speaking events and referrals, I can engage and serve people who, in turn, invest in their coaching success and my business offering.

Thirty ongoing coaching clients will require forty to fifty hours per month (not per week!), or roughly four to six full days to serve. Working with clients a maximum of three days per week will sufficiently allow me to deliver quality coaching in a manageable (a.k.a. sane) time frame. The other four days per week, I am free to market, build, plan, speak, or simply enjoy my life and my family. The fall, winter and spring are more intense periods and most people would rather enjoy leisure activities in the summer than engage in intense coaching, anyway. Demand for my face-to-face time slows then and can be managed with fewer focus days. During July, I stick to my coaching and a limited small event schedule and in August I only serve via phone/video conference.

I build my work life around being able to do that. A decade ago, I would work ten-hour days for five to seven days per week, in order to hopefully fund our holidays during the kids' school vacation time. I was succumbing to an archaic system and working to live. That is, living only when work allowed.

Then I made the proclamation, "This is what I want to do with my life. This is where we want to live. This is where we want to play, and this is the epic shit that we want to do." Then I asked, "What do we need to do to achieve it? What can we do in between today and our ideal life to ensure that the next year and the year after that, we build a business that allows us to continue to enjoy that freedom?"

The focus is on developing a quality business that operates in a way to support your pursuit of happiness and the experiences of life. It allows you live a life that matters, with impact for you, your family, and the community and the world around you. Build those personal life experiences first and have your business, your career, your enterprise work to support that.

When we are working less, but working right, we can be just as passionate, innovative, and creative in our businesses. In fact, as a result, we get more accomplished and make more money. This is because of the time we spend out of the business, not what we spend in it. We get out of our heads and into the experience.

Anyways, what is my epic shit? Besides snowboarding, hiking and travel, one of my epic shit things to do is Downhill Mountain biking. I've been doing it a lot. We ride in all kinds of different locations. We get to travel and see wonderful trails and new horizons all the time: animals, scenery, landscapes, mountain ranges, rivers, lakes, creeks, everything. Also, I scare the living shit out of myself occasionally. It is a singular, focused effort. There's only one thing I could possibly process in my mind while riding and that is to be successful, safe, and secure on the way down a hill going forty or fifty kilometers an hour while navigating rocks, trees, bumps, and jumps. Doing it brings all my attention to that moment, experiencing flow and immersive focus. The epic stuff I do un-clutters my brain, allows me freedom to think outside of the activity, and ponder bigger, better things for myself. It allows me to be more creative.

My epic stuff is a little bit scary - snowboarding, mountain biking, traveling, seeing new sights, new experiences, and mostly experiencing it with my family. It is the most epic thing possible because we're giving our children something that they'll cherish for the rest of their lives. We know our years with only them are limited in terms of our time spent together, so we're taking advantage of it while we can. Our work life and our business are being created to support an ideal lifestyle, not the other way around. We're not just going to "fit it in" around our work.

GROW GET GIVE

19. Exercise Your Mind

John Assaraf, author, entrepreneur and the star of 'The Secret' movie, is working on mental rejuvenation, rehabilitation, and mind programming. He calls the idea of exercising your mind "innercise", not exercise. We head out to the gym to exercise our bodies, Assaraf wants us to take our brains to the neuro gym. This is priming your brain for success by exercising your mind through visualization.

Innercise involves acknowledging the obstacles that you are facing in life and in your mental programming. Then priming your brain for the vision of your future in order to develop subconscious patterns. By doing this, it will allow you to readily act in better ways to think optimistically and positively, pointing you in a direction that will move you forward, closer to your goals and objectives. This focus on reprogramming your subconscious will guide you to the vision you have for your future life.

It is one of the most interesting investigations of health in this century. It is a literal exploration of unknown worlds within us. Neuro health, staving off illness, managing mental health, and what it takes to recover health from a damaged brain are part of the 21st century's biggest horizon for advancement in people's well-being. Consider the re-wiring of the neurotransmitters and neurons in your brain as you fight the deleterious effects of dementia or Alzheimer's, and all types of brain diseases that are basically brain-wasting diseases. They waste your life in terms of your cognition, mental awareness, and ability to function. It is believed that by exercising your mind and keeping active mentally, you can prevent and even slow or stop the onset of such illnesses.

Even concussion research where treatment protocols go back and forth all the time is now directing recovery by activation of your brain, not locking yourself in a dark room without stimulation. Stimulus is needed by your brain cells so they will function to produce energy and neurochemicals to fire across the neurotransmitters, the synapses, in your brain. This activity in your brain and the energy released rebuilds those compromised pathways.

Rebuilding and continually constructing new pathways and new programming of neural networks, of neurochemicals and transmitters in your brain, requires activity. This is the greatest understanding of neuro functionality that is evolving. The cells of our brains are living, breathing organisms, but they also can self-heal. They are growing, constantly learning and reprogramming organs. Our brains can be reprogrammed, and they can be trained.

If that is the case, then working on your brain is critical. Starting with negative versus positive thoughts for rewiring of your neuro pathways to pave the way to higher performance. A friend of mine, Duff Gibson, former Olympic skeleton racer and one of the oldest Canadian gold medalists (he was 39 when he slid to victory), shared his story at one of my coaching summits. He spoke about the very real effect of thinking and a culture of positivity versus negativity on performance - high performance. He shared how it manifested in him.

Duff was training with the Canadian Olympic bobsled team in the '90's. He was working hard to become a top Olympian in that sport, but there was a very negative environment in the training. There were a lot of borderline abusive comments and a lot of negative pressure. In fact, the macho behavior that was misguidedly intended to push one another created a bullying culture, constant negativity and adverse pressure on the various performers. Even the basic mandatory testing protocols year in and year out would be a negative experience versus an achievement-oriented one. Duff found that his results were not improving at a good enough rate - in fact, he was regressing. He was struggling to keep up. He was just about to abandon his dreams of becoming an Olympic athlete completely. "This is enough. I can't do bobsled anymore," he told himself. As word got out that he was quitting his pursuit to be an Olympic bobsledder, the coach of the national skeleton and luge team approached him. He saw that Duff needed a change of scenery and culture and he urged him to join the team.

The coach of the skeleton team said, "Come with us and try what we do. Try this positive environment that we encourage, this culture we have as athletes." What Duff found with them was a culture of athletes who were uplifting and positive. It was a joy to be back training in the gym and on the track. There was importance placed on the mental health, goodwill and positivity throughout the organization and the team. Duff noted in the mandatory testing that next year that his physical performance improved incrementally 30% to 50% over year for the same things he was testing in bobsleigh.

Imagine that. A 30% to 50% improvement in the near-dozen different things they test for: strength, physicality, endurance, power, agility, etc. He'd been training every year with the bobsled team for four or five years and of course he was progressing, albeit slowly, until his step backward. The year after he joined the skeleton team, enjoying a positive environment and removal from the constant pressure of a negative environment, Duff experienced a setting where people were optimistic, supportive and connected. Improvement for his physical performance dramatically increased and he went on to excel at the sport. While I acknowledge this is one anecdote and not a large scientific study, it is a dramatic account. Duff was going nowhere in bobsled and shifted to a better, more positive environment and quickly began to win on the world stage and ultimately an Olympic gold medal.

20. Give For Happiness

It truly is better to give than to receive. Study after study has shown that the

...happiness derived from giving has a significant measurable emotional

and physical benefit for the giver.

A study done by British researchers, published in the *Journal of Social Psychology,* looked at acts of kindness. In a ten-day experiment, they formed three groups: one to perform a daily act of kindness, the other to do something new each day, and the last had no instructions. In the follow-up satisfaction survey, the subjective measurement of happiness was the greatest in the group who had performed random acts of kindness. Researchers at Harvard Business School and the University of British Columbia published their findings online in the *Journal of Happiness Studies.* Beforehand, they had given their participants sums of money and asked that they choose to either spend it on themselves or on someone else in such a manner that made them happiest. They had already provided their recollection of what both acts felt like to them from their past. At the conclusion of the study results were reviewed. The first important discovery was the fact that the strongest happiness memories were following giving to someone else. The next very interesting finding was that those who recalled happiness from giving in the past were most likely to give in the present (and future). This implies somewhat of a feedback loop of giving and happiness. Anecdotally, we've heard that what we give comes back to us. This study confirms this statement and suggests we feed off this energy.

Further evidence of the giving effect on happiness was found by researchers (Aknin, L., Barrington-Leigh, C., Dunn, E., Helliwell, J., Burns, J., Biswas-Diener, R., Norton, M.) published in 2013 in the *Journal of Personality* and *Social Psychology* (page 635-652). Here are their comments from their study named *Prosocial Spending and Well-Being: Cross-cultural Evidence for a Psychological Universal*:

"Human beings around the world derive emotional benefits from using their financial resources to help others" (prosocial spending).

"Prosocial spending is associated with greater happiness around the world, in poor and rich countries alike."

"Our findings suggest that the reward experienced from helping others may be deeply ingrained in human nature, emerging in diverse cultural and economic contexts."

While two parties (or more) benefit in the act of giving, there can be a disproportionately larger benefit to the giver (benefactor) than the recipient of charity (beneficiary). There are chemical effects that occur as endorphins are released that provide a bit of a high when we perform the pleasurable act of goodness. Our brains are well tuned to reward us when our pleasure centers are affected. As well, there are social benefits to philanthropy as those who give can consider themselves as contributors (versus takers) within society. Lastly, there are also financial benefits from giving. From tax benefits, to access to events and activities and direct recognition, there are all sorts of financial benefits and incentives available to donors.

Establishing an ongoing or long-term giving strategy for you and your business will allow you to experience that happiness repeatedly.

Additionally, you are making available the gift of giving to your customers and stakeholders too. If given the choice of buying services or products from companies which support charity versus those which do not, consumers will support those who do give. In fact, a Forbes article from December 15, 2010 showed that 83 percent of consumers polled believed that companies should support charities and non-profits, and as such, consumers would be more inclined to buy from those companies. Wouldn't you want your customers to be happier as a result of their support of your company over others?

GROW GET GIVE

20b. Allow Happiness To Rise

Contemplate that phrase for a moment. "Allow happiness to rise". Allow it to rise within you and the people around you. Don't crush a good thought with a "but if" or an "if only". Don't feed yourself, or anyone, shit sandwiches by wedging the bad or doubtful between the good. Don't encourage others to share only their "if-only's" and their "I could have's." Don't kill other people's optimism with a "but if...", or a "what if...", "oh, but wait a minute..." Those are limiting beliefs. They are <u>self</u>-limiting beliefs.

Kristen Hadeed wrote, in her book "Permission to Screw Up", about how she built a successful maid service called Student Maid. She hired many college students to work for her. One of her early approaches to human resources, when dealing with discipline issues, training or even firing, was serving up what she referred to as a shit sandwich. In fact, she did it so much with others, that she even began serving herself a few now and again. This was a method of leading the conversation with something positive, then giving the bad news and then following it up with another layer of praise. Don't butter the fresh baked bread and then jam some crap in between the slices. It's not a pleasant way to deal with things when you can simply deal with people at a human level, at a genuinely caring level, and an honest level. Praising someone and then crapping on them, then giving a handshake and a smile is simply disingenuous and downright mean.

When you are direct and honest in a caring and considerate way, people will respect it; they'll appreciate it. Not everyone will thank you and they may not like it that moment, but at the end of the day, it will be much easier to swallow. Deal with people with the integrity you would hope they would deal with your grandmother. You wouldn't sugar-coat things, because your grandma's smart and wise. You would speak to her truthfully and plainly. Your grandma's not going to take bullshit from anybody, so it's no use glossing over something that is not positive.

Just get to it, be kind and respectful, and deliver bad news or criticism with integrity.

Authentic input delivered in a manner that is open, constructive and leading – even when you are covering things that need improvement or are unpleasant – will offer the recipient a chance to rise to the occasion and decide what their best choice of action might be. By allowing happiness to rise and encouraging the happiness to rise in others around and beyond you, it reflects brilliantly on you.

Happiness can be found in many places, but giving it a bit of a push is even better. When you are dealing with challenging circumstances, try adding some humor or lightness to the conversation. People know when things aren't working. They also know they are uncomfortable talking about it or hearing something they perceive will be negative, so be honest and address the seriousness with a bit of levity. This will help you deliver a necessary message to a more receptive audience. As much as this works when trying to convince, the same can be said when you are trying to sell.

I heard T. Harv Eker say this, and many have said before him and afterwards,

"If you want to make more money, be funny."

It is true - "More funny equals more money". What that means is you are also giving people permission in your life, even in your sales pitch, to be happy, to release their inhibitions and concerns and allow their happiness to bubble to the surface. Never prevent others from embracing it.

Don't hold back anyone from enjoying the endorphins by keeping that chemical away from them when they so deserve it. Choose to unleash happiness as an act of abundance, not repress it with scarcity. Allow happiness to rise. As it rises within you and it rises within the people around you, so too will your success and enjoyment of life.

GROW GET GIVE

21. Give Your Time

Time. The most valuable thing we have. Ahead of health, there is nothing more precious. Giving it away is one of the most generous things you can do. When you give time to others or to causes that matter to you, it is wise to make the most of it. Here are some things to consider when giving this precious commodity.

As a business owner, you can do this yourself. When you choose to give time personally, you should reflect on your strengths, and then make decisions that make the best use of those skills. You might be suited for doing the labor, governance, management or even fundraising. If you aren't best suited to help "on the ground", then maybe joining advisory boards or boards of directors is sensible for you. You could take on a committee lead role or lead an event or campaign.

While volunteering your time is as valuable as any funding could ever be, your participation in this capacity will likely give you a greater sense of pride and understanding of what exactly the charity faces in terms of challenges and opportunities. This knowledge can improve the effectiveness of your future philanthropy.

As an employer, you can encourage your staff to give their time, or you can challenge your peers to volunteer their time. Consider offering one day per month (or per quarter) to your employees to spend serving charity, on a paid basis. This is something major your business can do to help charity directly and it will build increased loyalty among your employees. In fact, as a twist, canvas your employees for the top five charities they would like to support and then place them in a rotation for the year. Make this known publicly, and then challenge your competitors or vendors to do the same.

Giving time returns valuable experience to you.

In one simple act of volunteerism, you gain knowledge of the cause, you learn about people you might not have ever met, you gain a perspective that will likely be from their point of view, and you might even gain a new understanding of the challenges faced by leaders who are trying to make an impact.

I have volunteered in many ways over the years. So many, in fact, that I have lost track of all the roles I've served and time I've committed. From organizational and event committees, to boards of directors and roundtables, to sorting food at the local Food Bank and serving meals to the homeless, it has been a lot. The one thing I did for a decade, and cherished, was the role as a volunteer coach of my daughter's soccer teams. A three to five day per week (evenings and weekends) commitment for all those years is quite an investment. Sport has so much to offer for mentoring and coaching. The learning that happens for youth in sport and on teams lasts a lifetime. Only lately, years later, have I been able to understand how significant an impact that giving had. I had the chance to see a few of the girls, whom I had known since they were five years old, exit high school and enter their adulthood, post-secondary education and the workforce. I am proud of who they have become. I only hope that some of the lessons I taught them helped shape their lives for the better.

The rewards that mattered for some of the girls were the coaching or skills, for others it was the lessons of habit and discipline they learned. A few of them were able to achieve more than they ever expected with the guidance and support provided, and others simply needed a father figure in their lives. Whatever the impact, it was a tremendously rewarding experience.

Committing your time in such a significant way might not appeal to you. Your schedule might not be conducive to it. However, if you can volunteer your time in an impactful way with whatever cause that resonates most, you will find incredible rewards in the effort.

GROW GET GIVE

22. Give Money

As I said, time and health are the most precious. However, society places an emphasis on money. It is something you gain, spend, lose, or give away. You can hoard it, save it, invest it and earn it. When you give it away, you receive things in return. When you give it away, you can obtain it again. Money it is not nearly as valuable as your health or your time and it is not finite. Interestingly, in a lot of cases, your money matters less to you than it does to others. Therefore, when you consider giving, you must consider sharing your money. Your wealth is more than just money.

For the owner entrepreneur, too often our resources seem scarce or tight. There's always another opportunity to invest in, more marketing to do, payroll to address, etc. Of course, there are also our families. We want to be able to re-direct our money to our lives and our families. It is easy to think that money is also a scarce resource. Believe or not, you have plenty of sources of money to choose from. These assets include human capital, business profits, personal funds, employee funds, supplier funds, customer support, sponsorship, etc. Money is found as product or service equivalents that you might contribute. All should be considered when deciding to make a financial gift.

There are many strategies to give. Some will be simply reflected as a line item or expense or tax credit, others might be infrastructure investment or marketing funds. Entertainment or event fundraising is also possible. Here are a few practical considerations and strategies you can use to give:

Corporate Giving

Giving through financial sponsorship, profit-sharing (donating a fixed percentage of profits), or funding infrastructure development for a cause or charity can be ways for your company to give. Think of funding the purchase of computer systems and hardware for a charity. This links your business directly to the effort and provides meaningful assistance and a strong community message. It is also an effective way to provide funds directly to a charity and most likely will offer a useable taxable expense for your annual filings.

Engaging employees and customers can be done as well. You might organize your own customer appreciation event with all proceeds going to a single charity or multiple charities. You might even promote contests, auctions or challenges that encourage customer buying or promotional activities by offering to match or donate a portion of their purchases. You could even reward them with a donation in their name and recognize them for simply being a customer or renewing or upgrading a purchase. In my early days as an advisor, when I was more actively transacting securities in my financial investment business, I launched a birthday "thank you" promotion, where I would donate to my charitable fund $5 per transaction for every transaction made by my clients in their birthday month. I sent a simple birthday card that had the statement, *"Giving back to the community — in your honour"*, sent a birthday wish and provided a personal note with their "donation amount", as well as details of the promotion. It was something our clients appreciated very much.

There are many other ways I affected giving directly through my business, such as giving back the occasional speaking or professional fee as a charitable gift, and sharing proceeds of my book or event sales.

When thinking about pooling charitable funds from events, promotions, etc., for your corporate giving, you might even wish to consider establishing a formal foundation which will manage the charitable giving aspects and reporting. If your funding is substantial you might set up a foundation; if it is not, a Donor Advised Fund at your local community foundation or investment firm would do. Your company would collect the funds allocated to charity, then make a single regular donation to the foundation and receive its tax receipts, then the foundation would be responsible for the disbursements. This also streamlines giving methods like profit sharing by directing a percentage of profits to the foundation monthly or quarterly, and then granting to multiple charities or causes throughout each year.

When you add a foundation, you separate the tax decision and the giving decision. You also have an added ability and time to make strategic decisions on how you grant funds. A giving strategy can be constructed more methodically within the foundation's framework. This can be a very public way for your company to express your philanthropy, while simultaneously supporting causes that matter to you and your company and providing customers a means to further identify with you at a personal level. Lastly, there is a simple tax credit earned for the corporation at the time when the gift is made. Thus, a foundation also adds to the tax planning options for your business.

Personal Giving

In my role as a Legacy Planning Advisor I was able to assist families in redirecting over $12.5 million to charitable causes in just over six years. These people were mostly baby boomers planning retirement and succession of their wealth. They were effectively done creating wealth and were looking to live off it, protect it and pass it on. Seeking even more leverage as I shift my energy to business coaching one of my audacious goals is to help entrepreneurs make more money and thus increase their capacity to give. In fact, I hope to coach entrepreneurs to help them collectively make a billion dollars in revenue that will allow them to re-direct as much as $100 million in profits to charity over a decade.

Encourage giving through your business on an ongoing basis, but also look at your personal situation to investigate where giving fits in your life. Will you give now, or give later? Or both? What will you give? There are many ways to give; from gifts of cash or securities, to assigning charity as the beneficiary of an insurance policy. You can also setup a private foundation, Donor Advised Fund, even your own endowment or scholarship. Most importantly, sophisticated financial planning is required. Take the time to properly plan and execute your philanthropy. We are motivated to give because it is important to us and we have a sense of responsibility and altruism. It is true there are great ways to do this and there are poor ways. You work extraordinarily hard for your money. You have taken risks and you do your due diligence when taking on new initiatives.

Do not allow anything less than the highest level of care when planning your giving.

Determine how you will give the most to impact the best possible outcome for the charities or causes your support. Planning can be a powerful tool when contemplating your philanthropic giving and it will increase the effectiveness of your gifts. It will also help you ensure succession of your family wealth. Using philanthropic giving incorporated into your personal or corporate tax planning and the succession of your wealth will uncover ways to give much more than you ever thought possible, while reducing or removing the impact of income and/or estate taxation. There are some incredible advisors who understand planned giving. Seek them out to help you. Through my legacy planning business, I taught entrepreneurs and baby boomers how they could plan for a zero-tax estate, while passing on their estate intact to their heirs. While we did a lot of good work together, the subject of conversations was often about missed opportunities in planning or the inability to use effective tools. What they did not know or care about when they were younger were things they desperately could have used in older age. I gained a lot of knowledge about the hindsight baby boomers were able to provide. That wisdom is something I am trying to share with younger entrepreneurs now. It is never too early to begin planning to take control of your philanthropy. Seek an expert to help you with these decisions.

GROW GET GIVE

23. Give Influence

When you are a business leader in your community, people look up to you and respect your decisions. As such, you are capable of influencing people and their behavior.

When you direct attention and act to support important causes or activities, you can create big impact in your community.

Be clear about the causes that are important to you and your customers. Use your platform and status as a business leader to raise awareness. Engage your peers and networks in the charitable activities you do and the events you hold. While your focus might be on your business, connecting your actions to a philanthropic goal can influence others to be moved to act. This does not require you to volunteer, or even give money; it is something more intangible.

I have spoken about Oprah Winfrey as a role model philanthropist on many occasions. Her biggest charitable contribution reaches far beyond the money she has directly or indirectly shifted to causes, but it has been her understanding of the position she is in. The "Oprah Effect" is all about influence. People focus on the incredible monetary gifts and the millions raised for various causes and charities when they think about Oprah's giving. In fact, she did more for literacy than almost anyone in America. It was her influence that changed the way people approached reading and turned authors into heroes — and success stories. Her Angel Network, established in 1997, raised millions of dollars for charity, funded scholarships, and built homes. None of this happened by accident. Oprah always understood that one of her biggest assets was the media platform from which she had incredible reach. Influence is what she leveraged to make a huge impact in this world.

24. Give Now And Get Help

This concept is so simple it seems trivial. Do not overthink this! As you know, smart and successful entrepreneurs make decisions quickly. As I have stated, they set criteria, check the boxes in their minds and act decisively. Giving can be done in the same way.

There is no reason to delay your philanthropy.
Give back now and plan to give more in the future.

Start something important and get it moving right away. Naturally you will want to plan things through to ensure you will have a big impact. This work can be done on an ongoing basis. In my first book, *Philanthropy; An Inspired Process*, I highlighted very clear, shared steps along the journey of philanthropy that were shared by the great philanthropic icons of our time, and then followed it up with another book, *Big Impact Giving*, to guide anyone to affect giving through each of those steps.

Let's review the upside of giving. The first big impact is that someone or something benefits from your philanthropy. Next, you can make that impact and build your legacy. Third, you get to experience more happiness. Yup - that simple.

There is also a business and financial case. You can use charitable giving to reduce or even eradicate one of the biggest threats to your wealth — TAXES. Estate taxes will steal from your heirs and reallocate your financial resources to the bureaucracy of government. You must take control of your money and your legacy and re-direct your social capital towards the causes and institutions that are most important to you and your family. As you do this, the government rewards you with tax credits. When citizens directly control their social spending, governments are not required to do so. Charities know they are not receiving more funding from government. Tax credits are the rewards put in place to encourage people to support causes in which government involvement would create more red tape.

There are intelligent financial planning tools that you can use, especially at a younger age, such as insurance. In fact, insurance combined with charitable giving can even help you achieve a zero-tax estate if the approach is right for you. It is possible to pass on your family wealth to the next generation and support the cases that matter most to you while reducing or eliminating the impact of taxes. Seek the assistance of a qualified expert to help develop the plan and identify the right strategies and tactics for your family.

One last threat to your wealth is a bigger concern than even taxes. The taxman will threaten your wealth and your heirs' inheritance, but health problems will threaten your life and steal your impact. While you are still healthy, you must act. Plan to give now, or at least, set giving in motion. You might know the old Chinese proverb asking:

> "When is a good time to plant a tree? Twenty years ago. If not then, when is the next best time to plant a tree? It is today."

Implementing philanthropy with the help of professionals is important. Seeking the advice of experts will help you do anything you don't understand entirely. Unfortunately, most financial and/or investment advisors won't necessarily educate you on this topic. They are in the wealth-hoarding industry, not wealth-sharing. Implementing charitable giving is often unknown to them and even perceived as a threat to their business. It is viewed as counterintuitive. They are fearful they will lose assets (they usually are compensated on the assets they manage) and there is a perceived lack of compensation connected to charitable giving. They are also concerned you will re-direct your attention from their agenda — which should, but might not always, be consistent with yours. Most likely, they lack knowledge in the area of legacy giving. Planned giving is not widely understood in the investment community. A lot of advisors don't even want to have the important, yet uncomfortable, conversation about mortality with their clients. They are either afraid to ask about planning for death or are simply uncomfortable with the topic. They might even be concerned you might want to engage them in a deeper, more personal conversation that they are not equipped to handle. Finally, and not to be dismissed, is the fact they just do not really care to get involved with this side of your financial life.

While deciding to act on your philanthropic intent might be a simple step, finding the expert to guide you through this journey could be slightly more challenging. Don't be dismayed, there are plenty of credible and knowledgeable specialists who can help you. To find them, you can ask your local community foundation, the charities you support, or larger organizations such as the Canadian Association of Gift Planners. It is important that you do your homework to find them.

GROW GET GIVE

25. Plan To Give Later To Leave Your Legacy

Commit to give back for the community - for you, and for your legacy. This is the planning part. Beyond an immediate gift, it takes planning now to give big in the future. During a decade when I focused on helping families re-direct their taxes to giving, with strategic thinking and using he right tactics, we were often able to turn a $5,000 annual gift to planned giving into one that was that was ten times larger ($50,000). In some cases, even one hundred times larger ($500,000)! When I met with any family who wished to plan their estate succession and legacy giving, I asked them to imagine their own ideal or Norman Rockwell painting of their future. This was their vision of what they wanted for themselves, how much they hoped to pass on to their heirs, and the impact they wanted to achieve through charitable giving. You must focus to envision your ideal outcome in future terms, because most people will view their own future through current lenses. In order to put people in the right frame of mind, I encouraged them to view their legacy through their grandchildren's eyes.

Proper planning starts with the right strategic financial advisor or planned giving professional. You know you have the right expert if they begin by listening to you and guiding you through a values discussion that helps them understand your vision of the future. The right person does not lead with a product idea or transaction! A strategic advisor will help you determine the goals for your four "P's": personal, provide, protect, and preserve. They will build goals for the four "P's" based on your vision and values.

"Personal" goals most directly reflect your values. They can include the things you hope to do, experience, buy, give, etc. Travel and lifestyle, volunteering, giving back, health, and creative pursuits are most often reflected here.

"Provide" covers income and funding for your current and future lifestyle. Your goals will identify how your assets will provide the cash flow you need to pay for the necessities and the things you hope to do.

"Protect" insulates you, your family and your wealth against the five biggest threats. They include health, litigation, creditors, marriage dissolution, and taxes. Quantifying what these will cost you, as well as identifying the structures and tools you can best use to insulate you and your family from the threats, will be discussed. When taxes come into the picture, succession and legacy soon follow.

"Preserve" is all about preserving your wealth in succession. This involves planning to pass on your wealth to heirs while reducing taxes in the process. When I worked as an advisor, we were able to plan zero tax estates for people. Philanthropic giving makes this possible.

There are three decisions to make when considering your succession goals:

1. **Do nothing**, pay your "fair share" of taxes and pass on whatever's left to your heirs,

2. **Give charitably** to re-direct your tax dollars away from the government to causes that are important to you and pass on the rest to your heirs, or

3. **Use tools**, such as insurance and planned giving strategies to give charitably, eliminate the taxman completely and pass on all your wealth, intact, to your heirs.

Number three is the preferred strategy of the well-advised wealthiest families in North America. Insurance planning delivers the succession outcomes for your goals by replacing estate assets. In fact, adding charity as the named beneficiaries of your life insurance will allow you to earn tax credits that could match your estate tax obligations, allowing you to pass on your wealth in its entirety.

GROW GET GIVE

26. Reflect

Giving back also means reflecting on the things in your life that you have experienced, acquired, invented, or built. Instead of always charging forward, take a moment to reflect on the good you do and have done.

It is important to appreciate your contribution.
It will energize you and refocus you on your purposeful life.

Use reflection as an opportunity to learn from your successes and missteps. Taking a moment to reflect demands that we free up time, as well as mental and emotional space to contemplate our lives and everything around us. Reflection is the first step toward gratitude. This review is vital, yet when I work with successful people, whether they're entrepreneurs, business owners, professionals or senior executives with high-profile firms, I've noticed they invariably focus on what's next. They are so driven, they rarely take the time to look at what they've accomplished today, let alone what they achieved last month, last year, or five years prior. I appreciate and applaud their commitment to looking ahead as they plan, push, and inspire themselves and those around them to do more and do it better, but I rarely see them pause to truly reflect on their results or really celebrate their victories.

Looking back is important in business, but also in life and philanthropy. It allows us to recognize the results of our efforts and actions in order to further develop the experience, expertise, and confidence required to maintain the momentum and focus on new targets.

GROW GET GIVE

27. Take Time For Wonder

Ask why. Jeff Hoffman, former founding partner of Priceline.com, has a lot of wisdom to offer. His TED talk, "The Power of (Childlike) Wonder", tells a great story about when he and his five-year-old daughter spent the day together. With a story about a day trip they took and her inquiries about everything, right down to why there is weather stripping and a frame around the car windows and was there a name for it? Jeff demonstrated how asking why is so natural for young kids and illustrated the wonderment of asking why. 'Why' leads to knowledge. The wonderment of seeing your life through the eyes of a five-year-old becomes a guide for investigating the world as an adult. Seeing everything like it was your first time and at every turn asking why.

This concept is something Jeff promotes, but he also stresses that you must "leave your industry" when wondering. This will help you learn one new thing that you don't <u>need</u> to know. When you write what it is you learned, you can combine that experience with all the other learning experiences you get and assemble the pieces like a puzzle. It will help shape your attitude and understanding of the world through your own immersion in it.

Ask these questions: Why this? Why does that work? Or, why do you do it that way? Or, what is this for?

The most successful people in life absorb the information from a broader world than others and thinking with that childlike wonderment is the key. They study innovators worldwide. "Info-Sponging" is a word that Hoffman used to describe it. Smart and successful people behave in the way that a five-year-old would with the world. If you need confirmation of that, just look at Elon Musk.

Elon Musk is driven by questions starting with "what if" and "why". Why couldn't we burrow a tunnel, like a vacuum tube, under LA to transport people through the earth? What if it would be cheaper than doing it above ground? What if it were quieter than the futuristic idea of having thousands of "flying cars" in the air at once? What if it was safer than having the risk of those flying cars dropping out of the sky due to accidents or pilot error? When you begin to ponder these questions, you must deal with all the ramifications of that inquiry and arrive at a conclusion or at least take another step and ask another question. Consider one concept – a hyper-loop train - and then layer it onto the tunneling idea and "The Boring Company" is envisioned. The conclusion was that it wasn't a terrible idea. It could work. In fact, in December of 2018, the first three-kilometre test tunnel for a hyper-loop train under Los Angeles was tested. It was crude and clunky and a bit of a farce in some people's eyes, but the test demonstrated the possibilities and some drawbacks. It could turn out to be a transformational moment for transportation or simply a distraction and failed attempt to confirm a hypothesis. There is merit in bringing incredible speed with low environmental impact and a capacity to move thousands of people daily without any disruption or noise pollution above the earth. Accidents would be virtually eliminated.

One idea is followed by an even bigger one. You can see wonder in the eyes, words and actions of visionary entrepreneurs like Musk, Sir Richard Branson, or Jeff Bezos. They use their kindergarten selves to think stuff up, and then use their evolved, adult selves to make it happen, or at least give something a genuine shot. Sometimes things simply don't work out. But with courage (and a lot of capital), you might ask, "Why can't we put a person or a spaceship into the atmosphere then launch from there to the stratosphere?", and then do it at various locations in space, and ultimately fly to Mars. What if we could do that? How about if we could make the rockets re-usable? Embracing those whys, those childlike whys, that look at the obvious things and yet aren't so obvious, isn't for everyone. Some people are simply not prepared to deal with the what-if once they've asked why. Maybe that is why most people don't indulge their inner five-year-old. They are too worried about the implications of what-if that result from asking why.

Asking why, being prepared to deal with what comes next and embracing the unknown wonderment of the world is what successful people do. Taking that step is what innovators and leaders do. I love the idea of and the word "Info-Sponging" because it indicates exactly what it is. It is being a human sponge for information wherever and however you can absorb it, in order to learn what the world has to offer. Learn from smarter people and the places you didn't know existed have to teach you. That's a big deal. Take the time to ask why. Enjoy experiencing the world with childlike wonder.

GROW GET GIVE

28. Raise Your Emotional Awareness

This is your emotional IQ. A great friend of mine and doctor of psychology, Dianna Campbell-Smith, wrote a helpful book called "Skills for a Life of Ease: Sharpen Your Emotion Awareness and Skills Edge". It is about mastering the concept of becoming emotionally aware and how the impact of doing so can powerfully transform, modify, and improve your behaviors. When you are aware of the thinking processes that go into your behaviors, you can change your outcomes and ultimately your success. Focusing your attention to become aware of opportunities, challenges, limiting thoughts, and hurdles allow you to overcome them. You can identify whether the challenges lie within, such as your personal belief systems and ideological reference points, or are external, such as how circumstances elicit your reactions.

It's like the first step in dealing with addictions. If you don't admit you have a problem, you can't fix the problem. Denial and negative self-talk are not a productive part of your thought processes. If you become aware of when it arises, or understand where it arises from, then you can take actions to reduce the incidence of these occurrences. When you're trained to become more aware, you can start applying techniques and tools to improve how you manage or deal with those thoughts and patterns. This enables you to change things that have become habitual and unconscious.

Developing these tools allow you to live a life with ease. Removing obstacles, rewiring thought patterns and focusing on positivity and success will allow you achieve great things.

Emotional hurdles can hold you back. They can manifest themselves as sabotage. One can experience self-sabotage when you're just about to succeed and things look like they are progressing, then for some reason something goes wrong, or a client leaves, or a prospect walks out of the conversation for reasons you simply don't understand. You take inventory of what happened and write it off as something to do with them. Then it repeats.

This was something I have dealt with in the past. There were some things that were holding me back and preventing me from closing business at a rate that I was accustomed to. In my last couple of years working in the financial services industry, it was how I dealt with new prospects. While it would have been logical to grow my business quickly and as large as I could in order to sell it at a higher price, deep down, I felt that it was disingenuous of me to attract new people who looked to me for help, build relationships with them, and then leave them soon after. I had a prospecting model that was effective and continual, thus I regularly met many families who might have been a good fit as clients, only to fail to convert them to clients. When it was happening, I thought it was my mistake for marketing to the wrong prospects, but when looking back at it, I realized that I was sending messages to the prospects that they weren't welcome as clients! I would intentionally price my services too expensively or appear aloof or so successful or too knowledgeable (beyond their needs) or give the impression that I really didn't want their business. At the end of the day it was clear that I was sabotaging my success. There were other instances of this throughout my life that Dianna helped me become aware of and thus better equipped to deal with some things. A lot of it was subconscious success sabotage.

It was hardwired into my life. My father had lived with mental illness all his life. He managed to successfully manage his illness with medication and therapy. He is a good father and a productive member of society and was high functioning in the roles of responsibility that he was given at work. I received programming at a young age though. Every time my father achieved greatness or rose to the top of whichever company, sales role, or business he was in, he checked out. The pressure and stress of the role was too much for him and he had to quit. Then, he would restart something new. His illness created an inability to deal with greater work stress. It was not because he wasn't deserving or capable, but he simply couldn't cope. The unpredictability of his mental health reduced his functionality when pushed to achieve more. What I learned was that when success came knocking, he dialed things back. It wasn't sabotage for him so much as it was a pattern. He just got to a point where he couldn't handle the increased pressure, but what I got was a subconscious hardwiring that it was natural to rise to success and then step away.

During the past thirty plus years, I found myself doing very similar things in sports, in school, and in business. I wasn't aware. As I rose to some level of success, I would do small things that would be self-sabotage. It wasn't the same as my dad. He would just up and quit every time, but what I would do is create these self-sabotaging incidents that shifted the opportunity and then stepped away from it. Once that step occurred, there was negative self-talk, that convinced me that the situation was wrong, so I determined it was better to be out of it.

The result was some incredibly poor selection of role models, partners, and business opportunities. But having learned how to identify and pay attention to the signs and the cues, I was able to make a shift. I added great mentors and coaches and surrounded myself with great people. I was able to overcome making those mistakes or having those situations repeat.

Now, as a coach, I help people understand how they can grow their business, get more freedom and give back. I have become more emotionally aware and have not repeated the past. The tools I've acquired and the lessons I've learned allow me freedom from repeating how I was hardwired to behave. I sought Diana's help. She confided that, "The fact that you even are aware that there could be a problem, even if it is or isn't a problem today, is a critical part of fixing it". She gave me techniques to identify when these circumstances arose, to deal with them and acknowledge what's going on at the time. That way I could bring it to the surface, deal with it, and move forward.

Emotional intelligence or emotional awareness is something that everyone must strive to become more in tune with. It takes rehearsal and it takes practice. We cannot address that which we do not acknowledge.

29. Unlock Your Brain's Subconscious Power

Digging into your subconscious is another level of emotional awareness. You might consider looking to hypnosis for keys to unlock that subconscious of yours. Part of releasing or unleashing the subconscious power of the mind is also becoming aware of the negative patterns that you've built over a lifetime and just tearing them down, reprogramming your brain, creating positive neural networks or completely dismantling old established patterns that aren't helpful. Doing these will allow you to release the power of your subconscious.

When you consider how we get mental rejuvenation or rest, you can look to sleep. If you're sleeping properly, if you're meditating and finding mindfulness, you're able to draw that subconscious power. One of the most powerful things about allowing your subconscious to become conscious is awareness. For anyone who experienced a mental or creative breakthrough or an innovation, it never occurred when they were deeply mired in the work or business. When they were deeply entrenched, it never happened. When they stepped away and were able to think about other things, they could allow their mind to process what it needed to deal with and the things that had to be sorted. In effect, when left alone to function optimally, your mind could come to its own conclusion of creativity, innovation, and solving problem-solving.

Our minds are extraordinary. We have the capacity to solve problems, envision future potential and assemble the strategies and tactics needed to succeed. Rational thought and extrapolation of ideas are uniquely human traits. But your brain needs time to work. It needs quiet - to be away from the noise of forced thought patterns and habitual activities to allow it to sort, file and process all the inputs and variables that it's aware of.

When you allow your brain to have that time, you give it the opportunity to create and innovate. It allows those subconscious thoughts to work themselves to the surface so that you can apply them.

30. Express Gratitude

"Piglet noticed that even though he had a very small heart,
it could hold a rather large amount of gratitude." — A.A. Milne,
Winnie-the-Pooh

Gratitude allows us to be thankful for the experiences we have had. Sharing your gratitude with others is important. When good things happen in any endeavor, you must acknowledge them and then share those successes with your colleagues, family, and friends. Being openly grateful and expressing it can be challenging for some, and I think business leaders find it extremely challenging. Some people perceive expressing thanks as giving up control and revealing vulnerability - not something a leader wants to reveal. However, sharing gratitude connects you with people and attracts them. They see you as giving and helpful. So express it whenever you can.

What makes it so special is how it feels to receive the true gratitude of someone who expresses it from their very inner core. Here are five things you can do every day to show gratitude:

1. Say thank you — this small phrase packs a ton of meaning. A simple thank you to anyone who has offered themselves in any way to you deserves this much. You deserve to share your appreciation for them.

2. Thank your family — every day you share with your family (parents, spouse, partner, children, grandparents, etc.) just how

much they matter to your life. Thank them for their unconditional love and share yours.

3. Acknowledge those who help — making a point of showing your gratitude for the work someone does is important to them. Additionally, sharing your appreciation with their peers or social networks is a compliment of gratitude that will lift them up in the eyes and minds of others.

4. Focus on the joys of what you have accomplished — remind yourself daily of the things you have done to get where you are. Be grateful that you have accomplished a life of experiences that have shaped who you are. The things you view as minor or simply a part of your life could be considered tremendous accomplishments. Give yourself the gratitude of a job well done.

5. Be grateful for the challenges that lie ahead — embracing life's challenges and not shying away from them emboldens you to succeed. Opportunities on the horizon help you grow, learn, and expand the fullness of your life.

31. Treat Role Players Well

How do we treat role players? We all have people in our lives that include fellow employees, partners or family members and friends. These are the primary players in our lives. Then there are secondary players who you could call the supporting cast. These are people we interact with daily, like the barista at the coffee shop that we frequent, the gas station attendant, the server at the restaurants, even phone solicitors or the help lines for our online or technical needs. The delivery persona or cab driver - the list goes on. How we interact with everyone matters a lot. Sharing gratitude and kindness with others is just plain decent.

Think of how you treat the people who work for the people you want to serve professionally. Be aware of how you treat them. Think about it. If you're trying to build a relationship with or access the CEO of a company or if you're working with one the executives, you always must speak with their receptionist, or executive assistant. Those people matter great deal in the life of the person you are trying to connect with. You must acknowledge that they are important in their position and that you respect them. They protect and have the trust of your customer or your prospect.

Understand that just like you, they prefer dealing with people who treat them with respect, who acknowledge their importance in the business and their role. They are a gatekeeper, so if you're going to deal with them poorly and act like a buffoon, demand things or demean people; you aren't going to get very far, even if you're not outwardly rude. Maybe you don't look people in the eye, you look past them or you don't greet them with a smile and wish them a wonderful day. How do you think it's going to work out for you when trying to access that person you're hoping to reach? If you've already reached them, then belittled their gatekeeper, do you think you're going to get many repeat visits?

How you treat people in those roles says a great deal about your character. If you're willing to pass over the role players in your pursuit of the star, you send a message that you might cut corners, seek power over substance and ignore important signs when making decisions.

Earlier in this book, I mentioned talented people in the playing field of mastery. You have one star, and then there is everybody else. Think of the NBA. One Lebron James and then a team full of role players. Those role players across the entire league are damn good. They're the best at the sport in the world. They're the best 500 players out of the millions on the planet who play basketball. If you think you can treat them with less respect than you would treat the star, or if you think that they deserve less respect or attention, less care or connection than the star, then it says a lot about whether or not you're worthy of the star's attention.

I don't like dealing with anyone who doesn't treat role players well. If I hear it or see it, boy, you know what? They're not part of my world much longer. It doesn't take much energy to be decent to the role players.

I am always surprised by the look on the face of my server at a coffee shop when I greet them first and ask them genuinely how their day is going and if they're doing well. They are astonished I cared enough to ask. They are prepared to take an order and it sets them off. When I get that surprised look, I'll ask them if anyone else asks them how they're doing. And they'll say "No, not often." I find that sad.

Try asking your server or the janitor at the school or office, for example, how they are doing and show genuine interest. You'll find it amazing how far it goes to make a connection and how important that is for them and you, as human beings. That is giving.

32. My Give Back

The last secret for living a Grow, Get, Give life is to simply give back. This book is an extension of that. Everyone with a big idea, unique ability and vision for their future success deserves to be given the chance to see it through. They deserve to someone to support them, give them guidance to celebrate their achievements, and be their true champion. My goal in life and coaching is to be that caring person. The kind, yet objective coach who listens to you and hears when your voice gives away its excitement, when your eyes light up with joy and your face tells the world you are in the right spot. I have developed the tools, lived the experiences, succeeded, failed, succeeded, failed and succeeded again. Thankfully, I possess the knowledge to help. My sense of responsibility to ensure I help you is overwhelming.

In this series of books, I give people a recipe. Like life, there are many recipes for making similar dishes. I am sharing mine. It is a handbook sharing some of the secrets to a Grow, Get, Give life. It is a philosophy, a mantra, a credo and even a manifesto. I learned to achieve, succeed, and thrive by using mentors and coaches. When we are together, you will get the most from me and the best from those who I have learned from. You will also get me, completely unabashed, unvarnished me.

I'm not tidy or "clean". My words are simple, and I am plainspoken. Take me for what I am. I will do right by you. You deserve a good person with integrity who will serve you if you want to engage, commit, and connect to boost yourself, release your happiness, and unleash the success within you.

The secrets to live your own Grow, Get, Give life have been laid out for you. That's it. Act today.

Share This Book!

Share the Secrets to live a GROW, GET and GIVE Life!

Retail: $24.95

Special Quantity Discounts:

5 – 20 books

$19.99 each

21 – 99 books

$17.97 each

100 – 499 books

$14.95 each

To place an order, contact:

(604) 898-6340

GROW GET GIVE

Hire Mike

A professional speaker you can rely on

for your next event!

If you're serious about getting the most out of the people you serve, employ or entertain, then Mike is the ideal person for a keynote or training experience.

To book Mike to speak:

Grow Get Give Coaching

Squamish, BC

604-898-6340

info@mikeskrypnek.com

www.GrowGetGive.com

www.GrowGetGiveSecrets.com

www.Sea2SkySummit.com

GROW GET GIVE

Acknowledgments

Wisdom comes with time and experience, you might hold it within you, but the interactions of the people in one's life plant it there, nurture it and allow it to grow. My life has been enhanced and made purposeful by the love and energy others have given me. Their input, wisdom, guidance and mentorship have impacted my life in many ways. It is difficult to recall everyone to thank, and I apologize if I did not mention you by name. I am eternally grateful for you all. As I reflect on all your influences, I share my deepest and most sincere thanks with my family, Sherri, Madison, Coen and my parents, Don and Maureen and sister, Cheryl.

Without your love and support I am nothing.

Thank you to:

Leeza Gibbons, Dianna Campbell-Smith, Kevin Harrington, Jack Canfield, Alvin Libin, Paul Alofs, Jill Lublin, T. Harv Eker, Rudy Rutiger, Craig and Marc Kielburger, Richard Branson, Dr. Lynette Charity, Seth Godin, James Malinchak, Scott Keffer, Dan Sullivan, Blake Mycoskie, Andre Agassi, Kevin Eastman, Kevin Garnett, Kathy Kolbe, Oprah Winfrey, Jeff Hoffman, Duff Gibson, Steven Shellenberger, Donny Deustch, Lebron James, Kyle Wilson, Vaughn Pyne, Launa Germiquet, Kim Moody, Dexter Charles, Danny Secter, Kristen Hadeed, Malcolm Gladwell, Geoff Starling, Mihaly Csikszentmihalyi, Arianna Huffington, John Assaraf, John Franzky, John Spencer Ellis, Jenna Anderson, Sarah Rose Sinclair, Tony Little, Michael LePage, Biaggio Veltri.

GROW GET GIVE

GROW GET GIVE

Mike Skrypnek

Made in the USA
Middletown, DE
21 March 2020